"ELECTRIC ENTERTAINMENT" TIME

"GWEN VERDON IS PERFECTION-THE GIRL OF THE YEAR.

Sweet Charity

MAKES ONE VERY PROUD OF AMERICAN MUSICAL COMEDY." cue

2ND SMASH YEAR

Original Cast Album by COLUMBIA RECORDS

PALACE THEATRE B'way & 47 St., N.Y.C.

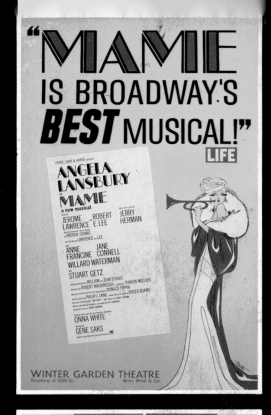

"MAMIE IS BROADWAY'S BEST MUSICAL!" LIFE

ANGELA LANSBURY in MAME a new musical

JEROME LAWRENCE • ROBERT E. LEE • JERRY HERMAN

ANNE FRANCINE • JANE CONNELL • WILLARD WATERMAN • STUART GETZ

ONNA WHITE • GENE SAKS

WINTER GARDEN THEATRE
Broadway at 50th St.    Mats. Wed. & Sat.

JOHN CULLUM

W9-CNG-4

ON THE TWENTIETH CENTURY

Betty Comden and Adolph Green • Cy Coleman

HAROLD PRINCE

TWENTIETH CENTURY

BEST MUSICAL–7 TONY AWARDS

THE WIZ

The new musical version of 'The Wonderful Wizard of Oz'

AT THE BROADWAY THEATRE
Broadway at 53rd Street. Mats. Wed. Sat. & Sun.

782.81 Got                    177339
Gottfried.
Broadway musicals.

DATE DUE

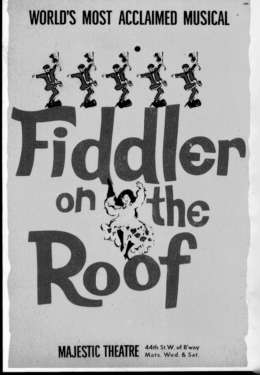

WORLD'S MOST ACCLAIMED MUSICAL

Fiddler on the Roof

MAJESTIC THEATRE    44th St. W. of B'way
Mats. Wed. & Sat.

The Playwrights' Company
PRESENTS

LOST in the Stars

A Musical Play

MAXWELL ANDERSON
and KURT WEILL

ROUBEN MAMOULIAN

TODD DUNCAN • LESLIE BANKS

WARREN COLEMAN
GEORGE JENKINS

MUSIC BOX    45th ST. W. of B'way
MATS. SAT. & SUN.

CHICAGO

Jules Fisher, The Shubert Organization & Columbia Pictures present

Dancin'

a new musical entertainment
directed & choreographed by Bob Fosse

Broadhurst Theatre
235 West 44th Street, New York, New York 10036

MARTIN GOTTFRIED

# BROADWAY MUSICALS

HARRY N. ABRAMS, INC.,
PUBLISHERS, NEW YORK

FOR JANE

Second Printing 1980

Project Editor: Robert Morton
Editor: Lory Frankel
Designer: Nai Y. Chang
Research Editor: Lois Brown

Library of Congress Cataloging in Publication Data

Gottfried, Martin.
    Broadway musicals.

    Includes index.
    1.   Musical revue, comedy, etc.—New York (City)
I.   Title.
ML1711.G68          782.8′1′097471          78-31297
ISBN 0-8109-0664-3

Library of Congress Catalog Card Number: 78-31297

Printed and bound in Japan

# CONTENTS

# INTRODUCTION

*Joel Grey in* George M. *Drawing by Al Hirschfeld from* The World of Hirschfeld.

This book is devoted—in both senses of the word—to the Broadway musical theater. Its purpose is not to present an encyclopedic or historical account of musicals but to define, analyze, criticize, and celebrate them—to capture their spirit. Every musical will not be described, illustrated, or even noted, because a mere accumulation of data would include everything but the qualities that make musicals such a unique kind of theater: exhilaration, energy, color and size, the emotional kick in the pants.

This book is about the impractical ambitions and the actual constructing of musicals. It is about who makes them and what goes into their creation and why the result is so special. When any theater work is performed, it becomes a living organism with a life spirit of its own. With a musical especially, it is this spirit that matters most.

The facts of the musical theater will not be entirely slighted; they can remind us of grand shows of the past. But the essence of a musical is the magic made in performance, the onstage transformation of materials into an event. Here is one trick whose illusion isn't spoiled by an explanation, for not even the creators know why a combination of story songs, dances, direction, scenery, lights, and actors fails to breathe in one show and "works"—takes full life —in another.

It is this electricity generated by a musical—how the musical feels as it is happening—that is most important of all to catch. It is this electricity that has always eluded imitators outside New York. It is what movie versions of musicals have never captured: the excitement that prompted the movie sale in the first place.

Just what *is* a Broadway musical? It isn't merely a musical that plays on Broadway. Operettas, cabaret works, shows created abroad have been produced on Broadway. They are not of the genre. Broadway musicals are a unique kind of theater, the outgrowth of a taste, a tradition. There is a Broadway sound, a Broadway look, a Broadway feel to them. This "Broadway" quality is an inheritance from our past's rowdy stages. It is the rhythmic spiel of New York; it is the broad, basic, and gutsy approach of a theater meant not for art but for public entertainment.

Commercialism—an appeal to a taste as popular as possible— has not always proved a deterrent to producing musicals of quality. In fact, it is the very basis of their development. The pressure to be an immediate popular as well as artistic success is a pressure that those working in subsidized theaters suffer the lack of. It requires that the audience be reached and satisfied. The public does not always appreciate great art, but it knows what sterile art is. It can often separate the pretentious and sham from the direct and legitimate. Recognizing this, most producers realize the futility of trying to calculate popular appeal. Instead, they choose according to their own tastes, on the principle that what they like others will also like.

Other pressures caused by our commercial system—rewriting, adding songs, changing numbers, solving unexpected problems, all under a time limit as a show heads for a date with a Broadway opening night—these leave neither time nor money for self-indulgence and no room for the arty.

Yes, the musical is America's most significant contribution to world theater. Cliché or not, that's true. Musicals just didn't exist before. Though one can link them to prior works—John Gay's eighteenth-century *The Beggar's Opera* or the comic operas of Gilbert and Sullivan, for instance—such a genealogy would be contrived. Unlike our dramas, musicals are purely American as a stage form. What is a Broadway musical if not an outgrowth of vaudeville's basic song and dance?

But historic as their conception was, and as much as we love them, there have not yet been any musicals to rank with the great classics of the dramatic literature. There are many beloved shows—even great ones—but they are not works of art; their period qualities are obvious in revivals. We actually love them for their marvelous and timeless songs, not for their plots and productions. Many are amateurish, most are naive, and all are limited by shortcomings of technique.

Why shouldn't our old musicals be imperfect? Even on the rare occasions that a form of art is invented whole, its technical perfection takes time. No masterwork can be created on a basis of immature technique. Broadway musicals are still in the process of becoming, and that must be understood if our appreciation of them is to be reasonable.

Yet spirit can overcome technical shortcomings. How many marvelous works the musical theater has given us! These are already more than transient entertainments. Let the dramatic theories fly, audiences need no one to tell them to appreciate musicals or how to. Musicals are self-justifying. They are all the show the theater is supposed to be.

The musical is an art both popular and fine, sharing roots with our vaudeville and burlesque. Spirit, lunacy, energy, and practicality—exuberance and show savvy—these are what energized the naive variety shows and the musicals of the early days. They still energize the increasingly artistic musicals. It is this flamboyance and showmanship that have created the mystique of Broadway musicals. It is this emphasis on entertainment first—on a show's theatrical viability—that has paid off in artistic depth and validity. The shows work not for what they say but for what they are.

When the houselights go down in a big Broadway theater, the plush St. James or the Majestic or the Alvin, and the pit band strikes up the overture, the audience hushes its buzz of anticipation. It isn't concerned with or even aware of the huge backstage team about to run through a complex operation. It waits for the energy to flow, not with a critical attitude but expecting only to be entertained and in a very big way. The houselights dim. The curtain rises. The ride begins.

*Ray Bolger in* All American. *Drawing by Al Hirschfeld from* The World of Hirschfeld.

Overleaf:
*Ann Reinking in* Dancin', *choreography by Bob Fosse.*

# THE ELEMENTS
## OF A MUSICAL

# THE BOOK

Of a musical's three elements—the book, the music, and the lyrics—the book is the most important. The book or text of a musical is the basis of the show's existence. It is what the show is *about*. It is the first part that is written. It is what the music and lyrics and dances are set to. It is the reason a musical is produced in the first place. Ultimately, it is the reason a show succeeds or fails.

Paradoxically, the book is also the *least* important element in a musical. A musical, after all, is *called* a musical. The main attraction is the song and dance. The details of a plot are soon forgotten. The glitter of music and dance pushes the story into the background. Because the book is so overwhelmed, few musical makers have grasped its significance and few writers have concentrated on becoming adept at writing it. The book is crucial and it is unappreciated. Consequently, it is hardly surprising that "book trouble" is the bane of the musical theater.

Book trouble is the problem of every musical faltering on the road; any show that isn't working is said to have book trouble because weak songs and dances are replaceable but the whole script isn't. If the replacements don't work, the book must be to blame. What is book trouble? One episode isn't leading clearly to another; the funny business is getting no laughs; leading characters look awkward, having nothing to do; scenes are not playing smoothly and musical numbers aren't properly set up; in short, one way or another the book isn't working. Show doctors look on such defects as things to be "fixed." They rewrite in sections, tinkering with the faults, adding, dropping, and combining characters as if playing with tin soldiers. Seldom having more than a few weeks in which to do this, they gloss over the problems, hoping to hide them.

Book trouble is not always the result of poor writing. Sometimes it is also the result of material that is unmusical. Certain stories and subjects and settings have natural musical references. *The King and I,* for example, has them in the exotic sounds and gestures of Siam. The story for *The Music Man* is also itself musical, dealing as it does with marching bands and the rhythm of the salesman's spiel. Other subjects may not seem musical until that quality is brought out. Rodgers and Hammerstein tried and gave up on musicalizing *Pygmalion.* Lerner and Loewe then found rhythm and lilt in British social manners, and used these musical qualities to transform *Pygmalion* into *My Fair Lady.* On the other hand, there have been shows that dealt, somehow successfully, with unmusical subjects such as labor unions (*The Pajama Game*) or corporate politics (*How to Succeed in*

*Business Without Really Trying*). Still, the musical that has song and dance quality in its subject matter has a head start over the musical that does not. If the material doesn't suggest dancing and singing, it means that the musical sequences will have to be manufactured. Odds are, they will clash with the dramatic sequences, and the audience will become restless between numbers. The original choice of material is to blame.

Book trouble is also caused by the musical's creative process itself. Unlike a drama, a libretto is usually written on order—as an assignment given by a producer or song-writing team. It is not written with the personal dedication given to a play, and the professional librettist tends to think of his work as less an art than a craft. Books are therefore rarely good plays, but then they shouldn't be plays at all. They should be custom-designed for the musical theater's particular needs, conscious of musical usage, conscious of dance staging, conscious of dances and the presence of dancers, *conscious of being musicals.*

The fact that the book is usually written before rehearsal puts more distance between it and the rest of the show, which is assembled on its feet. The book then has to catch up with what's being created in the studio, but by this time the book writer has lost control of his own script. When the composer and lyricist go to work on it, they pull and twist at it in order to set up, frame, and enhance their songs. Immediately after he hands in his script, the book writer drops to the bottom of the creative totem pole. He is the first one blamed if the show is a failure and the last to be credited if it is a success.

What musicals need, then, are books written especially for them: texts tailored to the form and style of the musical theater and to a particular show. Such books require an understanding of the musical's chemistry. Playwrights are unlikely to share the mentality of choreographers and directors of musicals because they are word people. Special writers must be developed if the musical's book is to match the character of its songs and dances. Librettists must work with the composers and choreographers and directors *while writing* so that the songs and dances and musical staging are not tacked on but built into their scripts.

Inevitably, librettos must gravitate toward original stories rather than adaptations. This is not a matter of principle. There is nothing immoral about an adaptation. It's just that its source was not devised for the musical stage, so the show is starting out with a strike against it. The original libretto, on the other hand, can be created with a musical in mind and can even be based on a musical production idea—such as *A Chorus Line*, which uses the concept of a dance audition. This makes for an organic relationship between text, song, and dance.

Because its practitioners have been slighted and its importance ignored, book writing, then, is the least developed of the musical theater's disciplines. There are no career book writers to rank with Broadway's celebrated composers and lyricists. Herbert Fields, for example, wrote twenty-two books over a thirty-five-year career, but there wasn't an essential difference between his first show, *Dearest Enemy*, which he wrote with Rodgers and Hart in 1925, and his last, *Redhead*, which he and his sister Dorothy wrote with Albert Hague in 1959. Dated, clumsy, or just plain silly books are the main reasons why so many shows with great scores cannot be revived.

The Red Mill *was one of Victor Herbert's most popular Broadway operettas, running 279 performances in 1906 and then enjoying a popular revival in the forties. Herbert's shows blurred the distinction between operetta and the twenties musical comedy. The farcical plot of* The Red Mill, *and its catchy songs (including "Every Day Is Ladies' Day with Me"), enchanted audiences and opened the door for the Broadway musical as we know it.*

*The style of musical comedy books was set by Guy Bolton (left), who collaborated with P. G. Wodehouse (center) and Jerome Kern on the legendary Princess Theater musicals. With various collaborators, Bolton wrote more than fifty librettos for Broadway and London shows over a fifty-year career.*

Although the term "book musical" has come to mean a conventional show, it originally meant the musical with a story, as opposed to a revue, which is a series of songs and sketches. "Book" derives from the Italian "libretto" ("booklet")—the script of an opera. The librettist wrote every word of dialogue and song. Some of Broadway's librettists, like Oscar Hammerstein II, continued to do all a show's writing: the play *and* the lyrics. But almost at the start, we had specialists: lyricists and librettists. So, "libretto" and "librettist" have come to refer to the book—the script of a musical—rather than the lyrics.

Guy Bolton and his collaborators on Jerome Kern's Princess Theater musicals (1915–1918) were the first to break with the operetta tradition, writing breezy stories that did not call for massive companies and opulent costumes. Their settings were contemporary and their main characters were usually two lovers and a comedian. Vaudeville had bred a peculiarly American comedian, the wisecracker, and it was he who provided the comedy in musical comedy. He did it in more ways than one, for he usually wrote his own lines, interpolating his routines into his part.

The first librettist—perhaps the first *person*—to take the musical theater seriously was Oscar Hammerstein II, an active librettist for *forty years*. His career spanned most of our musical theater's phases. When operetta was in the twilight of its vogue, Hammerstein collaborated with the established composers of the genre, writing *Rose Marie* with Rudolf Friml and Herbert Stothart and *The Desert Song* with Sigmund Romberg. Even the book for his acclaimed *Show Boat* in 1927 has distinct ties to operetta, but it opened the door to serious American musical theater: It deals with serious subjects and even has elements of tragedy; it is not a musical comedy but something new—a *musical play*.

In adapting Edna Ferber's popular novel, Hammerstein began with a Deep South environment that had natural musical echoes. The specific setting of a show boat provided a logical reason for the presence of singers and songs, but Hammerstein's crucial innovation was integrating the book with the lyrics, thereby creating the "book song." A book song relates to and even furthers the plot, functioning as dialogue set to music. Early musical comedies hadn't plot enough to support such relevant lyrics. Hammerstein provided his musicals with a substantial story line and linked the music with the story through relevant lyrics. Though this may seem obvious now, in 1927 it was a major advance. Not until *Show Boat* was any musical taken seriously as theater.

*Show Boat* also introduced the scenic changes of operetta into the Broadway musical theater, for so much detail of plot necessitated many settings. This resulted in a format of episode, song, set change, episode, song, set change, alternating for the duration of the show. Shows were built to have short scenes building to song cues, after which the buildup began all over again. Ultimately, distracting the audience during set changes came to dictate the form of a musical as much as did the desire to keep the musical numbers coming.

Considering its age, Hammerstein's libretto for *Show Boat* has held up amazingly well. It is certainly superior to the American plays that were being written at the time. Even Eugene O'Neill's works of the same period are more stilted and melodramatic than *Show Boat*. Yet it wasn't until after sixteen years and fifteen shows that Hammerstein wrote another book as serious and achieved another success of its stature: *Oklahoma!* Between these two, he had his share of failures. In 1943, following the sensational debut of *Oklahoma!* he took out an advertisement in *Variety* reminding his colleagues of the theater's unpredictability. Listing all his recent flops, the signed advertisement concluded, "I did it before and I can do it again."

Beginning with *Oklahoma!* Hammerstein and Richard Rodgers established and then specialized in musical plays—naturalistic dramas with songs. Daring at the start, Hammerstein's books became ever more conservative, dealing with safe, sentimental material. All were adaptations except *Allegro* in 1947 and *Me and Juliet* in 1953. Although Rodgers and Hammerstein's musicals are among the most beloved of all, there is no sense pretending their books are literary gems. They resemble the dramas of their time—*Tea and Sympathy*, *Mister Roberts*, *Picnic*—and have not aged well. When *South Pacific* opened in 1949, the script was considered good enough to stand on its own as drama. Today it seems as dated as a wartime movie.

The trouble with Hammerstein's scripts is that his technique of setting up songs makes them too episodic. They are also too earnest; they are preachy. But, in their time, they were better crafted and more professional than other books. The best of them, *The King and I*, is the finest and most revivable of all Rodgers and Hammerstein musicals. Here is a superior example of the musical drama and it is worth studying in detail.

*The King and I* is based on Margaret Landon's book *Anna and the King of Siam*. It opens on the deck of a ship docked outside Bangkok. We are introduced to Anna Leonowens and her teenage son Louis. Anna admits to her son that she is sometimes frightened and sings "I Whistle a Happy Tune."

We are given more information: She is the widow of a British

Overleaf: Oklahoma! *may look dated now, but in its time it was truly original, well-crafted, and exhilarating. Richard Rodgers's songs reflected, in their wholesomeness, his switch in lyricists from Lorenz Hart to Oscar Hammerstein II. In a style new to him he created one of the great Broadway scores. Up front and from left to right are Celeste Holm, Betty Garde, Lee Dixon, Ralph Riggs, Alfred Drake, and Joan Roberts.*

Army officer and she is to be the schoolteacher of the King of Siam's children. Then there is the first of many scenes "in one" (in front of the curtain while the set is being changed behind). This is an awkward device that stifles a production's flow. Though it was used by virtually all musicals at the time, it's hard to understand why Hammerstein used it for this show since, two years earlier, all of his *South Pacific* set changes had been made in full audience view. It may have been because *The King and I*'s sets were too elaborate to change openly. In this particular scene in one, the court dancers are dressing and there is no dialogue.

The second scene is set in the King's library. Lun Tha, an emissary, brings the slave girl Tuptim to the King as a gift from Burma. The King examines her and exits. The Prime Minister tells her the King is pleased with her and leaves followed by Lun Tha. It is a blatant cue for Tuptim to sing sarcastically, "He is pleased with me!/My lord and master." The King and Anna enter and meet for the first time. This is one of the book's longer scenes, taking time to develop the main characters. Anna is refined and cerebral, the King authoritarian and physical. They spar about her quarters, which are in the palace. Anna insists on the private house she was promised. The King refuses and leaves. His head wife, Lady Thiang, tells Anna of Tuptim's love for the young man who brought her. There seems only one purpose for this: so that Anna can sing "Hello, Young Lovers." After the song, the King reappears, announcing that the children are to be presented to the schoolteacher. Within four lines of dialogue, "The March of the Siamese Children" begins. Though this seems a contrivance it plays smoothly, and the number is marvelous.

There is another scene in one while the setting is being changed. In front of a painted curtain the King and the Prince briefly discuss the difference between Anna's teachings and Siamese lore. The son leaves. The King, confused about the role of a monarch in a changing world, sings "A Puzzlement." The next scene is just as brief but it has a full setting because more than one song will be sung in it. It opens with Anna teaching her students geography. "For many years, before I came here," she says, "Siam was to me that little white spot. Now I have lived here for more than a year. I have met the people of Siam. And I am beginning to understand them." With this flimsy cue, she sings, "Getting to Know You." After the song, the King enters, and once more he and Anna argue over her quarters. This dispute is the first act's key element because it symbolizes Anna's challenging of the King's absolute, arbitrary authority. Hammerstein's use of it is excellent. During this particular argument, the King angers Anna by telling her she is his "servant." She storms out, and everyone else leaves, evidently just to allow Tuptim and Lun Tha, the subplot lovers, to enter and exchange four lines to cue "We Kiss in a Shadow." You'll notice it's usually the ballads that give Hammerstein (and most book writers) setup problems.

After still another scene in one—this many really should have been avoided—the setting is changed to Anna's bedroom, where she is still furious over having been called a servant. She sings the superb soliloquy, "Shall I Tell You What I Think of You?" Then a completely new plot development is introduced in the space of eight lines of dialogue. The King's head wife, Lady Thiang, stops by to tell Anna that the British are considering making Siam a protectorate unless they can be convinced that the Siamese are not barbarians.

*Here, in* The King and I, *is one of the musical theater's most thrilling moments—"Shall We Dance?" with Anna (Gertrude Lawrence) teaching the King (Yul Brynner) to polka. Lawrence had brought the idea of the show to Rodgers and Hammerstein. (It was to be her last; she died of cancer during the run.) In 1976, twenty-five years after its premiere, Brynner recreated his original role opposite Constance Towers, and the show proved its durability with a two-year run—astounding for a revival.*

She asks Anna to forgive the King and help put his court into European shape, for a British legation is coming to see things for themselves. Lady Thiang sings about the King's specialness—"Something Wonderful"—and Anna is convinced, understandably, for the song represents ideal integration of lyrics and plot, making a most compelling argument: "He may not always say/What you would have him say/But now and then he'll say/Something wonderful." Hammerstein uses this song just as effectively in the following scene in one, after Lady Thiang tells the Prime Minister she's convinced Anna to help the King. For this time, when she sings a reprise of "Something Wonderful," the implication is not of her love for an imperfect King but of Anna's, which is then budding. This is excellent dramatic manipulation on Hammerstein's part.

In the final scene of the first act, Anna and the King are unconsciously playing courtship games and it is quite nice. The scene and the act then end uncommonly, not with a musical number but dramatically, capitalizing on the device that had been set up over the previous hour and a quarter: The King prays to Buddha for success with the visiting English, promising in exchange for that success that he will give Anna the private house she has been pleading for. Unlike most musical act endings, it is upbeat.

The second and weaker act opens with the King's wives dressing in Western style and singing "Western People Funny," but when the British arrive, they panic. This condescending treatment of Orientals, evident throughout the show, is typical of both Hammerstein and the period in which he was writing. Anna dances with one of the Englishmen, a former beau, making the King jealous. The show's most crudely structured scene follows: Lady Thiang tells Tuptim that her lover is being sent away. The couple plans to flee together. They sing "I Have Dreamed." Anna comes across them, they tell her of their plans, and she reprises "Hello, Young Lovers."

Next comes Jerome Robbins's ballet, "The Small House of Uncle Thomas." Presented as an entertainment for the Englishmen, Tuptim has devised it to describe her own situation: a slave and her lover fleeing a tyrant. It is an excellent, textual use of ballet and the dance itself is a classic. Following this is a wasteful section setting up the minor "Song of the King," but it leads to one of the show's highlights: Anna teaching the King to polka. "Shall We Dance?" logically belongs several numbers earlier, after the King had been made jealous by Anna's dancing with the Englishman. Placed here to strengthen the second act's latter half, it is virtually uncued but it remains one of the enthralling moments in American musical theater, a blue-chip showstopper.

The dance is interrupted by Tuptim, who bursts in, pursued by the King's men. She was caught fleeing and will not tell where her lover is, though he will soon be found dead. The King is about to whip the girl when Anna challenges him on the point, calling him a barbarian. He backs down but realizes that in doing so his time as king has passed, and he flees from the room. "You have destroyed King," the Prime Minister tells Anna, in the Pidgin English that Hammerstein uses throughout the play when dealing with the Siamese.

Hammerstein squeezes too many events into the end of his book. The King is mortally ill, and Anna is preparing to leave. Receiving a deathbed letter she returns to the King's side and agrees to stay and teach the children. The King asks the Prince, his heir, what he would do if he were to succeed to the throne. As the son practices being a monarch, and as the orchestra plays "Something Wonderful," the King dies. The curtain falls. It is an extremely moving finale.

Hammerstein's playwriting in this script is practical but it is also often inspired; certainly, it is his best writing. The show worked in 1951 and will always work because of its drama and its emotional appeal. The libretto is sometimes obvious about its song cues and tends to rush from scene to scene, but it deals forthrightly with the problem of combining dramatic with musical theater. It is also, not incidentally, a book with great musicality of subject matter—a model of its kind. With such work, Oscar Hammerstein II made book writing respectable.

One can accuse Hammerstein of taking the fun out of musicals but not of taking them lightly. He was a lifetime student of the musical theater, from the heyday of operettas until the *West Side Story* era. He came to the musical theater when it was naive, and when he left, it was grown-up. He had much to do with that.

Hammerstein's book-writing colleagues in the early part of his career were Bolton, George Abbott, Herbert Fields, and Howard Lindsay and Russel Crouse. They specialized in the musical comedy, essentially modeled on Bolton's Princess Theater shows, that we now find so inane. Abbott took the genre a step further. Previously established as a director and writer of plays, he brought to musical comedy the breakneck tempo of farce, and that became his trademark. More important, he also brought practicality and professionalism to the musical theater. George Abbott's business was show business and his product was the functioning musical comedy.

Along with Abbott, other prominent librettists of this period included director-writers such as Abe Burrows and George S. Kaufman. They were reluctant to follow Hammerstein's progress from musical comedy to musical drama. Instead, they, and Abbott in particular, took musical *comedy* into its second generation. The second-generation musical comedy made a passing attempt at being a play and at integrating book with lyrics. Much like Hammerstein's drama, it too used episodes to link one song with the next, like the velvet ropes that string one stanchion to another in a theater lobby.

*Guys and Dolls* (1950) has a strength of character in its book because Abe Burrows, the author, grasped the originality of Damon Runyon's short stories. Yet, despite the mythic quality of the material, the book has a conventional structure; it is basically a second-generation musical comedy. *Guys and Dolls* is so firmly established as a classic Broadway musical, however, and has so wonderful a Frank Loesser score that criticism of it seems beside the point.

Other successful musicals of the era—*High Button Shoes*; *Kiss Me, Kate*; *Call Me Madam*; *Wish You Were Here*; *Kismet*; *Wonderful Town*; *Plain and Fancy*; and so on—have been more seriously dated by their books. Very entertaining in their time, their broad senses of humor hold them to that time. Even worse, *Finian's Rainbow*, though it has one of Broadway's crowning scores, tied itself to social relevance with a story about a union organizer, the redistribution of wealth, and Jim Crowism. It remains hopelessly locked in its political era.

Some of the books written during this time proved to have lasting power. Abbott retained enough of Brandon Thomas's classic farce, *Charley's Aunt*, to make the 1948 *Where's Charley?* a musical good for all time. It has the simplicity, the energy, and the consistency of the original. Sandy Wilson's *The Boy Friend*, a rare British musical on Broadway during the fifties, is also true to itself. Its mimickry of twenties musical comedy is so straight-faced that the show can almost be taken sincerely, and its mockery is affectionate rather than snide. Though verging perilously on the collegiate, it is close to being a perfect musical because its book and lyrics are written in such matched tones of voice. Wilson wrote *The Boy Friend*'s music and lyrics as well as the book, a rarity. Frank Loesser also wrote the book, music, and lyrics for *The Most Happy Fella*, Noel Coward did the same for *Sail Away*, and Meredith Willson wrote everything for both *The Music Man* and *Here's Love*. The triple-threat man may well be jinxed on Broadway. Nobody ever succeeded at it more than once. In fact, the talented Sandy Wilson never had another Broadway show.

Contrary to most, who considered musicals light entertainment and wrote comedies for them, Joshua Logan tended more toward the Hammerstein style of musical play. As a director-librettist, he had a streak of hits from 1951 to 1954—*South Pacific* (co-written with Hammerstein), *Wish You Were Here*, and *Fanny*. *Fanny* had the best story, based as it was on Marcel Pagnol's trilogy of plays about life in Marseilles. It is a good standard musical play.

Among the librettos of musical plays, *My Fair Lady*'s is in a class of its own, based as it is on one of the most charming romantic comedies ever written, George Bernard Shaw's *Pygmalion*. Alan Jay Lerner's uncanny fidelity in adapting the original paid off in perhaps the most interesting, touching, and literate story a Broadway musical has ever had. And still his book dovetails neatly into Frederick Loewe's magnificent score.

Lerner has been a prolific librettist, writing not only with Loewe, but with such other major composers as Kurt Weill, Burton Lane, and André Previn. Lerner's other librettos have not been as graceful as *My Fair Lady*'s, however, leading to the inescapable conclusion that without a Shaw original to draw from, he is but an ordinary book writer in the Hammerstein manner. He wrote many musical books, but his great strength is as a lyricist.

On the basis of experience, Lerner is a professional librettist and yet, in this strange field, halfway between the written word and musical production, quantity and consistent competence do not seem to go hand-in-hand. A professional book writer does not have to be an artist; he does not have to come up with a success every time out. But he should be reliable and sure. He should know his business; he should be confident with the peculiar needs of a musical's script and always be able to come through with at least a *presentable* book every time.

Such consistency somehow eludes career librettists. Arthur Laurents wrote both *West Side Story* and *Gypsy*. While neither book was a work of art, they gave a solid underpinning to the two wonderful shows. He seemed the musical theater's most significant librettist since Hammerstein. Yet his later books—for *Anyone Can Whistle*, *Do I Hear a Waltz?*, and *Hallelujah, Baby*—did not hold up. Joseph Stein wrote the excellent book for *Fiddler on the Roof*, but not many others of its caliber.

Laurents and Stein, like Lerner, wrote musical plays in the Oscar Hammerstein tradition. Betty Comden and Adolph Green, on the other hand, were heirs to George Abbott's style of musical

An import from London in 1954, The Boy Friend *poked affectionate fun at American musicals of the 1920s (notably Rodgers and Hart's* The Girl Friend). *It introduced a nineteen-year-old Julie Andrews (right). Author-composer-lyricist Sandy Wilson described the show as a "new twenties musical," meaning that he was not mocking the genre but rather duplicating it so that it mocked itself. "Won't You Charleston with Me?" (below) was his version of the most famous of all twenties dances.* The Boy Friend *is virtually perfect in succeeding at what it intended.*

comedy, having gotten their start under his direction. They were among the busiest of all librettists during the fifties and sixties, but the period charm of their *Bells Are Ringing* and *On the Town* gave way to pushiness and excess comic breadth. The Comden and Green scripts of this period perhaps typify the dangerous dating of the musical comedy during its second generation. They continued to write such scripts into the seventies, until in 1978, they came up with a fresh and funny book for *On the Twentieth Century.*

A third generation of librettists matured in the sixties but the increasing cost and declining frequency of production gave them fewer chances to show their work. Writing six produced musicals between 1960 and 1976 was writing a lot for this time—enough to make Michael Stewart the most prominent librettist of the period— and four of his shows were hits: *Bye, Bye, Birdie, Carnival, Hello, Dolly!*, and *I Love My Wife.* They not only established him but established him as a true professional. Stewart was among a new generation of librettists applying Hammerstein's seriousness of approach to the writing of funny musicals. His book for the 1964 *Hello, Dolly!* is one of the best our musical theater has ever produced. As the book of a comic musical, it also deserves more thorough study.

Producer David Merrick's decision to adapt Thornton Wilder's 1954 play *The Matchmaker* to the musical stage was a brainstorm to begin with. *The Matchmaker* is a stylized work. It has an elevated reality, harmonious with that of song and dance. The story is set in turn-of-the-century New York, a time and place with musical associations. The comedy and romance of the story are playful, the mood whimsical, qualities with dance connotations. These characteristics are rare in the sources usually chosen for musicals, though they are the ones that should be looked for first.

Oddly enough, it is unusual for a musical to open with song and dance before a word of dialogue has been spoken. *Hello, Dolly!* does. As the curtain rises, the company is arranged in a tableau that resembles a period greeting card. The performers come to life as if from a movie's frozen frame and sing "Call on Dolly," which sets the show's tone: stylized, turn-of-the-century elegance. After the first of this song's three parts, Dolly Gallagher Levi makes her entrance and establishes a running joke of having business calling cards to suit any occasion, though she is primarily a matchmaker. Dolly, the widow of Ephraim Levi, has been engaged by Horace Vandergelder, "the well-known half a millionaire" from Yonkers, to arrange his marriage. Most conventional musicals will have a few lines of dialogue in the midst of a song but this opening number has full speeches, which establish Dolly Levi's comic longwindedness at the start.

In the number's second part ("I Have Always Been a Woman Who Arranges Things") and third part ("I Put My Hand"), the audience learns that Dolly also wants to help Vandergelder's wailing niece, Ermengarde, marry Ambrose, the impoverished artist she loves. It also learns that Dolly herself intends to marry Vandergelder, quite frankly "for his money."

With but one exception, all the scene changes in *Hello, Dolly!* are made in full audience view. To avoid *full* sets for every scene, the superb designer Oliver Smith made "olios"—drop curtains well upstage (at the rear). They do not pretend to imitate sets but look like illustrations from turn-of-the-century rotogravures, consistent with the show's style. The first of these olios takes Dolly—in the midst of this opening number—to Grand Central Station for the train to Yonkers.

At Vandergelder's combined home and feed store (a two-level set), the tiny Ermengarde is bawling as usual, though warned by the cantankerous Vandergelder not to "cry in front of the store." Vandergelder is planning to go to New York for the Fourteenth Street Association Parade and will leave his two clerks—Cornelius and Barnaby—to tend to business. He speaks of marrying the young widow Irene Molloy and sings "It Takes a Woman," describing the role of a wife as a menial. Dolly arrives, eager to discourage the marriage to Irene Molloy that she'd arranged ("All my congratulations and sympathy . . . according to all known facts her first husband passed on quite naturally"). She alludes to another available girl for him, an heiress named Ernestina Money. Vandergelder agrees to meet Ernestina and Dolly's plan to snare him is working. The lights dim on them and go up on the set's lower level, where Cornelius is bemoaning to Barnaby their restricted life. They will go to New York, he says—they will stink up the store with exploding tomato cans so that it must be closed—-"We're going to have a good meal, we're going to be in danger, we're going to spend all our money, we're going to be arrested . . . . And we're not coming back to Yonkers until we've each kissed a girl!" As the cans start to explode they sing "Put On Your Sunday Clothes."

Upstairs, Dolly, Ambrose, and Ermengarde are also dressing to go to New York, for Dolly is going to enter them in a polka contest at the Harmonia Gardens Restarurant so that with the prize—a week's engagement as a dance act—they can afford to get married. So these three join in singing "Put On Your Sunday Clothes" while the set becomes the Yonkers railway station. A big, steaming locomotive and train arrive for everyone to board and as it pulls offstage, the hat shop of Irene Molloy pulls on. Irene's assistant, Minnie Fay, can't open the door but Irene arrives to cut stage fiction with the breath of reality: "It's stuck? Then push!" The two revolve the whole set, transforming the store's facade into its back wall. Irene tells Minnie she's marrying Vandergelder because she's tired of "being suspected of being a wicked woman with nothing to show for it." Trying on a hat she sings "Ribbons Down My Back" which, like all ballads, is hard to cue and defies musical staging. Cornelius and Barnaby show up, hiding from Vandergelder, who is waiting outside the shop to meet Dolly. When he comes in, bringing Irene chocolate-covered peanuts (unshelled), the boys hide. Vandergelder realizes someone is hiding there ("No man that hides in ladies' closets can frighten me") but Dolly, who has arrived a few minutes earlier, distracts him by singing "Motherhood." Once Vandergelder goes, Irene tells the boys to leave or she'll call the police, but with her usual perverse logic, Dolly suggests that Irene and Minnie dine with them first. "It's the way things are done in the law. Dinner first, dungeons afterwards." Believing Dolly's description of Cornelius and Barnaby as playboys, Irene suggests they all eat at the plush Harmonia Gardens, but the impoverished Cornelius begs off, claiming he can't dance. Presenting her dance instructor's card, Dolly insists that "absolutely no sense of rhythm is one of the primary requirements for learning by the Gallagher-Levi Method." The dance lesson becomes a full-scale waltzing number, "Dancing."

This almost cinematically dissolves, again through the use of an olio, into Dolly's old neighborhood. She tells her dead Ephraim that she's had enough of independence: "I've decided to rejoin the human race, and Ephraim . . . I want *you* to give me away!" That is, she wants a sign of approval for her plan to marry Vandergelder. The scene exists primarily to cue the first-act finale, "When the Parade Passes By," but it enriches Dolly's character and works with great feeling. At the parade, Vandergelder fires Dolly as his match-maker, convincing her "he's as good as mine," and the first-act curtain falls. Here, again, is that rarity, a dramatically effective, cheerful first act finale.

The second act begins with Irene, Cornelius, Minnie, and Barnaby walking to the Harmonia Gardens because, according to the penniless boys, "really elegant people never take hacks." This becomes the stylish song and dance "Elegance." As they all exit, Ambrose and Ermengarde enter, practicing their polka for the dance contest. They pass, too, while Vandergelder finally meets Ernestina Money, a very fat young lady indeed. This all happens "in one"—the only use of this device in all of *Hello, Dolly!*, and it is used because the subsequent Harmonia Gardens setting is too elaborate to be moved in full audience view, by remote control. Now the light bleeds through behind this scrim (a painted drop curtain that becomes transparent with such lighting). At the Harmonia Gardens the waiters are being told that in honor of Dolly's return after a ten-year absence, the usual lightning-fast service will be sped up. Cornelius, Irene, Barnaby, and Minnie are shown to their private dining room and they shut the curtains. The dance number "Waiters' Galop" begins. Vandergelder enters with Ernestina, so embarrassed by her obesity that he tells the headwaiter she's his personal physician ("That's enough rouge, Doctor!"). He pulls the curtains around *their* private dining room. There is more of the "Waiters' Galop"—ice buckets, trays, and skewers flying through the air. Barnaby and Vandergelder are caught up in the frantic dance and lose their wallets. Each winds up with the other's, so that the boys have lots of money and Vandergelder has none. Meanwhile, everything is building toward Dolly's grand entrance and this, of course, is the big show-stopping number, "Hello, Dolly!"

Ernestina disappears from the scene, and Dolly moves to a center-stage table with Vandergelder to watch Ambrose and Ermengarde's polka. A fine comic scene has Dolly getting Vandergelder's mind onto the subject of marriage. As she sits and eats, the polka contest gets out of hand, a riot follows, and everyone winds up in court with the drop of an olio. Dolly is still seated at her table.

Dolly's opening remark as everyone's attorney is that "the defense rests!" Still, Cornelius rises in his own behalf and sings "It Only Takes a Moment," declaring his love for Irene. This whimsical cue only momentarily stirs the dead air created by almost any ballad in almost any musical. Dolly then surprises Horace—who has been suspecting her of looking to get married—by singing good-bye to him ("So Long, Dearie"). When he next sees Dolly, back in Yonkers, he is startled into a proposal, in the midst of which he unknowingly quotes Dolly's beloved late husband ("Money is like manure. It's not worth a thing unless it's spread around, encouraging young things to grow"). So, in a very touching way, she has the approval she wanted ("Thank you, Ephraim") and with Vandergelder reprising "Hello, Dolly!" the curtain falls.

This show marked a sharp break with Broadway's musical comedies. Demanding more of a book, Stewart made it much more classical in its style of farce, less direct in its sequences, and generally classier. Most of its songs are related to the story and also to its style,

*One of the most spectacular moments in all of Broadway musical theater is Dolly's entrance at the top of a staircase to sing the title song from* Hello, Dolly! *Though many other stars played Dolly Levi, the role will be forever identified with Carol Channing. As with all great stage numbers, this one is a transaction directly between the performer and the audience. When Channing sang it, the audience never failed to cheer throughout her performance.*

*Overleaf: An example of impeccable staging by Gower Champion, "Put On Your Sunday Clothes" is thoroughly consistent with the dramatic, scenic, musical, and choreographic style of* Hello, Dolly!—*from the steaming locomotive to the greeting-card setting, the ladies' feathered hats and the men's spats.*

*Sid Caesar kicks up in* Little Me.

and few of their cues are arbitrary. The central plot deals not with a romance between a standard hero and heroine, but, rather, with an antiromance between a conniver and an object of ridicule. The basis of Stewart's libretto is actually *style,* and in that respect *Hello, Dolly!*'s story is consonant with its stage production. The show deserved every one of its 2,844 performances. Revived ten years after its opening, a dangerous age, it showed no sign of dating. It seems a classic. It is also a truly funny musical, one of several produced in the sixties. The musical theater was unmistakably graduating from the adolescence of musical comedy.

Matching Neil Simon with composer Cy Coleman and lyricist Carolyn Leigh for the 1962 *Little Me* was inspired. Patrick Dennis's satiric novel, *Little Me,* is a mocked memoir of a been-around actress. In adapting it, the challenge lay in converting the story to one with a starring male role. Simon, along with co-directors Cy Feuer and Bob Fosse, accomplished this by having the lead (Sid Caesar) play all seven men in the actress's life, beginning with her lifelong love, Noble Eggleston, a young aristocrat so rich he attends both Harvard Law School and Yale Medical School.

*Little Me* has one of the best of Broadway musical books. Though it ran for only 247 performances, the show has developed a cult following and is better remembered than many greater hits. Perhaps the eccentricity of its comedy was ahead of its time. The show will doubtless prove revivable because of its unique, smoothly written, and deliriously funny script. The score is also wonderful but, again, the lasting power of a Broadway musical is always determined by its book. Musical scores can endure but they cannot overcome a weak script.

Neil Simon wrote other successful musicals: *Sweet Charity* in

28

1966, and *Promises, Promises* in 1969, and *They're Playing Our Song* in 1978. He will never make a structural breakthrough; he lets the director worry about musicalization, the composer and lyricist worry about song spots. But with *Little Me* he found an exuberance and comic lunacy that he did not often display in even his most successful comedies. The unreality of a musical freed him.

It is hardly coincidence that as examples of excellent books, both *Hello, Dolly!* and *Little Me* are comic musicals. Comedy has much more in common with the musical theater than drama does. It trades in nonsense, in anarchy; the stylization of *Hello, Dolly!* and the madcap humor of *Little Me* lead comfortably into the exaggeration of characters who sing and dance.

Another example of the superb comic librettos written in the sixties is Burt Shevelove and Larry Gelbart's *A Funny Thing Happened on the Way to the Forum* (1962). Written for Phil Silvers, announced for Milton Berle, and opening with Zero Mostel, as its title suggests, it was a tribute to comics. This was a freewheeling compilation of Plautus's Roman comedies, celebrating the classical qualities common to ancient comedy and America's burlesque stage. The combination paid off handsomely. *A Funny Thing Happened on the Way to the Forum* has a rowdy wit about it. It is without doubt the most intellectual of all our musical books, but its brains are applied to showmanship. It is tempting to say that of all the books ever written for the musical theater, *Forum*'s is the least likely to date. No other book succeeded as well in accomplishing its intentions.

The man responsible for the musical book's most dramatic change after Hammerstein's development of the musical play was not a writer but a director. Harold Prince created the musical theater's first production-oriented scripts—the scripts for concept musicals, correlating text with performance. These made no attempt to be ordinary plays. They became drastically shorter as more book weight was shouldered by music, lyrics, and dance. Prince's name has never appeared on a program as an author. Yet he has been the dominating collaborator on every musical he has directed.

Prince's major work began with *Cabaret* (1966). Since the concept musical was still in a formative stage, this was a schizophrenic show. One-half of it was an orthodox musical play whose story unfolded in dramatic scenes with duly integrated book songs. The other half, however, startled and changed Broadway.

As adapted by Joe Masteroff, *Cabaret* was based on John van Druten's play *I Am a Camera* as well as Van Druten's source, several stories by Christopher Isherwood. It is set in Germany in the early 1930s and is about the romances and adventures of a young singer (Sally Bowles) and a writer (Clifford Bradshaw). Prince devised a production concept as a staging background for this story: a Berlin cabaret—the Kit Kat Klub—symbolizing the decadence that spawned Nazism. His production image was drawn from the German expressionist George Grosz's paintings, which the great designer Boris Aronson translated into striking scenery. The settings for *Cabaret*'s book sequences were more conventional and naturalistic.

The parts of *Cabaret* set in the Kit Kat Klub were grotesque and perverse sequences in which the show didn't tell a story or talk about its subject—the Kit Kat Klub *was* its subject. Likewise, the John Kander–Fred Ebb songs for these scenes did not involve characters singing plot to each other. They were presentational numbers, sung

*The difference between a comic musical and a musical comedy is that a musical comedy's story is modeled on a conventional stage comedy and then adapted by inserting cues for songs and dances. It remains essentially dramatic rather than musical, and the dramatic style is farce. A comic musical, on the other hand, creates its own comic style or vision. This style sets the tone for the entire production, even its songs and dances, and sometimes it dictates the show's very form: The elements are integrated by the sense of humor. Little Me is a wonderful example of a comic musical, possibly the funniest made until its time. Although extremely talented contributors were involved—Bob Fosse and Cy Feuer (co-directors), Cy Coleman (music), and Carolyn Leigh (lyrics)—its overall tone was set by the librettist, Neil Simon. Little Me shows an unusually whimsical and even bizarre Simon, freed by the essential unreality of musical theater from the logic that is usually at the center of stage comedy, especially farce. Little Me is truly zany and surreal. It was tailored to Sid Caesar's performing personality, which is why Simon was asked to write it in the first place. He had been one of the comic's television writers and knew by heart the style of Caesar, perhaps the last of our great stage clowns. Like the Patrick Dennis book on which it is based, Little Me mocks the as-told-to memoirs of famous actresses. In the flashback episodes comprising the life of Belle Poitrine ("Poitrine," of course, is French for chest), Caesar plays a variety of men in her life. In the photograph opposite, he is Val du Val, a Maurice Chevalier-like nightclub performer who befriends Belle early in her show business career. Val eventually marries her but dies in a shipboard accident when he loses his memory, forgets how to swim, and drowns.*

*Overleaf: Caesar plays Prince Cherny at the Monte Carlo casino, betting his bankrupt country on one spin of the roulette wheel. Belle, now a famous movie star, changes the Prince's bet from 36 Black to 19 Red. The winning number, of course, is 36 Black and the Prince, in despair, draws a gun. "It's the only way," he says. But he points it at the casino manager. "This is a stick-up."*

by nightclub entertainers. But unlike musical numbers in other shows that used floor shows as excuses for songs, these are the tapestry into which *Cabaret* is woven. Here, the "book" of this musical is not just text but its realization. The door to concept musicals was open.

Prince did not fully capitalize on this development until 1970, with the first of his collaborations with Stephen Sondheim, *Company*. This show was revolutionary. George Furth, the librettist, drew its script from a group of his one-act plays, each presenting a couple coping with marital problems. Prince supervised their assembly into a cinematic script arranged so that the stories intertwined, overlapped, and flashed forward and backward. Ultimately, *Company* has no plot. It studies a group of relationships and, ingeniously, fashions them into a dramatic structure. It also has no chorus of singers or dancers. The "company" of actors does everything. This book exemplified a way of writing specifically to the needs of the musical stage. Had it no songs at all it would still seem a musical, and that is the acid test for any musical's book. Furth's book for *The Act*, written seven years later, shows how great a part Prince played in the writing of *Company*. *The Act* is also a concept musical, but its book has none of the assurance with this new form that *Company* has.

Prince refined his approach to musical books while doing *Follies* and *A Little Night Music* with Sondheim, but his next major book development was for the 1976 *Pacific Overtures*, written by John Weidman with additional material by Hugh Wheeler. Set in 1853, its story begins with the impending and uninvited visit to Japan by Commodore Matthew Perry. This simple situation, the West coming to the East, is expanded to include the corruption and tragedy of a minor samurai, representing the corruption of all Japanese tradition by Western influences. It is constructed to be performed in a way that brings the storytelling into the same dimension as music and dance. *Pacific Overtures* was the first musical that never stopped being musical when involved with plot. For it is written to be presented as if it were a Japanese production—that is, its staging concept—with the rites and mannerisms of Kabuki theater, which have the colors and rhythms and fantasy of musical theater. Like Kabuki, it is performed by an all-male cast, using such devices as The Reciter, stageside musicians, and "invisible" stagehands swathed in black robes. Yet, it does not pretend to *be* Kabuki theater. It is a Broadway musical in the Kabuki style, a musical as the ancient Japanese might do it and that reflected its very subject: the Westernization of Japan.

The show was a predictable Broadway disaster. It was too esoteric and its very idea denied the warmth and exhilaration that audiences demand of musicals. The writing of its book, however, marked the most advanced use of libretto the Broadway musical had yet achieved. There has never been so theatrically conceived a musical script. It may seem unfair to credit it to Prince rather than Wheeler and Weidman, as it may seem unfair to credit him with the books of *Cabaret* and *Company*, but even if Prince never wrote a word, in shaping and dominating these scripts he was most responsible for them. Inherent in the scripts of Prince's shows are their look and performance, the unification of their music with their movement and their textual content—their entire mode of presentation.

The show that most benefited from Prince's developments was *A Chorus Line* (1975), directed by his protégé, Michael Bennett. This fabulously successful musical could never have happened without the progression of concept musicals behind it, starting way back with *West Side Story* and leading through *Fiddler on the Roof, Cabaret, Company,* and *Follies.* Indeed, Bennett, who "conceived, choreographed and directed" *A Chorus Line,* had been *Company*'s choreographer and *Follies*'s co-director. The book of *A Chorus Line* does not have the ingenious structure that *Company*'s book has, nor the conceptual authority of *Pacific Overtures*' book but it organically includes song and dance as a series of pools and undercurrents flowing throughout the body of the show. Taking music and dance, as well as the book, into account—and their roles in the show are written *into* the book—*A Chorus Line* was the most successful of all the concept musicals up to its time. It was a monster hit, and that was because *A Chorus Line* had the excitement and emotional clout that successful Broadway musicals always have and always must. So its book is worth detailed study as an example of the book of a concept musical.

*A Chorus Line*'s book was written by James Kirkwood and Nicholas Dante, though Bennett formed the show in rehearsal before a word of dialogue had even been written. The script was based on tape-recorded conversations between the dancers and Bennett. The book was begun, then, with the production already getting on its feet. The script opens with action: the sound of a rehearsal piano. The lights go up on a dance studio. Zach, a choreographer, is leading twenty-eight dancers at an audition. He chants the directions over and over: "Step, kick, kick, leap, kick, touch ... Again." The orchestra goes to full blast. Brief spurts of dialogue between the dancers tell the audience the basic facts of such rehearsals and what these "gypsies" (chorus dancers) are like as people. A song with the repeated lyric "God, I hope I get it!" is interwoven with the dialogue. The "it" is the jobs they're all after. Among the dancers, Zach personally knows only Cassie.

The "story" doesn't start in earnest until after ten minutes of this dance and dialogue. After eliminating several dancers, Zach tells the sixteen remaining dancers to step up to the "chorus line"—the white adhesive tape on the stage floor. When they are in a row he asks each dancer to give his name and age and to tell a little about himself. While they do so, he moves to the rear of the auditorium, behind the audience. Then, Zach explains that he is looking for a "strong dancing chorus" but thinks it "would be better if I knew something about you." (Nothing of the sort happens at real auditions.) He tells them he is going to hire four males and four females. Mike, asked to begin, talks about his childhood introduction to dancing. This becomes a song and dance for him, "I Can Do That." Bob talks about his past but, behind him, the company resumes the chant they repeated earlier, this time asking, "What should I say?" Bob finally continues his story and then Sheila, who has been established as the wisecracker, the show's comic relief, takes her turn. This becomes another autobiographical song, "At the Ballet," but in the midst of it the others in the company sing individual lines about their own, similar pasts. With Kristine's turn to speak, her memories lead into a duet with her husband, Alan (also auditioning), "Sing!" (which is this character's problem—she can't).

As the individual reminiscences continue, a mini-opera begins. Mark starts telling a childhood story that fades into the company singing "Hello Twelve, Hello Thirteen, Hello Love." That refrain becomes the overall motif and frame for bits and pieces of different

stories centering on adolescence, some of them sung in part and others in full. The overall refrain changes to "Goodbye Twelve, Goodbye Thirteen, Hello Love." The sequence develops musical and narrative counterpoints; one or two sung lines; isolated lines from the dancers. Much of this is in the form of dialogue-lyrics:

> But then when I was fifteen
> The most terrible thing happened
> The Ted Mack Amateur Hour held auditions in St. Louis
> And I didn't hear about it till after they had gone
> And I nearly killed myself.     (*A Chorus Line*)

This is the integrated lyric verging on recitative. The refrain of "Goodbye Twelve" resumes, building against the various counterpointed stories. The entire number takes a full fifth of the show's entire script.

Zach calls the shy Paul out of the line but the young man is reluctant to speak, and so the choreographer excuses him and calls a break. It leaves the stage empty for a personal scene between Zach and Cassie. The book's only "story" as such involves them, and the writing here changes decidedly. What had sounded like actual conversation (and probably was, mostly), now takes on a very "written" sound.

We learn that Cassie had been a featured dancer but was never able to become an actress. "There's nothing left for me to do. So—I'm putting myself back on the line." The authors are reaching for metaphor here. "Line" refers to (a) the chorus line, (b) the line of tape on the stage floor, and (c) sticking one's neck out. Zach may not be looking for featured dancers in the show *he*'s casting, but the makers of *A Chorus Line* want Cassie to have a featured spot and they give it to her at this point with "Music and the Mirror." Since star dancing is in Cassie's past, this may be excusable as her autobiography but the excuse is tenuous. Is she really dancing there in the studio or is she imagining it? In terms of plausibility and overall show logic, this is the weakest moment in *A Chorus Line*.

After Cassie's turn, Zach tries to talk her out of dancing on the chorus line; being a featured dancer, she can't fit into a chorus line because she doesn't dance like everyone else. She insists on trying for a job and exits. Paul is then summoned and Zach talks briefly with him. The young man launches into a long soliloquy about his childhood, his homosexuality, and his humiliating experience as a transvestite in a drag show. He concludes his story by telling how his parents showed up unexpectedly at a performance, and his father accepted him. Paul is the most fleshed-out character in *A Chorus Line*. His speech is extremely moving and it is expertly followed up—capitalizing on the audience's sigh—with the rhythms of the resumed dance rehearsal.

The dancers begin to rehearse a number that will actually be done in the musical the choreographer is casting for. This is called "One" and it is an archetypal Broadway song—a modified bump and grind showpiece for a lady star, on the order of "Hello, Dolly!" Of course it is minus the leading lady. It is also minus the lyrics at the start, as Zach drills the company. The complexity, the repetition, the perfectionism, the uniformity, and the sheer drudgery of chorus dancing is laid out in this exercise: "Hat to the head, step, touch, step, up, step, up, plié, kick, plié, tip the hat, plié, tip the hat,

*Although* A Chorus Line *presumably had no stars, the actors with the larger and more affecting roles were inevitably outstanding. From left to right are Sammy Williams as a vulnerable dancer; Pamela Blair, singer of "Tits and Ass"; Donna McKechnie as a soloist trying to get back into the chorus; Robert LuPone as the choreographer; Kelly Bishop as a tough dancer and comic relief; and Priscilla Lopez, the singer of "What I Did for Love."*

plié . . . right, ball change, kick. Hat, no hat, hat, no hat, hat, hat, hat, hat. Now, let's do the whole combination, facing away from the mirror." When the company turns to *do* this number facing the audience, the rush of emotion crosses the footlights once more. Bennett is a master of such emotional manipulation, and when it is used knowingly there is no talent more powerful.

Zach puts the girl dancers on a line (dancers are treated as children, always called "boys" and "girls"). As they rehearse he gives Cassie a terrible time. What he (and the authors) are really doing is teaching the audience the difference between a featured dancer and a chorus dancer, for everything that Cassie does wrong for a chorus dancer is right for a star. "Don't pop the head," "Too high with the leg," "You're late on the turn," "Dance like everyone else." This is a telling moment but it is marred by a return to the subject of Cassie and Zach's romance ("Why did you leave me?"). While the company dances ghostly, in the manner of *Follies*, she talks of his obsession with show business. The scene is clumsy, exposing the problem of the concept musical's book: Should there actually be a story? If so, how should it be told? (*Pacific Overtures* and *Company* demonstrate how.)

Juxtaposed against Cassie and Zach's exchange is the company's singing of "One." In a few lines between Cassie and Zach, the main point of *A Chorus Line* is made:

ZACH (Pointing to the LINE): Is this what you really want to do?

(THEY both look upstage at the LINE as it slowly comes to life. The music builds.)

CASSIE: Yes . . . I'd be proud to be one of them. They're wonderful.

ZACH: But you're special.

CASSIE: No, we're all special.

It is now time for Zach to make his decisions: Who's to be hired? He breaks the company down into pairs and they do tap dance combinations. Paul slips in the midst and damages his bad knee. His career is probably over. The event is striking and we realize a truth about dancers' dependency on physical luck, but it is used to lead into the show's one irrelevant song, "What I Did for Love." Though this is a good ballad, it is a blatant try by composer Marvin Hamlisch and Edward Kleban for a hit (they got it). It detracts from a score otherwise scrupulous in its devotion to the show's purposes. This song is followed by Zach's announcement of his selections. His speech is brief. He asks those whose names he calls to step forward. These are the ones *eliminated*. (The dramatic device is lifted from the movie *The Red Shoes*.) Cassie is among the chosen. In reality she would not have been. The emotional effect of her being rejected would have been strong—but also perhaps depressing, which is why the decision was made otherwise. As the lights dim, Zach tells the remaining eight dancers that they have jobs.

In Zach's final speech he says the words these dancers have been dreaming of hearing, the answered prayer in the show-business litany: "Rehearsals begin September 22nd. We will rehearse for six weeks with a two-month out-of-town tryout," and so on. The chosen dancers are overcome with emotion. One weeps. Another reaches for the rafters. The moment is quite moving.

*A Chorus Line* is a concept musical, as opposed to a musical play or comedy, because it is based on a staging scheme rather than a narrative story. The Cassie-Zach relationship and the choosing of dancers are its only "plot." It uses music and dance functionally, not decoratively; its book is expressed through the media of music and dance as much as through dialogue. It is not written in episodes but in overlapping layers. Its dialogue and time are not sequential. While the lyrics and songs are integrated and relevant to the story, they are not narratives or "book songs." The music is virtually continuous, and includes snatches of melody and several melodies built into a musical mosaic. Most of all, the difference between such a concept musical and an orthodox one is that the production is built into the script. The book is of the *musical* theater and couldn't possibly be staged without the songs and choreography.

There is no sense demanding that all musicals be written this way. The theater has room for anything that succeeds on its own terms. But there can be little question that *A Chorus Line* made definite a great step forward in the development of scripts unique to the musical theater. Moreover, it was a huge popular success; the concept musical was no longer a special show for people with refined taste.

It would be naive to expect the Broadway musical theater to promptly capitalize on such a breakthrough. Such copies as *Working* and *Runaways* grasped only the surface of *A Chorus Line*. In 1978, Bob Fosse's *Dancin'* followed *A Chorus Line*'s example in creating an entire show during rehearsal before any book was written, but no book ever did develop and it was essentially a dance program, not musical theater. The commercial failure of the less exciting but more significant *Pacific Overtures* did not encourage many to try to understand the theories behind concept musicals. For musicals must justify themselves financially if they are to set practical precedents. The success of so conventional a book show as *Annie* in 1977 created a reactionary mood among producers. Yet, once taken, steps cannot be withdrawn. It was sixteen years between the breakthrough of *Show Boat* and *Oklahoma's* confirmation of its advances. It may be a while before the Prince developments that led to Bennett's work take hold. How can one possibly relate them to the primitive beginnings of musical book writing as established by Guy Bolton for Jerome Kern's Princess Theater musicals? What in the world do *Pacific Overtures* and *A Chorus Line* have to do with the musical comedies of George Abbott and Comden and Green or with Oscar Hammerstein's musical plays? Yet, they *all* have much to do with each other. All librettos, whether featherbrained or virtuoso demonstrations of theatrical know-how, share the basic problems, purposes, and flavor of the Broadway musical. *A Chorus Line* is, after all, a tribute to conventional musical comedy, drawing upon the musical theater's root mythology. If many shows are not revivable because of silly books, remember that the revivable ones owe it to excellent books. The musical theater has never taken one step of progress that didn't relate to books—as it moved from revues to book musical comedies to musical plays to concept musicals. In more ways than one, then, the book is where a musical starts.

# MUSIC

Music is the key to musicals and yet were it strictly the music that epitomized the feel of musicals, we could sit at a piano, play a show's songs, and get the kick we get at the theater. It is a score as it is performed that characterizes our musical theater. In tracing the music's journey from its composer's piano to the stage, perhaps we can understand the process, if not the magic, by which a show sparks to life.

The score for a musical is not merely a series of numbers. Were that so, a musical would be merely a play with songs. In fact, dramatic scenes absorb little more than half the running time of even the most traditional musical. There is almost continuous music, from the overture through the entr'acte (the overture before the second act) to the walkout music played as the audience leaves. Besides the song and dance there is underscoring—music played under dialogue—to lend a musical flavor even when there is no musical number.

A show's "composer" is really only one of its composers. He usually writes just the songs. An army of specialists—an orchestrator, a rehearsal pianist, a dance pianist, a vocal arranger, a musical director, and, in recent times, a sound engineer—completes the score and readies it for performance. Seldom is a Broadway composer master of these various disciplines. At one end of the spectrum is Leonard Bernstein, a fully trained musician schooled in classical music. Irving Berlin, at the other end, could play the piano in only one key—and there have been Broadway composers who couldn't even do that. Most Broadway composers are slightly schooled pianists who can write rudimentary piano arrangements, or lead sheets, notating melody and indicating basic chords for the harmony. Some composers go a step further and write three-staff arrangements. These state the song in the upper staff (or row of lines on which music is written), and then give a complete piano arrangement of the accompaniment in the bottom two staves. It can pretty much state what kind of orchestration the composer has in mind—voicings, harmonies, counterpoint, and so on. Ideally, the composer should do his own orchestrations. It makes the music personal and whole. Some, including Bernstein and Kurt Weill, have worked on their own orchestrations. Gershwin, of course, orchestrated *Porgy and Bess*. But few Broadway composers are trained for it, and most claim that the breakneck production schedule leaves scant time for it or anything else besides replacing songs. Harvey Schmidt, with lyricist Tom Jones, wrote over a

39

*Peter Howard, conductor of* Annie.

hundred songs for *110 in the Shade* before the final choices were made.

The composers begin their work when the first draft of the book is finished. With that in hand, the composer and lyricist make the first of the crucial decisions that will ultimately affect the show's success: They begin to place the songs. That is, they decide at which points, by which characters, and for what purposes the songs will be sung. The process is sometimes referred to as "spotting" the songs. The decisions will determine the flow, the musicality, the very sense of the show.

The composer and lyricist look for dramatic or comic climaxes. They plunder the script for ideas, dialogue, even whole scenes to be converted into musical numbers. They sometimes write songs for characters who don't exist or for situations not in the story. Such inspirations might unnerve the author of the book. However, as the least influential of the show's creators, he has no choice but to rewrite his script to fit their songs.

Having been placed, the songs are then written. Usually, but not always, the music comes first; occasionally lyrics are written first (Hammerstein almost always did this). Some composer-lyricist teams work simultaneously. For example, the lyric for the main part of a song (the chorus) might fit the music perfectly but the lyricist may have thought of a middle part (release) that does not. If the composer can be convinced of the lyric's quality, he will write new music for it. So the songs grow through a process of give-and-take.

The songs written by the composer and lyricist at this stage are rarely, if ever, the final ones. The practice of spotting songs, like so much in the musical theater, is neither consistent nor organized. It is

*The only one of George Gershwin's theater works to benefit from his mastery of orchestration was* Porgy and Bess, *on which he's shown working, in 1935. A composer's own orchestrations are different in kind from those of hired orchestrators, for the entire body of the music—melodies, rhythms, counterpoints, harmonies, instrumental makeup, and texture—springs from the same creative source.*

40

affected by spontaneous problems, immediate needs, even simple ego. When Ethel Merman heard the marvelous "There's No Business Like Show Business" for *Annie Get Your Gun,* she insisted that it be hers to sing. Richard Rodgers, who was co-producing the show with Oscar Hammerstein II, agreed with her but wondered how she could fit into the spot the song had been written for. After all, the number was supposed to be an attempt by the operators of a wild west show to convince Annie Oakley—Merman's role—to join up. Why would Annie sing it?

Dorothy Fields, the musical's librettist, solved the problem. The operators of the show, she suggested, would sing the first chorus and then Merman would say, "You mean—?" and proceed to do the rest of the number. Berlin translated this into the lyric, "There's no business like show business/If you tell me it's so." Even as late as 1946, then, when musicals were presumably growing up, such stuff and nonsense was common. In fact, stars still demand good songs for themselves or deny them to others. So, song spotting is not always reasonable. Moreover, the most unreasonable spot can be overwhelmingly successful.

If a director is involved with a musical early on, he too will work on song placement. With the growing importance of the director in musical theater, this initial involvement is becoming common. Indeed, the director is usually the ultimate judge of which songs go where.

Once these songs are approved by the director (assuming that the show has been sold to a producer), the composer tape-records a piano version of the score for the orchestrator, the choreographer

*Written simply to keep the audience occupied during a scene change in* Annie Get Your Gun, *"There's No Business Like Show Business" became the Broadway musical's anthem.*

*Because the making of a musical is so complex, its different parts are rehearsed in different places and often not seen by all the contributors until finished. Here, Cy Feuer (the co-producer, right) and Abe Burrows (the director) watch a rehearsal of Bob Fosse's number "Coffee Break" for* How to Succeed in Business Without Really Trying.

and dance pianist, the set designer, and the costumer—the latter two so that their work can reflect the show's tone.

Then the choreographer and dance pianist go to work. The dance pianist accompanies the choreographer at dance rehearsals. When the dance steps and tempos are settled, he puts the dance music together. He works from the composer's melodies and does not write new ones unless the composer is unusually liberal. So it is the choreography that determines the dance music rather than, as in classical ballet, the other way around. This music is called a "dance music arrangement," an arrangement of the show's melodies for the dances.

The dance pianist is a middleman between the composer and the choreographer. If he favors the composer, he protects the score's integrity while fitting it to the evolving dances. If his allegiance to the choreographer is greater (often the case when the choreographer is also the director), he may distort the composer's intentions to accommodate developments at dance rehearsal. Unless the composer keeps a wary eye on this process, he may find a theme of his overextended, a mood misunderstood, a tempo or rhythm changed.

Broadway dances have, on occasion, been choreographed to original, prewritten scores. Those composers competent to write their own dance music claim there just isn't time to do it in the pell-mell of preparation, but that isn't the time to do it anyhow. Dance music could be composed before rehearsals begin. Agnes de Mille usually asked for and was given original ballet scores for her shows, as did Jerome Robbins. Bernstein composed most of the dance music for *West Side Story,* and Sondheim some for *Anyone Can Whistle.* Jule Styne wrote the "Keystone Kops Ballet" for *High Button Shoes.* When a choreographer can demand it, a composer *will* find the time. Michael Bennett had Marvin Hamlisch work that way on *A Chorus Line*, and had Billy Goldenberg do it for *Ballroom.* Their work was worth the effort; these shows had unusually good dance music. But they are the exceptions. Broadway dance music is usually a hodgepodge of melodic snatches from a score.

When the dance music is arranged to fit the final choreography, it is ready for orchestration. This is an awesome job. The orchestrator will eventually turn all of the show's music from piano to orchestral scoring. He must be able to experiment with and select all the combinations of instruments in his imagination. He must know every instrument's capability and how to write for it. He plays a crucial role in the making of a musical, for he, more than anyone else in a show's musical family, is responsible for the way the music sounds to the audience. And the moment the company of a rehearsing musical hears its orchestra for the first time is one of the great thrills of show making.

Broadway orchestrators work under an absurd handicap: They are obligated to employ the precise number of musicians, specified

*Ballet and modern dance are choreographed to existing music. But in the musical theater, dance music is extemporized from tunes in the show while the choreography is being created. That is why most Broadway dance music is so shallow. Agnes de Mille, here rehearsing her dancers for* 110 in the Shade, *was the rare choreographer who regularly insisted on pre-composed dance music.*

in the musicians' union contract, in each theater—twenty-six in the Imperial Theater, twenty in the Alvin, and so on. These are minimum figures, but producers are not inclined to spend for more. The real problem arises when a composer or orchestrator wants a smaller sound. The only solution is to use the desired number of musicians while paying the required others to be idle. It has been done, but producers don't like it.

However, the orchestrator is free to write for any instruments he chooses, and in this his musicianship and imagination are challenged. If he is interested in the music he can find harmonies and sounds the composer never thought of. If he is bored or tired, he may merely grind out yet another Broadway-sounding score. Many theater orchestrators take a workaday attitude toward their assignments because they don't respect the music they are working on. Yet a sensitive and sympathetic orchestrator can be a composer's alter ego, as Robert Russell Bennett was for Richard Rodgers and Jonathan Tunick for Stephen Sondheim. Even in such cases, however, the result is only an approximation of what the composer might have done for himself.

The songs cannot be orchestrated until they've been routined and rehearsed. Routining is the actual conversion of a song into performance. It is the laying out of how a song is sung; the number of people to sing it and the number of choruses to be sung; whether it should be fast or slow, loud or soft; what key it will be sung in; if, when, and how to use a chorus behind the singer; if there should be dialogue inside the song; how to voice the chords (that is, writing the harmonies for the chorus if it is not to sing in unison)—and so on. If the composer does not voice the chords, a vocal arranger will. Sometimes, a musical number so dominates a scene—a finale, for example—that the entire sequence, including dialogue, is routined.

46

*Jerome Robbins's "Keystone Kops Ballet" for* High Button Shoes *established the comic ballet on Broadway. At the time (1947), ballets were considered serious business, but Robbins showed that dancing could be fun. This ballet, which included the comic mugging of Phil Silvers, became so renowned that thirty years later, when Gower Champion was staging a musical about Mack Sennett (Mack and Mabel), he didn't dare show any Keystone Kops, though they were the first thing anyone thought of when the subject of Sennett came up. Champion just didn't want to remind anyone of Robbins's famous ballet, and certainly didn't want any comparisons with it. You couldn't blame him, for it has remained one of the brightest dances from any Broadway musical.*

Since the orchestrator's fee—a sizable item in a musical's budget—depends on how soon he can begin and how fast he can finish, the director tries to keep the songs routined and rehearsed one step ahead of the orchestrator. In addition, the score for each musician in the pit band is copied by hand—a laborious task— rather than printed. If song changes and slow rehearsals force the orchestrator to go out of town with a show, and he and the copyists end up working around the clock, orchestration can triple in cost, to as much as $100,000 in 1977.

Underscoring is the music played beneath dialogue and between scenes to accent mood and to provide continuity. It is usually left for last. Before microphones came into use, only light instruments—strings or flutes—could be played while actors were speaking or else their lines would be inaudible. Choreographer-directors are especially music-conscious and want continuous music. Amplification of the voices has made that possible. Underscoring has grown much more elaborate, especially when musicals have many scene changes. Then, this music is used to cover the din and must be precisely timed.

Underscoring is written by the composer if he is able and willing; it is not as challenging as writing original dance music or doing the orchestration. Pieces of the songs are more apt to be used than original themes. More often than not it is the hard-working dance pianist who does it. Usually the orchestration of the underscoring is postponed while a show is on the road. The composer or dance pianist will meanwhile improvise it for one or two pit musicians to play.

The quality of the orchestra is naturally of critical importance. The musicians who are to play in New York are hired by a "contrac-

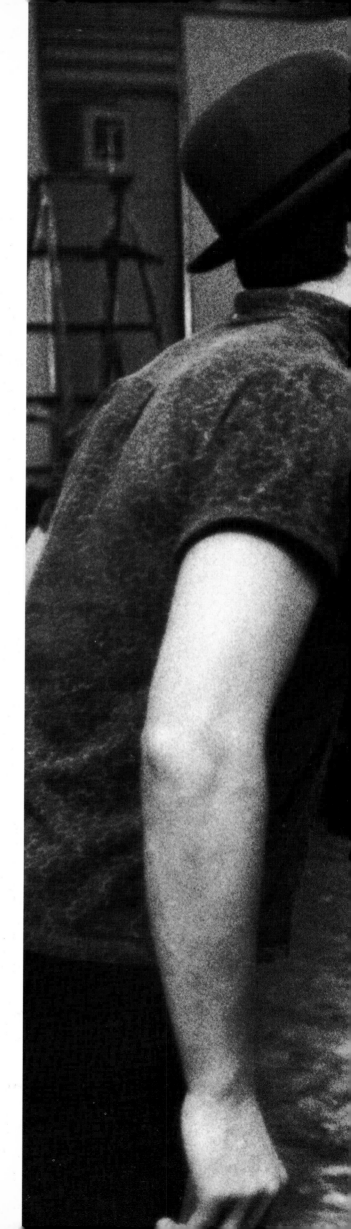

tor" with the show's management, though the more experienced composers take a hand in the selection. When the score is difficult, good instrumentalists can make the difference between finesse and chaos. New York's first-class pit musicians are at a premium and there is fierce competition over them.

The pit musicians are led by a musical director who, despite his title, is not the show's musical director. (That role is really the composer's.) He is a conductor. Yet he too is an important figure because he is the only member of a show's musical team who is present at every performance and who is an active participant in the daily running of the show. It is the musical director who keeps the musicians and singers in balance and up to standard; he who keeps the tempos right—the musicians synchronized with the singers and dancers; he who makes sure numbers don't slow down or (more likely) speed up as the show goes into a long run.

Finally, there is the sound engineer. When musicals introduced microphones and sound amplification in the late forties, an audio engineer was added to the theater personnel. By the time of rock musicals, composers were seeking to emulate the fabulous tricks of studio engineering that had been developed by the pop-record industry. Burt Bacharach, a composer whose experience and success had been with pop records and movie music, hoped to bring to the theater their tricks of over-dubbing, sound mixing, and isolated amplification when he did *Promises, Promises* in 1968. Bacharach brought a first-rate recording engineer into the theater along with a sound-mixing console. The engineer was placed in the midst of the audience at the rear of the house and has since become a familiar sight in theaters.

Audio engineering can lead to abuses in the theater. There have been shows—*Follies*, *A Chorus Line*, *The Act*—that used prerecorded tapes while the actors synchronized their lips to the recordings. This was necessary for hectic numbers in which the actors have to sing and dance simultaneously. However, prerecording can destroy the most important quality of the theater: human presence.

Sound engineers have vastly improved amplification in the theater. Unamplified voices are wonderful in principle but cavernous theaters may lose them, causing audiences in the balcony to miss much of a show. The primitive amplification of the forties created an artificial-sounding metallic timbre and sometimes appeared to separate an actor from his voice. Today, most sound engineers are influenced by directors to conform their work to a particular theater's needs. The result usually has been an evenly balanced sound that simulates presence while boosting audibility for those in the furthest reaches of a theater.

So, creating and producing a musical's music is a process involving a large team of talented professionals. The wonder is that, despite their differences in training and function, all these people can work together toward a common goal. Their combined efforts create the musical theater's music, with its blessedly exhilarating effect. The composer, who sets this elaborate process in motion as he writes the tunes at his piano, might well have imagined at the outset a full-fledged Broadway musical dancing on his keyboard.

*Overleaf: Leonard Bernstein, composer of* West Side Story, *drills the women's singing chorus and co-star Carol Lawrence (leaning on the piano) accompanied by twenty-seven-year-old Stephen Sondheim.*

# LYRICS

Weary of repeated references to "Ol' Man River" being Jerome Kern's song, the wife of Oscar Hammerstein II finally said that Kern hadn't written "Ol' Man River" at all. Kern wrote "Da-da-da-da," she said. "Oscar Hammerstein wrote 'Ol' Man River.'"

A song is music *and* lyrics. Without words, it would be only a melody. Lyrics give the music expression and body. They identify it, they make it singable, they make it whole. They make it a song.

> Once I laughed when I heard you saying
> That I'd be playing solitaire,
> Uneasy in my easy chair.
> It never entered my mind.  (*Higher and Higher*)

Richard Rodgers's melody for this song, "It Never Entered My Mind"—from the 1940 *Higher and Higher*—is one of his most exquisite. There are doubtless many lyrics that might have been written to it and served it well. But in this lyric of Lorenz Hart, the words are so mated to the music that one cannot say which better serves which. Each complements the other, by now each *sounds* like the other. Examining Hart's technique, we find the internal rhyming of "playing" with "saying" (an internal rhyme occurs within rather than at the end of a line and is not emphasized by a musical pause); the contrasting of "uneasy" with "easy chair"; the imagery of a lonely game of solitaire; the start of the song with a warning, "Once"; and the final, ironic use of a lighthearted expression, "It never entered my mind." These are devices well known to lyricists. But Hart's use of them in this perfect song is so fine that we don't notice them as devices. His imagination and technique serve the greater purpose of a lyric: conveying a thought, a feeling, and even a story within the restricted form of a song.

In the modern musical theater, more is demanded of lyrics. They should be relevant to the plot, and even further it; they should be consistent with the character who is singing; they should be integrated with a show's style and structure. Yet most theater lyrics have been merely serviceable and many are not even technically adept. Such work is tolerated because, of the basic elements in a musical—the book, the music, the lyrics—the lyrics are the least crucial to success. The book is the basis of the show's existence. The music is what makes it a musical. If both of these are strong, then even mediocre lyrics can pass because a musical presents such a barrage of entertainment (songs, lyrics, dances, sets, costumes) that

*In a crowning moment from* My Fair Lady, *Rex Harrison, as the exultant Professor Higgins, accepts the acclaim of his household staff and his colleague Colonel Pickering (Robert Coote) after successfully passing off the former flower girl, Eliza Doolittle, at a society ball. One would think this an obvious place for a song but a lyricist less gifted than Lerner might not have chosen to write directly (which is always the best way for a lyric),* "You Did It."

most audiences can't grasp the lyrics on first hearing anyhow. No show ever failed because of poor lyrics.

Yet there could be no musical theater without lyrics. They make the music sensible. They are the link between the book and the music. Dialogue, after all, is as different from music as air is from water. Having musical and verbal qualities, lyrics provide a common denominator for the two. They make the meeting of dialogue with music a harmonious one, for in their very form and symmetry, their rhyme and rhythm, lyrics approach the quality of music. They are *lyrical.*

When lyrics are mundane, they simply present the music. When they are well made, they can also be appreciated in themselves, providing two pleasures for the price of a song. But when they are theatrically conceived, they can elevate the entire song into a dramatic experience.

An example of such theater making occurs in *My Fair Lady.* Professor Henry Higgins, intent on proving that only poor speech separates commoners from the elite, has coached Eliza Doolittle in elocution for weeks, eliminating her Cockney accent. Trying to pass her off as a duchess, he and his friend Colonel Pickering take Eliza to a grand ball where she not only speaks high English but actually convinces Higgins's rival phonetician that she is a princess. Arriving home, Higgins is triumphant and Pickering bursts into song:

Tonight, old man, you did it!
You did it! You did it!
You said that you would do it,
And indeed you did.
I thought that you would rue it;
I doubted you'd do it.
But now I must admit it
That succeed you did.          (*My Fair Lady*)

As much as Frederick Loewe's music—*more* so, I think—Alan Jay Lerner's lyrics make this moment because they give it not just theatrical size and contagious glee but also dramatic complexity. The men burst into song because they are, well, bursting with pride. The repeated short phrases, "did it," "rue it," "do it," "admit it," convey their excitement. But after first sharing this exultation, we are angered by it, for *Eliza* is the one who did it and she isn't even singing. We realize that these men are egotistical and insensitive. The story's sympathies are shifting, from Higgins to Eliza, and Lerner has made the song a pivot for that shift. Because of his lyrics we grasp the situation in a musically heightened way.

In making the first choice of where to put a song in a show the lyricist must consider who is singing, why is he singing, what is he saying, and what is the character's style of speaking and thinking? Stephen Sondheim has criticized his own lyric for *West Side Story*'s "I Feel Pretty" as being too clever for Maria. According to Sondheim, the character, a teenager from New York's slum streets, would never have said, "It's alarming how charming I feel," and would hardly have used an internal rhyme. Sondheim may be too hard on himself—all characters use rhymes in lyrics and we accept expressions in a song that we wouldn't accept when spoken—but his point is correct. She *wouldn't* talk that way.

If a number is to be comic, it must of course deliver the punch line, ideally serving it up at the end of the song (if the punch line comes at the start, the audience ignores the rest of the lyric). It must grasp the kernel of the comic situation and then play with the elements that make it funny.

Having first concentrated on the contribution of the lyric to the show, the story, and the character, the lyricist must then fit it to the music or, if writing before the music is composed, write with music in mind. This calls in the craft of lyric writing and it is a very strict one. Writing to Sir Arthur Sullivan's music, W. S. Gilbert established the discipline that Broadway's lyricists follow. The Savoy operas set out standards of prosody (the faithful matching of pronunciation and accent to musical time values), rhyming, singability, verbal dexterity, literacy, and felicity of expression. The prosody must be immaculate and the rhymes accurate. The use of waste words (*"And, you will note,*/There's a lump in my throat") or artificial abbreviations ("'cause") is cheating. Words can't be wrongly accented or stretched to follow a beat. Archaic or obscure pronunciations are forbidden. Because the singer has to be considered, open sounds ("ah") rather than closed ones ("em") should land on high or low notes; consonants are difficult to hold on sustained notes. Words should be separable, especially in a fast song ("half from," sung quickly, becomes "haffrum"). Rhyming is a science in itself. If repeated consonants precede final sounds they create not rhymes but repeats, or "identities" ("solution" and "condition"). There are "masculine" and "feminine" rhymes. A masculine rhyme has a final accented syllable, for example "hope" and "grope." It is used to "put a button" on a melody, to be strong and final ("I'm in love with a wonderful *guy*"). A feminine rhyme is multisyllabic and is not accented on the last syllable. It is used to create a soft, transitional feeling ("Your looks are laughable, unphotographable").

W. S. Gilbert's lyrics set our theater's style of cleverness:

Ever willing
  To be wooing,
We were billing—
  We were cooing;
When I merely
  From him parted,
We were nearly
  Broken-hearted—
When in sequel
  Reunited,
We were equal-
  Ly delighted.     (*The Gondoliers*)

Gilbert made such virtuosity and wit the hallmarks of stage lyrics and if he had any heir on the American stage, it was Cole Porter.

Let's throw away anxiety, let's quite forget propriety,
Respectable society, the rector and his piety,
And contemplate l'amour in all its infinite variety,
My dear, let's talk about love.     (*Let's Face It*)

Celebrated as Porter is for such verbal pyrotechnics, he is just as noted for romance:

*Donald Oenslager's Art Deco liner setting for Cole Porter's* Anything Goes *seems as quintessentially thirties as the waving chorines. The show included "You're the Top," "I Get a Kick Out of You," "All Through the Night," "Blow, Gabriel, Blow," and the title song. Ever after this dazzling score, Porter complained, critics would review his show songs as "not being up to his usual standard."*

Flying too high with some guy in the sky
Is my idea of nothing to do,
Yet I get a kick out of you.     (*Anything Goes*)

The drama contained in these lines is abetted by rhyme. There are six "i" sounds in those first two lines (including the wrongly accented "idea") and they frame the melody, set the mood. Porter was a master of such purposeful rhyming, using it elsewhere to underline his dramatic rhythms ("Do do that voodoo that you do so well"). But he also knew when to be simple:

So good-bye, dear, and amen.
Here's hoping we meet now and then.
It was great fun,
But it was just one of those things.     (*Jubilee*)

That's the Porter we're crazy about. Porter's work, with its meeting of thirties' sophistication, literacy (it was in style then), and technical mastery, was emulated by a generation of lyricists. Sometimes, Porter went too far:

When ev'ry night the set that's smart is
Intruding in nudist parties
In studios,
Anything goes!     (*Anything Goes*)

Rhyming "intruding," "nudist," and "studios" is marvelous but the song moves at such a clip that the words can hardly be comprehended. These lyrics are *too* clever, too "lyric-y."

It might seem odd to bring up Oscar Hammerstein's lyrics at this point since they are so contrastingly homespun, but content is only one aspect of song lyrics. Hammerstein was as smart a technician as Porter and used rhyme just as purposefully. But where

56

Porter wanted internal rhymes noticed, either for rhythm's or rhyme's sake or just for their own sake, Hammerstein camouflaged them for a different purpose. He wanted his inside rhymes to create a subtle musicality in support of Richard Rodgers's music, which was more rhapsodic, more flowing, and less rhythmic than Porter's. Here is an example of such rhyming in Hammerstein's verse for "People Will Say We're in Love" from *Oklahoma!* The end rhymes create form because they are followed by pauses and so are noticeable, while the internal rhymes (in italics) create musical texture because they are hidden:

> Why do they *think* up stories that *link* my name with yours?
> Why do the *neigh*bors gossip all *day* behind their doors?
> I have a *way* to prove what they *say* is quite untrue;
> Here is the *gist*, a practical *list* of "don'ts" for you.　　(*Oklahoma!*)

Hammerstein knew this was to be a list song (one whose lyrics give a series of examples) and even said so in his lyric. His thoughts are saccharine, but, except for "gist" (of what?), these are excellent examples of internal rhymes that are ingenious without being senseless, and they are not showy. We will find that *too* many good lyricists want their tricks noticed. Sometimes we enjoy the fun. Other times we tire of its triviality.

Songs do not always call for rhymes. In Lerner's wonderful "I Talk to the Trees" from *Paint Your Wagon*, the only true rhyme comes on the final line:

*Monarchs of a mythical land, Melville Cooper and Mary Boland celebrate their silver anniversary in Cole Porter's 1935* Jubilee, *just as the King and Queen of England had recently celebrated theirs. Porter wrote this show while on an around-the-world trip with Moss Hart. Nobody had more fun writing musicals.*

I talk to the trees,
But they don't listen to me.
I talk to the stars,
But they never hear me.
The breeze hasn't time
To stop and hear what I say.
I talk to them all in vain.
But suddenly my words
Reach someone else's ear;
Touch someone else's heartstrings, too.
I tell you my dreams
And while you're list'ning to me,
I suddenly see them come true.        (*Paint Your Wagon*)

Lyric writing was almost as virginal a territory at the start of our musical theater as composing was. Jerome Kern worked with many lyricists who clung to the ornate expressions of operetta. Otto Harbach, for example, used words like "forsooth" (in "Yesterdays") and "chaff" (in "Smoke Gets in Your Eyes"). In P. G. Wodehouse, however, Kern had found a lyricist for a new kind of song writing:

But along came Bill,
Who's not the type at all,
You'd meet him on the street and never notice him;
His form and face, his manly grace
Is not the kind that you would find in a statue.        (*Show Boat*)

These are not exemplary lyrics. "Form and face" and "manly grace" are each awkwardly sung to notes played in rapid succession. The first phrase, having three words, makes for uncomfortable singing; "manly grace" is better. "That you" is wrongly accented not only for the sake of a musical beat but to rhyme with "statue," but they rhyme only if you pronounce "statue" as "stat-yew." Still, for 1927 Wodehouse's lyric was refreshingly colloquial and it presented a neat solution to a lyric-writing problem. Facing up to three extra notes of Kern's—and Kern was never a composer to change *anything* to accommodate a lyricist—Wodehouse wrote:

I love him
Because he's, I don't know,
Because he's just my Bill.        (*Show Boat*)

The "I don't know" not only fills Kern's notes but is the key to the lyric's success. It turns the song conversational and frank and reveals its singer as helplessly in love. "Bill" was interpolated into *Show Boat* but its straightforwardness is consistent with the other lyrics by Hammerstein.

The informal style of "Bill" presents a second strain in our musical theater's lyrics and perhaps a more American one. For instead of deriving from the cool wit of the British Gilbert, it is drawn from our own warm and sunny Stephen Foster. Foster was surely the first of the great American songwriters. In his brief career (he died in 1864 at thirty-eight), he wrote the music and lyrics for folklike songs of heartbreaking simplicity.

Weep no more, my lady,
Oh! weep no more today!

We will sing one song for the old Kentucky home,
For the old Kentucky home, far away.

These beautiful words of "My Old Kentucky Home" and their melody create virtually an art song. At his death, Stephen Foster left a total estate of thirty-eight cents in his pocket, and these words scribbled on a piece of paper: "Dear friends and gentle hearts." Probably for a song, the words were indeed a legacy, for they could very well have been written later by either Berlin or Hammerstein. Hammerstein especially admired the simple quality in Irving Berlin's lyrics and, as you might expect, Foster was Berlin's idol.

Such heartfelt lyrics led to a rich body of song, less Continental than American. In later years, lyricists tried to combine these two historical strains. One who particularly followed the Foster-Berlin-Hammerstein tradition was Jerry Herman:

We'll join the Astors
At Tony Pastor's
And this I'm positive of:
That we won't come home,
That we won't come home,
No, we won't come home until we fall in love!     (*Hello, Dolly!*)

There is no time limit on such straight, uncomplicated lyrics. These (from "Put On Your Sunday Clothes" in *Hello, Dolly!*) are set to a rather ambitious musical sequence, so if the word approach is old-fashioned, the theatrical intentions are modern.

Like Porter, Lorenz Hart belonged to the school of lyric writing established by Gilbert. It can be said with little risk of challenge that Porter and Hart were the supreme lyricists of the American musical theater, at least as it existed in their day. Hart was twenty-three when he teamed up with Richard Rodgers in 1918, and but for trivial exceptions he never worked with anyone else. His lyrics were tender, witty, sophisticated, original, and word-sensitive. To implement his feelings, he had the necessary technique: perfect choices of simple words. They were also devised to be comfortably sung:

Looking through the window you
Can see a distant steeple:
Not a sign of people,
Who wants people?     (*On Your Toes*)

This is beautiful because it is romantic and straight and *musical*. Given the comic possibilities of a faster song, Hart's technique could be dazzling:

The furtive sigh,
The blackened eye,
The words "I'll love you till the day I die,"
The self-deception that believes the lie—
I wish I were in love again.     (*Babes in Arms*)

In his earlier works, Hart would write two and even three verses (introductions) before as well as in the middle of a song. In Hart's time, lyricists traditionally showed off their virtuosity in the verses. Late in his career Hart took to writing many choruses. Surely that was because of changing song-writing fashions and a developed show wisdom (you don't sing a verse for an encore). But it also reflected the turn of his life, for a verse only introduces a subject. The chorus gets to the point and expresses feelings. As he grew older, Hart held in less and let out more unhappiness, so he wrote more choruses. His pain finally ended in 1943, when he died at forty-eight of alcoholism and despair.

Ira Gershwin enjoyed the ingenious rhyme too, but the lyrics for his ballads weren't as neurotic, let's say lovelorn, as Hart's. Reflecting his brother's confidence, Ira's lyrics always assumed that he would get the girl. There was no anticipation of being rejected in "Embraceable You" or "I've Got a Crush on You" or "Funny Face." Even his wistful "The Man I Love" wondered *who* would come along rather than, as Hart would have wondered, whether *anyone* would ever come along.

Ira Gershwin had a knack for setting solid, *landing* words to such joyous songs his brother was writing as "Strike Up the Band," "Fascinating Rhythm," and this example from "Love Is Sweeping the Country":

> Each girl and boy alike,
> Sharing joy alike,
> Feels that passion'll
> Soon be national.     (*Of Thee I Sing*)

"Boy," "joy," "passion'll," "national"—these are meaty rhymes. Gershwin was also fascinated with specific song problems. It wasn't ignorance of grammar that led to "I Got Rhythm." It was the daringly deliberate corniness of his brother's song (such as the music for the final lines, "Who could ask for anything more? Who could ask for anything more?"). "*I've* got rhythm" would have been all wrong for this song. Besides, Ira Gershwin had impish fun with lyric writing. The most celebrated example of this is his lyric for "'S Wonderful," with its repeated, invented contractions, "'s awful nice, 's paradise," and so on. There are many examples of Ira's inventing playful lyrics that are neither verse, prose, nor Gilbertian patter:

*Opening on the night after Christmas, 1931,* Of Thee I Sing *was George Gershwin's biggest hit. This was the first musical to win the Pulitzer Prize for Drama. But apparently the judges were so confused about having to take a musical seriously that they gave the award only to the librettists, George S. Kaufman and Morrie Ryskind, and not to George and Ira Gershwin.*

*A sexy and unbelievably electrifying Ethel Merman flashed to stardom at twenty-one singing "I Got Rhythm" in Gershwin's* Girl Crazy. *It was as nervy for lyricist Ira Gershwin to write "I got rhythm" as it was for his brother to compose so brazenly simple a tune. Merman's style of performance was as direct as the song.*

I know, know, know
What a beau, beau, beau
Should do, Baby;
So don't, don't, don't
Say it won't, won't, won't
Come true, Baby.  (*Oh, Kay*)

Perhaps all the "baby's" and "sweetie pie's" in Ira Gershwin's lyrics have come to characterize his work but they also characterize the *Broadway* feeling of his era.

E.Y. ("Yip") Harburg was Ira Gershwin's protégé, but though he began writing for the theater in 1929, wrote the classic "Brother, Can You Spare a Dime?," and did the marvelous lyrics for *The Wizard of Oz*, Harburg had no hit show until the 1944 *Bloomer Girl*. In 1947 he came up with his only other major success, the classic *Finian's Rainbow* with Burton Lane. Aside from the mildly successful *Jamaica*, Harburg's other shows did not do very well.

*Finian's Rainbow* made Yip Harburg's reputation. Its lyrics are so often cited as models by later generations of Broadway lyricists that he might be considered the most influential of all the masters. This is because he was one of the first to write lyrics to character and managed to combine our best lyric-writing traditions: the wit of Hart and Porter, the warmth of Hammerstein, the directness of Berlin, the spirit of Ira Gershwin. Working to Lane's rich *Finian* score, Harburg came up with a gimmick lyric that only Ira Gershwin could have so unself-consciously exploited:

*In* Lady in the Dark, *opposite Gertrude Lawrence, Victor Mature played a movie star who was "a precious amalgam of Frank Merriwell, Anthony Eden and Lancelot." Mature's song to Lawrence was the mock-ardent "This Is New," but one wonders whether Ira Gershwin's lyric was self-mocking or just plain overdone:*

> *"Head to toe*
> *You've got me so I'm spellbound*
> *I don't know*
> *If I'm heaven or hell-bound."*

> Thou'rt so adorish,
> Toujours l'amourish,
> I'm so cherchez la femme.
> Why should I vanquish, relinquish, resish,
> When I simply relish this swellish condish?    (*Finian's Rainbow*)

One could quarrel—"*vanquish*" *what*? But as a style of speaking for a leprechaun, this lyric is positively ingenious and it is a very early (1947) example of a character lyric. Again, the leprechaun speaks (in the anthem to the faithless, "When I'm Not Near the Girl I Love"):

> My heart's in a pickle,
> It's constantly fickle,
> And not too partickle, I fear.    (*Finian's Rainbow*)

Such paradoxical usages as "constant" modifying "fickleness" are irresistible. In such songs, Harburg's musical sense is impeccable, his poetry delightful, and his technique absolute. However, he can also be maddeningly inconsistent and his lyrics for other shows are not so neatly written.

As Harburg was influenced by Ira Gershwin, Howard Dietz was influenced by Hart. Yet Dietz wasn't just a lesser Hart. He had a special knack for inventing staging ideas with his lyrics, as in "Triplets":

> We do ev'rything alike—
> We look alike, we dress alike,
> We walk alike, we talk alike,
> And what is more we hate each other very much.
> We hate our folks,
> We're sick of jokes
> On what an art it is to tell us apart.    (*Between the Devil*)

62

Collaborating almost exclusively with Arthur Schwartz, Dietz wrote many love songs. Coming from such a witty man, they are curiously ardent—"You and the Night and the Music," "I See Your Face Before Me," and so on. A Dietz-Schwartz ballad that was more subdued, and consequently more affecting, was

> Dancing in the dark,
> Till the tune ends,
> We're dancing in the dark
> And it soon ends;
> We're waltzing in the wonder of why we're here,
> Time hurries by,
> We're here and gone.     (*The Band Wagon*)

This song is carried by the opening image of dancing in the dark. Alliteration is a sound-repetition device that usually only calls attention to itself. This lyric uses it repeatedly—first the title, then "till the tune ends," and finally "waltzing in the wonder of why we're here"—and in a rare, purposeful way. In other songs, Dietz uses technical devices in similarly wise ways:

> No one knows better than I myself,
> I'm by myself alone.     (*Between the Devil*)

As in Porter's "I Get a Kick Out of You," these multiple "i" sounds ("I myself, I'm by myself") are not merely for rhyme's sake. They underline the chromatic pattern on which Schwartz constructed and ultimately resolved "By Myself."

Howard Dietz had his success with revues and had little interest in relevant, plot-justified, or character lyrics. This left him behind when the theater moved away from revues and toward book musicals. We can sympathize with such lyricists. Writing to character and

*Though the device of offstage singers was made popular by* Promises, Promises *in 1968, as far back as 1931 Dietz and Schwartz's* The Band Wagon *featured such a number. It was the sensuous "Dancing in the Dark," featuring Tilly Losch and the Albertina Rasch dancers on a mirrored, revolving stage.*

plot means giving up wit, unless your show happens to be about some smart set. Otherwise, the wit is the lyricist's rather than the character's. Sophisticated and literate lyrics are among the great joys of musical comedy. Would we even have *wanted* Hart or Porter to write for character and deny their wit? But, except in the dwindling number of revues, by the fifties the musical theater had little room for clever subject matter.

We must not confuse character lyrics with relevant (or "integrated") lyrics. Relevant lyrics refer to and sometimes advance the plot. Hammerstein had originated them in *Show Boat*. Character lyrics are written in the conversational style of the character singing them. Hammerstein established them too. His contributions to lyric-writing progress are simply prodigious. It was his work for *South Pacific* that settled the trend to character lyrics. The songs for the aristocratic planter, Émile de Becque, are formal ("Some Enchanted Evening," "This Nearly Was Mine"). Those for the small-town Nellie Forbush are energetic and down-to-earth ("Honey Bun," "I'm in Love with a Wonderful Guy," "I'm Gonna Wash That Man Right Outa My Hair"). The chorus songs for the marines are manly ("Bloody Mary," "There Is Nothing Like a Dame"). These songs suggest that Hammerstein had stereotypes rather than specific characters in mind, but it was new to tailor songs this way.

Writing lyrics to character soon was standard Broadway practice. Dorothy Fields, who became Arthur Schwartz's partner when Dietz left for Hollywood, had a natural inclination to write character lyrics because she was a librettist-lyricist. Her work was influenced by Hammerstein, but it tended to be drier, and so a bit easier to swallow. She was at her best when writing affirmative, muscular lyrics, using colloquial speech. She was less concerned than her colleagues with fancy rhymes, though she certainly was precise. Her ear for patterns of speech, among all classes, made character lyrics come more easily to her than to other lyricists. In the 1951 *A Tree Grows in Brooklyn*, Fields wrote these for Cissy, a none-too-bright but lusty and appealing lady:

> He had respect and feeling
> All our married life.
> Just the thought that maybe he'd hurt me
> Cut him like a knife.
> So he never mentioned that
> He had another wife.
> He had refinement.     (*A Tree Grows in Brooklyn*)

These are in the character's style. The jokes are on her, so they make her lovable, and they are jokes that *land* (that is, they work). When Dorothy Fields wrote for ordinary people like Cissy, the people sounded not only legitimate but as if she liked them.

> The minute you walked in the joint
> I could see you were a man of distinction,
> A real big spender.     (*Sweet Charity*)

This was Fields writing, at sixty, for the dance hall hostesses in *Sweet Charity*. She never let slang developments pass her by. Set to Cy Coleman's music, these words are colloquial and on the nose as well as intelligible (as lyrics *must* be). They also support the melody, giving fat sounds for the music's big beats—"walked," "joint," "man," "dis-*tinc*-tion," and "real," "big," "spender." These are words we remember. *Why* do we remember one lyric rather than another? Not only because of repeated hearings. We've heard "Autumn in New York" dozens of times without learning the words. A lyric that leads gracefully from line to line, holding to a thought and expressing it succinctly while being sympathetic with the music, is the lyric that sticks. Managing all that and writing to character at the same time became a tougher challenge than the verbal fireworks that occupied Hart and Porter.

Once established, the character lyric took such firm hold that those without a knack for it got into trouble. A striking example of this is the career of Betty Comden and Adolph Green. They made their stage-writing debut with *On the Town* in 1944, as the second generation of musical comedy was coming into its own. Their cleverness and wit, unfettered by character demands, roamed freely:

> When I sit and listen to a symphony,
> Why can't I just say the music's grand?
> Why must I leap up on the stage hysterically?
> They're playing pizzicato,
> And everything goes blotto.
> I grab the maestro's stick
> And start in leading the band!
> Carried away, carried away,
> I get carried, carried away!           (*On the Town*)

*Lyricists Betty Comden and Adolph Green got their start as performers. Here they are as the anthropology student Claire de Loon and sailor Ozzie in New York's Museum of Natural History. The number is the exuberantly brainy "I Get Carried Away" from Leonard Bernstein's score for* On the Town, *lyrics by Comden and Green.*

This is the sort of delightful material that Comden and Green had written and performed in nightclub revues. It took perfectly well to the stage. In such subsequent musical comedies as *Wonderful Town* (1953) and *Bells Are Ringing* (1956) the team continued to be successful with this brand of satire, but the approach was beginning to grow creaky. By the time of *Do Re Mi* in 1960, the excellence of their technique could no longer carry such satiric writing that paid scant attention to character. Refusing to alter their style, Comden and Green continued to write essentially revue material, going without a Broadway success as lyricists until the 1978 *On the Twentieth Century*. Considering the unusual musicality of their technique, this dry spell was a particular shame, but that is how definitely the character lyric had established itself. Others unable or unwilling to adapt to it were similarly frustrated. Johnny Mercer, for example, was one of the most wonderful of lyricists:

> Days may be cloudy or sunny
> We're in or we're out of the money
> But I'm with you, Della,
> I'm with you rain or shine.        (*St. Louis Woman*)

These beautiful lines are typical of the talent that made Mercer one of the finest of all American lyricists. "Shine" is the final word in the song and it covers three of Harold Arlen's notes. A lyricist less oriented to singing would have set three syllables to the notes but Mercer, himself a singer, realized that Arlen's notes were meant to be sung as a blues slide and that individual syllables would have made the song too formal, too racially white. Exquisite as this lyric is, however, it simply isn't the sort that contributes to a show (the show was *St. Louis Woman*) because it is so anonymous. It is a pop lyric.

Less beautiful but more showmanly and also more "characteristic" were Richard Adler and Jerry Ross's lyrics for their 1954 *The Pajama Game*:

> Her is
> A kinda doll what drives a fella bats,
> Isn't her?
> Her is.        (*The Pajama Game*)

Those who crave literacy would hardly be satisfied with this, but their indignation would be narrow-minded. Much as we delight in Porter's trips to the moon on gossamer wings, the Midwestern factory worker in *Pajama Game* wouldn't speak that way. By the same token, Sheldon Harnick would hardly have had Tevye, in *Fiddler on the Roof*, singing of the moon growing dim on the rim of the hill in the chill, still of the night. That's Porter too. Tevye and his wife Golde would more likely sing:

> May God bless you and grant you long lives.
> May the Lord fulfill our Sabbath prayer for you.
> May God make you good mothers and wives.
> May He send you husbands who will care for you. (*Fiddler on the Roof*)

Not as flashy as the Porter, it is equally challenging. Harnick has written, for the most part, with composer Jerry Bock. Among the lyricists who emerged on Broadway in the late fifties with the third

*Eddie Foy, Jr. (left) was one of the few remaining burlesque clowns on Broadway in 1954. His eccentric comedy effectively deflated the sturdy leading man-leading ladyness of John Raitt and Janis Paige in* The Pajama Game. *It also gave lyricists Adler and Ross a specific comic personality to write for.*

66

generation of show composers, he has no superior in terms of character writing. A graduate of revues, Harnick is perfectly capable of the clever, but he appreciates the difficulty and the rewards of writing to character, to period, to style. His lyrics are tailored to each show: its story, the character, and the moment. They are fitted to the ward heelers and politicians of *Fiorello!*, the prissy citizenry of *Tenderloin*, the cognac and whipped-cream milieu of *She Loves Me*:

Couples go past me.
I see how they look—
So discreetly sympathetic
When they see the rose and the book.
I make believe
Nothing is wrong.
How long can I pretend?
Please make it right.
Don't break my heart.
Don't let it end,
Dear Friend.     (*She Loves Me*)

This is just gorgeous. Harnick has presented exactly the delicate romance of *She Loves Me* and this character's fear of being left waiting for "Dear Friend"—her lover-by-correspondence. By not rhyming ("right" and "heart") where rhyme would have seemed obvious, and then rhyming the uneven lines "Don't let it end,/Dear Friend," Harnick created sentiment without sentimentality, which was the main purpose of this show.

Fred Ebb, another among the third generation of lyricists, has taken a more active interest than most in show theory. Ebb considers Dorothy Fields his mentor and his lyrics reflect her directness. Yet at the same time, his technique is impeccable and he has an instinctive gift for song placement. Writing for such concept musicals as *Cabaret*, *Chicago* (for which he collaborated on the libretto), and *The Act*, Ebb was as much a man of the theater as a lyricist. *Cabaret* dealt with degeneracy in Nazi Germany. Given the show's visual sordidness and the irony of his partner John Kander's music, Ebb realized that the lyrics would most effectively contribute to the savage mood if they were sickeningly innocent against that background:

What good is sitting alone in your room?
Come hear the music play.
Life is a cabaret, old chum,
Come to the cabaret.     (*Cabaret*)

*Chicago*, built on the idea of a vaudeville bill, is about an adulteress who murders her lover. Ebb's "Mister Cellophane" is a song that her ignored husband sings in the costume of a gloomy clown:

Cellophane, Mister Cellophane,
Should have been my name,
Mister Cellophane,
'Cause you can look right through me,
Walk right by me,
And never know I'm there.     (*Chicago*)

The technical foundation beneath this lyric is secure—every word is clean, simple, and correctly pronounced on every beat. The words

*The production concept of* Chicago *was to retell the story of the 1926 play* Roxie Hart, *through archetypal vaudeville turns of the era. Here, Barney Martin sings the part of Roxie's betrayed and ignored husband. The Kander and Ebb song "Mister Cellophane," emulates such famous numbers as Bert Williams's "Nobody" and Ted Lewis's performance of "Me and My Shadow."*

are easy for the actor to sing. In keeping with *Chicago*'s concept, the lyric is modeled on a period number—Bert Williams's "Nobody"—and even its phraseology is in a period style. These lyrics accurately reveal the character and situation of the husband in *Chicago*'s story. There is a tremendous amount of work and mental concentration here and Ebb consistently practices at this level.

As modern and beyond cleverness as his lyric writing is, Ebb is also a traditionalist. Like most first-rate lyricists he insists on literacy and technical cleanness, and has a soft spot in his heart for such bypassed practices as introducing a song with a verse. He wrote a perfectly nifty verse for "Arthur in the Afternoon," a song in *The Act*:

> Though grim and obsessively sad was I,
> And never organically glad was I,
> Now life is the berries
> And cherries invaded my bowl.      (*The Act*)

Comparisons are useless but irresistible. Our theater has had lyricists the equal of Fred Ebb, but none the superior.

The third major lyricist of this generation is Carolyn Leigh. However, with only three complete scores—for the conventional shows *Wildcat*, *Little Me*, and *How Now, Dow Jones* — to her credit, she hasn't faced as many challenges as Harnick and Ebb. Miss Leigh works in the style of the classicists—Hart, Gershwin, Porter, and Harburg—and none of her contemporaries can write a gentler or more consistently metaphoric lyric:

> Right now I'm ridin' the tall hope.
> The ship that I call "Hope"
> Has me in the bow.
> Come tell me tomorrow
> To settle for small hope,
> I'm ridin' a tall hope
> Right now.      (*Wildcat*)

But, as with all lyricists, the comedy song brings out Leigh's ingenuity:

> So here's a good tiding
> If men you are killing
> A talent you're hiding
> To be a performer!
> So be a performer!
> And soon you'll be riding
> If God should be willing
> The crest of your life.      (*Little Me*)

The singers of this song from *Little Me* are a couple of old-time vaudeville bookers, which is why the argot is Jewish. The asymmetric rhyme scheme is not only ingenious but creates that speech pattern, underlining it with the final, unrhymed "life." "Tiding" is used both colloquially and literally (to agree with "riding" the "crest"). Finally, in its meaning and in its spirit, this lyric conveys the feeling of a couple of hustlers trying to convince someone to go on the stage.

Unlike most lyricists of her generation, Leigh has come to appreciate the Stephen Foster–Irving Berlin–Oscar Hammerstein tradition, which had been so long rejected for the wit of Hart and Porter. Simplicity is as valid (and certainly as difficult to achieve) as the complexity, dexterity, and felicity of Porter and Hart. Some of this aversion to cleverness was in reaction to the tremendous recognition that Stephen Sondheim won in the seventies. Sondheim's esteem as a lyricist was such that it was rather unfairly casting a shadow over the prodigious talents of Harnick, Ebb, and Leigh. Few of Sondheim's colleagues begrudge him credit for his unquestionably fabulous craftsmanship. But they *are* colleagues, and they, as much as Sondheim, have brought the Broadway lyric to its most genuinely sophisticated state.

If Sondheim's work has weaknesses, they are excess complexity and a lack of warmth. Yet he *is*, without question, the most influential lyricist of his time, because his work deals not merely with words but with the entire structure of a musical. Sondheim is attempting to do more with lyrics than anyone ever attempted. Because he is also a composer, and a figure of special importance, a separate section is devoted to him. Even his peers have been influenced by his theatrical approach to lyric writing. For he writes not mere songs but musical scenes, in a style peculiarly devised for the theater. While we may miss the simplicity and warmth of the plain *song* in his work, Sondheim is drawing music and lyrics toward a higher purpose than the freestanding song. It will be because of his work that a musical's lyrics will finally be recognized for being as important to a musical as the book and music.

# DESIGNING A SHOW

## SETS

*Scenery for a musical is among its most fundamental, theatrical—and expensive—elements. A Broadway designer must be architect, engineer, showman, and artist, as Robin Wagner's fabulous sets for the 1978 hit* On the Twentieth Century *demonstrate. Illustrated on the following pages are the phases of the musical's physical settings—from sketch to blueprint to scale models (below) to building and painting the real thing. This show was one of the most scenically spectacular ever produced. Replicas of the thirties streamlined train* The Twentieth Century Limited*—exteriors, interiors, even full-scale models—roared through the show. A train unfolded and closed, it raced toward the audience with Imogene Coca (left) spread-eagle on the engine front, it rotated and fled upstage with the same actress waving from the rear deck of the observation car. All this gave the show tempo and muscle, gave it a trademark.*

*Appearance isn't the only requirement of stage design. Designer Wagner had to allow floor space for actors and dancers; his sets had to fit and be stored not only in the St. James Theatre but also in the theaters to which the show would tour before and after the Broadway engagement. What is more, all the set changes had to be possible in full view of the audience, with no stagehands in sight, because that was the way Director Harold Prince wanted it. That was the way most directors of musicals had come to want it, making for a fluid, uninterrupted performance. There was a time when musicals restricted themselves to one set per act or, when changes needed to be made, they were made during blackouts or behind a curtain while the actors performed out front ("in one," as it's called). Today, set changes are made in view of the audience, the curtains and lights remain up and directors actually choreograph the changes of scenery. Indeed, a musical's set changes are part of the show—and with shows like* On the Twentieth Century, *they make a glorious contribution.*

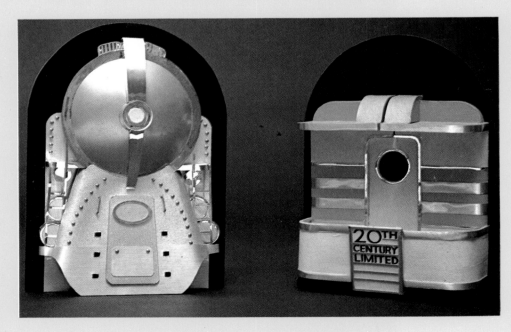

*Scale models of the engine front and the rear end and deck of the observation car.*

*Imogene Coca plays a religious fanatic who slaps "Repent" stickers on everything in sight on, and off, the train.*

73

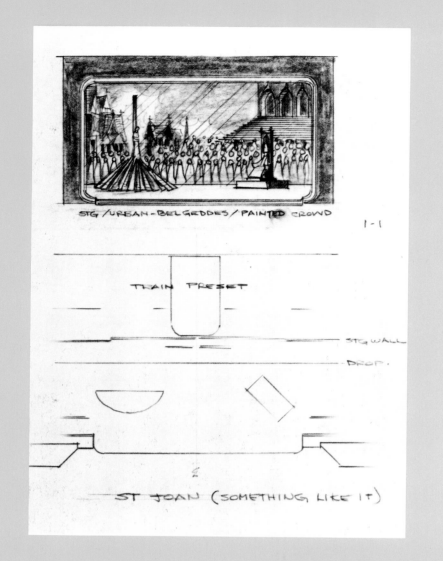

STG/URBAN-BEL GEDDES/PAINTED CROWD     1-1

TRAIN PRESET

STG WALL

DROP.

ST JOAN (SOMETHING LIKE IT)

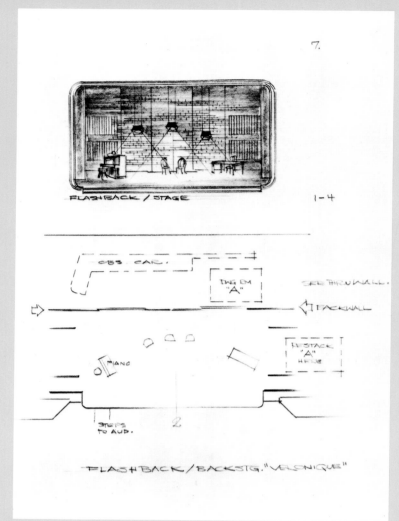

7.

FLASHBACK / STAGE     1-4

OBS CAR.

SEE THRU WALL.

BACK WALL

PIANO

STEPS TO AUD.

FLASHBACK/BACKSTG. "VERONIQUE"

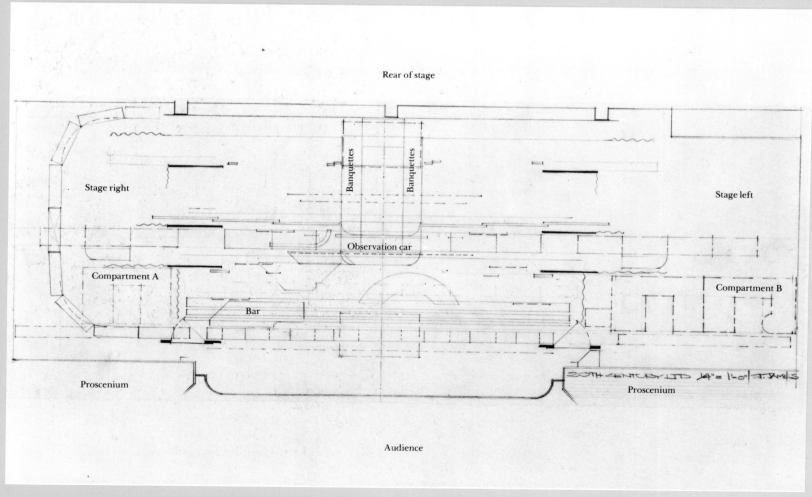

Rear of stage

Stage right

Banquettes    Banquettes

Stage left

Observation car

Compartment A

Compartment B

Bar

Proscenium     20TH CENTURY LTD ¼"=1'-0" T. JAMES     Proscenium

Audience

74

At the far left is Robin Wagner's sketch and ground plan for the first scene in On the Twentieth Century, *the climax to a terrible play called "The French Girl" produced by the flamboyant but down-at-the-heels Oscar Jaffe. Near left is Wagner's sketch and plan for the second scene that first represents backstage at the Chicago theater where "The French Girl"—a version of Joan of Arc—is about to close. Later, the setting is used as a flashback for Oscar Jaffe's discovery of the girl he makes a star, Lily Garland. At left (below) is Wagner's blueprint—a kind of bird's-eye view of the stage—showing outlines of the main pieces of scenery and indicating the intricate storage arrangements necessary for so much material on the stage of the St. James Theatre, where the show opened.*

*Wagner's painting for the scenic drop used as a setting for "The French Girl" (top right) takes off on Art-Deco-like designs of the thirties—the period of* On the Twentieth Century. *Notice that in his preliminary sketch (opposite, top left), he refers to "Urban/Bel Geddes," the names of two of the era's most influential stage designers.*

*The three photographs above show the vast, aircraft-hangar-like interior of Nolan Scenery studios, where the drops and other settings for the show were painted. Wagner's designs were scaled up on a grid system, marked off on huge pieces of canvas, and then painted by hand or with the aid of mechanical stencils. Some painted-canvas scenes were later hung on pipes and dropped from the "flies" of the theater; others—called "flats"—were mounted on frames, like fine art paintings, and stored in the wings to be slid onstage at the proper moment.*

75

The first thing the audience sees at Twentieth Century is the spectacular drop. Wagner made the model (above) fourteen inches high and two feet wide; its scale is one half inch to the foot. Later in the show (left), four tap-dancing redcap porters do "Life Is Like a Train" in front of it.

Wagner's sketch for the interior of the observation car lounge (opposite, top left) also shows a ground plan of the stage, with the lounge seen from above. Behind it, in dotted lines, is the observation-car set in its closed form. To the right of the drawing are two models of the Chicago train station with the rear end of the observation car in place at the center. In action in the show (right), the arches of the train station rise as the rear end of the train moves slowly downstage. It opens, revealing the interior of the observation car. All this takes place while the actors scurry about as they prepare to board the train. During the rest of the show, on the journey to New York, Oscar Jaffe will attempt to convince the now movie star, Lily Garland, that she should return to the stage—and bail him out.

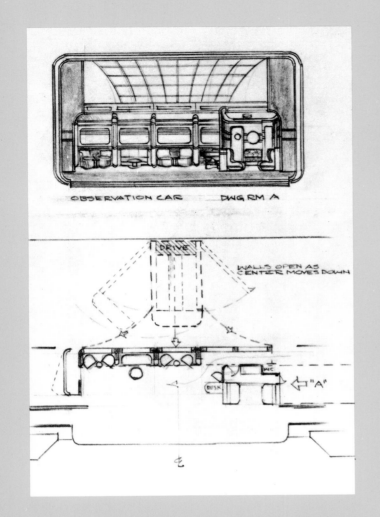

OBSERVATION CAR   DWG RM A

DRIVE

WALLS OPEN AS
CENTER MOVES DOWN

DESK

"A"

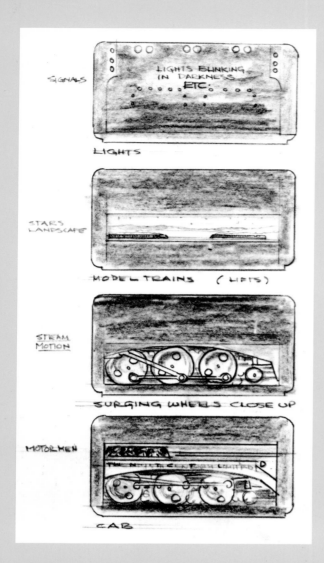

SIGNALS

LIGHTS BLINKING
IN DARKNESS
ETC.

LIGHTS

STARS
LANDSCAPE

MODEL TRAINS (LIFTS)

STEAM
MOTION

SURGING WHEELS CLOSE UP

MOTORMEN

THE NORTH CENT LIMITED

CAB

For the climactic second-act sequence in which the train itself becomes the principal actor in the show, Wagner sketched a cinematic build-up (left) of images. First (top), a dark stage with distant stars; then, on the horizon, two faraway trains cross in the night; suddenly, clanking wheels, thrusting pistons, and hissing steam fill the proscenium; finally, the entire massive engine is revealed. Below is his blueprint for the engine; at right is the scale model, five and a half inches high and seventeen and a half inches across. At the bottom of this page, craftsmen at Theatre Techniques Inc. build the locomotive.

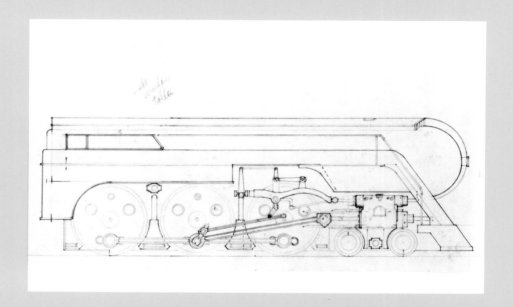

In its finished form (left) the vast New York Central engine throbs with life. Revealed in the engineer's cabin window is the intrepid Letitia Primrose (Imogene Coca) a loony lady ("She a nut, she's a nut, she's a real, religious nut") who is on a mad, train-long flight to elude the psychiatrists, conductors, and trainmen who are chasing her. Blithely, she waves from the cab. Blackout. The engine has been onstage for not more than fifteen seconds—a difficult, brief, and costly effect. And worth every penny.

*Most of the action of* On the Twentieth Century *takes place in the adjoining compartments A and B (below) and in the observation car lounge with its row of banquettes and half-round bar. Wagner's precise models, not more than five inches wide (right), were converted at the scene shop (opposite) into working units that roll on and offstage with apparently effortless ease throughout the performance. The designer's ground plan (page 74) shows where the units are stored when they are not onstage and the paths of their movements. The logistics of the show are highly complex, but the audience is never for a moment made aware of the stagehands' hidden work.*

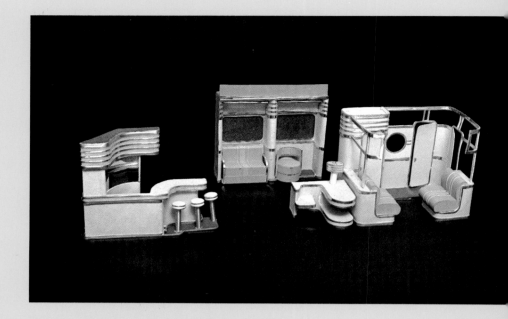

*The final scene of the show (right) spreads across the observation car lounge as Oscar Jaffe makes a last, desperate effort to get Lily Garland to sign the contract to do a play for him. Feigning death after a fake suicide, he lies sprawled on the bar. A woman doctor (whose play he has agreed to produce to earn her cooperation) pronounces him mortally wounded. As a last wish, he exhorts Lily to sign the contract for old-times' sake. She does so—and Oscar leaps up triumphantly. "Not so fast," she cries—"Look at the signature!" Not fooled at all by Oscar's theatrics, she has signed "Peter Rabbit." A shouting match ensues, but within minutes Oscar and Lily suddenly confess their love for one another; they embrace; the train arrives in Grand Central, and all ends happily.*

# COSTUMES

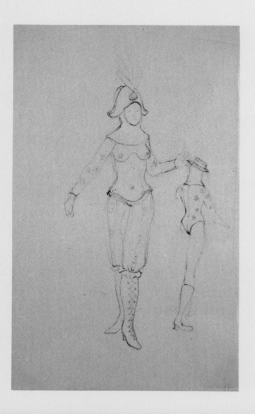

*Although costumes give musicals much of their color, the most beautiful ones aren't necessarily the best. A musical's costumes must first serve basic theater needs. They must be accurate to period, reflect the production's tone of voice, define each character for the audience: the man in red is vain, the woman in blue is sincere, the fat guy in plaid is the comic. Like scenery, the materials and colors must be chosen with stage lighting in mind. Then, a musical's costumes must fit a musical's special needs—they must leave enough physical freedom for dancing, they must be particularly durable because of the active movement and they must often be quick-changeable. For these reasons, and unlike costumes for plays, a musical's costumes can seldom be bought in stores. They must be custom-made.*

*Patricia Zipprodt has been one of the best and most active costume designers for Broadway musicals (*Cabaret, Fiddler on the Roof*). At left is her sketch for a female dancer in* Pippin, *and at right are some color renderings for* Chicago, *with the finished costumes beside them. For* Pippin, *Zipprodt had an unusual problem: The script called for armor but Director Bob Fosse warned the designer that his choreography wasn't going to be possible with dancers in rigid costumes. Zipprodt had to invent a new kind of armor. With some technical assistance she concocted a material made of layers of latex and cheesecloth topped with a flexible enamel paint. The*

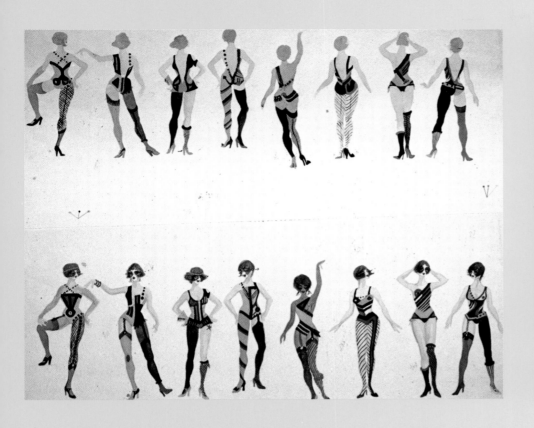

light and flexible material proved durable, easy to clean, and most to the point, it worked, as the photograph at left shows.

A more traditional approach to stage armor was taken by Tony Duquette and Adrian for Camelot. The show was a spectacle, and with little choreography, movement wasn't a problem. Below, Richard Burton tries on King Arthur's chain mail and helmet. At right, in a fitting room, Julie Andrews critically appraises her queenly look. On the following page is the finished effect. In the dozen years between Camelot and the 1972 Pippin, Broadway costuming had grown from orthodox realism and splendor toward a more creative approach to costuming.

# DIRECTING THE SHOW

The director of a play literally *stages* a script—he supervises the speaking of its dialogue, the acting out of its story, the transformation of writing into living theater. The responsibilities of a *musical's* director are not so clear-cut because he deals not only with dialogue and stage directions but also with songs and dances. He is the head of a creative committee that includes a librettist, a composer, a lyricist, a choreographer, an orchestrator, designers, rehearsal pianists, dance arrangers, and vocal arrangers. Presumably, he criticizes, sorts, apportions, and blends their work and then brings it all to life.

I say "presumably" because directors of musicals have not always wanted to or been allowed to do all this. A show usually has a center of power and this center has changed from era to era; it still changes from show to show. Who holds the center of power depends on who has the reputation, the prestige, the name; it depends on who finally attracted the producer and the investors. It can be a star performer or a star composer, or even the producer himself, but things are not right with a show unless the dominating person is the director, for his interest is the show as an artistic whole.

Directing a musical is so different from directing a play that few have been successful at both. At one time, directors of musicals actually staged only the dramatic scenes—the book—and merely supervised the musical elements, approving or disapproving the songs and dances as staged by the choreographer. It was inevitable that the choreographers would resent a drama person's control over their work. They felt that rather than the story, the songs and the dances were what made musicals popular, and that a musical person rather than a drama person should be in charge. Producers and composers tended to agree and so, in the sixties, directing began to pass from the writer-directors such as George S. Kaufman, Abe Burrows, Moss Hart, Josh Logan, and George Abbott to the choreographer-directors such as Jerome Robbins, Michael Kidd, and Bob Fosse.

When the choreographers first began to direct, they were handicapped by their inexperience with dialogue and drama. They didn't know how to deal with actors. Ultimately, those choreographer-directors who couldn't learn to "direct book" fell by the wayside. Those who could learn changed the power structure in the musical theater. The writer-directors had performed in a servicing capacity. They allowed the songwriters and the stars to dominate the musical theater. We identify shows from the past as Gershwin musicals, Kern musicals, Rodgers and Hammerstein musicals or as Jolson musicals, Mary Martin musicals, Bert Lahr musicals. How many of us remember who directed *Oklahoma!* or *Porgy and Bess*? (Rouben Mamoulian, both).

Now the musical theater was growing up. The show as a whole and not the songs or the star was being placed first. The writer-directors had accepted projects originated by composers or producers. In the sixties, the choreographer-directors began to dominate the projects, as Jerome Robbins did with *Fiddler on the Roof* and Gower Champion with *Hello, Dolly!* Finally, in the seventies, some of them assumed massive power. These men created their own shows, engaged composers and authors to write them, and went directly to investment sources, leaving producers out entirely. It was Michael Bennett's *A Chorus Line* and Bob Fosse's *Dancin'*. By then, there was no question but that the Broadway musical theater, once ruled by producers and personified by composers and stars, was being taken over by directors.

# MISTER ABBOTT

From the staging point of view, George Abbott *is* Broadway musicals. He perfected techniques, set standards, and laid down the pragmatic measure that still governs a musical: *Does it work?*

Abbott was the reigning director of musicals over the three decades in which they grew up, from the thirties through the sixties. Established as a director of drama and then farce, he worked on his first musical (*Jumbo*) in 1935 and over the next twenty-seven years staged twenty-six, of which twenty-two were hits! It was an extraordinary streak.

Abbott came to musicals when they were on the brink of adulthood. They were brash, they were energetic, they were tremendously popular, and they needed to organize themselves. Songs and fun had been their main reasons for being. The plot was just an excuse for jokes and pretty girls. By 1935 the musical comedy was ready to do more. Abbott introduced discipline. He insisted on a workable book: a script that could hold its own without songs and dances. The inclination was natural for him. He had meant to be a playwright. When circumstances led him to directing he became a rewriter, a reviser, a show doctor—for his own musicals and others.

His approach was utilitarian. A no-nonsense man who believed in theatrical law and order, he had no patience for artistic pretensions, dawdling scenes, or moments of mood. His values were drawn from farce: speed and structure. No scene could be too brief for him, so fearful was he of idle sequences that didn't further the plot and might lose the audience's interest. Such devotion to action and episodes led to the constant scene changes that so affected the look and rhythm of musicals during his heyday.

Abbott enlarged the physical scope of musicals and developed methods to handle their size. In many ways, this came down to traffic management—getting crowds of actors on and offstage, moving scenery in and out. But "traffic management" is too modest a term for all this. It adds up to the energetic, glossy, smooth flow of show making we identify with musicals. This has sometimes been disparaged as "slickness" but there is no sense blaming emptiness of content on aplomb of technique. Abbott made Broadway musicals professional, so professional that long before they were taken seriously they represented the epitome of production technique.

Abbott's kind of musical separated a show into songs, dances, and book. He left musical staging to choreographers, whom he seemed to consider alien but necessary creatures. Though he worked with three of the theater's greatest choreographers (George

Opposite, above: *At an audition for* Once Upon A Mattress *at the Phoenix Theater, the tall, bespectacled Mr. Abbott (center) does the casting.* Below: *The first day of rehearsals for* Flora, the Red Menace, *with producer Harold Prince looking thoughtfully over Mr. Abbott's shoulder. Traditionally on this day, the designer will show models or drawings of his sets; the cast will read through the script; the composer and lyricist will sing the songs. Traditionally, too, it is the most optimistic and exciting day this new family will have until six weeks later, when they will have their first dress rehearsal and for the first time hear the music played by an orchestra.*

Balanchine, Jerome Robbins, and Bob Fosse), his attitude toward dance never grew beyond toleration.

The director, as he saw the role, was essentially responsible for the quality and staging of a musical's book. Abbott considered the book his territory whether or not he was the credited author, no matter how the author felt about having his work rewritten. Abbott couldn't understand how librettists could disagree with him or fail to appreciate his improvements. He had problems with those who were resentful—especially when he neglected to consult them. Convinced he knew what was right and stimulated by the need to get it right in the bustle of a pre-Broadway tryout, he simply went ahead and did what he thought had to be done.

Abbott was chosen to direct *Jumbo* because Rodgers and Hart wanted him to have some experience before directing their *On Your Toes* (1936), Abbott's second musical. In the next five years he staged five Rodgers and Hart musical comedies, setting an everything-at-a-trot style that became his trademark. He ignored the more serious developments represented by *Show Boat* and *Porgy and Bess*. To Abbott, musicals were nuts-and-bolts commercial theater made under pressure against an opening night deadline. That was challenge enough.

Breaking with Rodgers and Hart in 1941, he found a talented new song-writing team in Hugh Martin and Ralph Blane and staged their collegiate musical, *Best Foot Forward*. Turning again to newcomers, he worked with Leonard Bernstein, Jerome Robbins, Betty Comden, and Adolph Green on their first show, *On the Town*, of

*Yes, that is an elephant dwarfed by Albert Johnson's mammoth set and Raoul Pène du Bois's giant clown. Broadway will never again be able to afford the likes of such spectacles as Jumbo. (Among other things, the huge Hippodrome theater is gone.) The show's story—a romance between the children of rival circus owners—was only an excuse for the acrobats, sideshows, horses, and, of course, a woman shot out of a cannon.*

1944. It was the first dance-heavy musical and encouraged Robbins to conceive *Look Ma, I'm Dancin'!*, a musical about a dance company that Abbott also directed. But he still spoke as derisively of seriously meant dance as he spoke of all stage ambitiousness. "Time and again," Abbott wrote, "the ambitious dance effort will fail whereas something conceived for practical purposes and on the spur of the moment will be a big success." That is true but Abbott seemed averse to any kind of aestheticism, accepting the appealing proposition that utility is pure art and anything else is just arty. Perhaps he resented dances because they took time from his book. He was not able to intimidate Robbins, however, and Robbins was meanwhile learning the fundamentals of staging musicals from him. The two worked together repeatedly. Abbott respected Robbins's talent and, consciously or not, he was training his successor.

*High Button Shoes* in 1947 set some sort of record for Abbott's seat-of-the-pants brand of show making. On the first day of rehearsal there were only eighteen pages of script in existence. Abbott sat down with the company and talked the plot through, making it up as he went along and encouraging the actors to improvise. This is how the show's book was ultimately "written." Because *High Button*

Jumbo *starred Jimmy Durante as a flamboyant press agent. It was produced by Billy Rose, with a book by Ben Hecht and Charles MacArthur, songs by Rodgers and Hart, and an orchestra led by Paul Whiteman.*

*Adolph Green, Betty Comden, and Robert Chisholm in a book scene from* On the Town. *George Abbott's experience as a director of plays made him thoroughly confident with a musical's dramatic moments. When choreographers began to take over the directing of musicals, scenes involving straight dialogue—without song or dance—were often amateurishly directed, or not even directed at all.*

*There were many dream sequences in Broadway musicals after* Oklahoma! *This one is from* On the Town: *One of the three sailors on shore leave in New York, Gaby (played by John Battles), fantasizes that he has finally found the sought-after beauty queen of the subways, Miss Turnstiles (Sono Osato), at the Coney Island amusement park, only to find the locale turn into a boxing ring. She knocks him out. Symbolism was big in 1944.*

The "Who, me?" look is classic Phil Silvers in High Button Shoes, *representing George Abbott at the peak of his musical comedy form. The gentleman at the far right, in tails, is Donald Saddler, later to be a prominent choreographer. At the left is Helen Gallagher, a chorus "gypsy" on her way to stardom. Between them are Broadway's too-soon-forgotten professionals— Mark Dawson, Jack McCauley, Joan Roberts* (the leading lady of Oklahoma!), *and Lois Lee.*

*Shoes* turned out to be a hit, Abbott continued treating musicals as paste-up affairs.

*High Button Shoes* was Jule Styne's first show as a Broadway composer. Abbott regularly worked with new composers and lyricists. He had introduced Bernstein to the theater, as well as Hugh Martin, Morton Gould (*Billion Dollar Baby*), Frank Loesser (*Where's Charley?*), Adler and Ross (*The Pajama Game*), Bob Merrill (*New Girl in Town*), and Stephen Sondheim (*A Funny Thing Happened on the Way to the Forum*). This may not have been altogether altruistic of him. The composer having his first show produced is not apt to be assertive. Novices can be counted on to be respectful. Abbott occasionally worked with established composers who could fight back, but his quarrels with Rodgers and Hart had made him wary. Helping newcomers get started had its advantages.

Turning sixty years old as the fifties began, he showed no signs of slowing down nor of interrupting his succession of hits. He directed musicals almost exclusively and was very successful with them. His taste agreed with the public's. It was a taste for the genre of "musical comedy"—theater meant simply to entertain.

We loved the Abbott musicals of the fifties and love them still. For many, those were the golden years of musicals. It wasn't just for their music, it was for their energy and spirit. This was a time when that excitement seemed perpetual and Abbott helped to keep it going by directing and co-writing one smash musical after another: *Call Me Madam*, *A Tree Grows in Brooklyn*, *Wonderful Town*, *The Pajama Game*, *Damn Yankees*, *Once Upon a Mattress*, *Fiorello!*.

1952 was Abbott's first year without a new musical in seventeen years! He was back the next year, however, and with two—*Wonderful*

*Town* and *Me and Juliet*, the former a hit and the latter a jolting first failure for Rodgers and Hammerstein. It proved to be an unhappy reunion for Abbott and Rodgers.

*Wonderful Town* contained the seeds of Abbott's approaching obsolescence. Bernstein's score was much more sophisticated than the book, which was an adaptation of the Chodorov-Fields play *My Sister Eileen*. Bernstein's music, as it invariably does, called for a dance show, a step forward from *On the Town*. Yet Abbott made *Wonderful Town* a standard musical and, although Robbins came in to help on the road, it could not be altered into anything else.

Having successfully tried musical plays with *A Tree Grows in Brooklyn*, Abbott now turned to them with increasing frequency. For Broadway was mistakenly thinking of progress in terms of content rather than in terms of form. The musical play simply was to be made the same way as a musical comedy; just without the laughs. For its lack of laughs alone, it was considered superior to funny theater. This is wrong in fact and in spirit. There is nothing closer to the stage's heart than making an audience laugh, and there are few greater challenges. Yet, in the change from musical comedy to musical play, laughter as a prime purpose was shunted aside. Development of form—which is the only real progress—was ignored. It was of course not the idea of laughter itself but the song-story-song scheme that made the musical comedy trivial. Some shows sought to be amusing but the fun had gone out of them. As the clowns went, so went the clowning. Perhaps the theater reflected the America of the fifties. There were few laughs.

The presence of vaudevillian Eddie Foy, Jr., gave Abbott's *The Pajama Game* (1954) some golden comic spirit but this show was essentially a musical play, and one with a most unlikely subject—

*An actor in female clothes maliciously pouring tea into a friend's top hat—this is the stuff of comic theater and perhaps our musical stage has strayed too far from such roots. Brandon Thomas's* Charley's Aunt *was a classic farce. And George Abbott's stage business for* Where's Charley?—*the play's musical version—was equally classic. Jane Lawrence is the real Charley's aunt and Byron Palmer plays the roommate standing behind Charley himself— Ray Bolger, of course, in his greatest stage success.* Where's Charley *was the first show presented by Cy Feuer and Ernest Martin, initiating an amazing streak of hits for the team:* Guys and Dolls *in 1950,* Can-Can *in 1953,* The Boy Friend *in 1954, and* Silk Stockings *in 1955. Feuer and Martin subsequently presented* How to Succeed in Business Without Really Trying *and* Little Me. *They came to be known as Broadway's classiest producers and their success in a theater fraught with chance made them legends in their own time.*

union problems in a pajama factory. Again, it exemplifies the fact that Abbott judged musicals not on their musicality but on their books. He was attracted to Richard Bissell's novel *7½ Cents* for its unaffected story and its adult treatment of romance. Here was no ingenue and juvenile but a serious working woman (movie star Janis Paige), a union representative no less, and a factory foreman (stalwart John Raitt). The characters' jobs instigated the kind of basic romantic conflict that Abbott appreciated in a play.

And *The Pajama Game* proved one of Abbott's best shows. The score by newcomers Richard Adler and Jerry Ross is catchy, muscular, masculine, and theatrical, all qualities valued by Abbott. Curiously, one doesn't get the feeling that he was particularly in love with music. He seemed to think of a score in terms of "numbers"—elements that serve a function—rather than as music. Perhaps he had no trouble changing song-writing teams so often or working with unproved teams because songs were just interchangeable cogs to him. If so, he came up lucky with *The Pajama Game* for it has a wonderful score, beginning, as hit shows invariably do, with a strong opening number: "Racing with the Clock." "Hey, There" is a fine ballad, by no means simpleminded. However, its staging as a duet sung by the hero to his tape-recorded voice is a sobering reminder of how time can make a bright idea seem foolish. The other songs in the score are almost all assertive: "I'm Not at All in Love," "Steam Heat," "Hernando's Hideaway," and a fine comic song that advances the story, "I'll Never Be Jealous." Overall, Abbott's staging of the show was sensible and straightforward. *The Pajama Game* is an excellent example of the book musical. It is revivable simply because its script is interesting and its score is so solid. Harold Prince was producing for the first time. This was the start of his long association with Abbott, from whom Prince learned the fundamentals of musical staging. Years later, after becoming eminent as a director of much more modern musicals, Prince frankly acknowledged his debt to Abbott.

*Damn Yankees*, which Abbott directed a year later, played like a sequel to *The Pajama Game*. Structural similarities created the echo. Abbott had staged so many shows that they were beginning to look alike. His cavalier attitude toward musical numbers and his willingness to force fit a song into a story situation had once been part of normal procedure. Constantly confronted with the need to find good excuses for staging dances, he created artificial devices which stuck out like the sore thumbs they were—in *The Pajama Game*, a union meeting entertainment ("Steam Heat") and a visit to a nightclub ("Hernando's Hideaway"), and so on. Such devices weighed down Abbott's musicals.

Mind you, Abbott was still king of Broadway musicals, still capable of hits like *Fiorello!* in 1959, but in 1962 Abbott, the ultimate show doctor—the expert called in to help shows ailing in tryout—himself needed a doctor for *A Funny Thing Happened on the Way to the Forum*. Jerome Robbins served this function, and not just in choreography. Robbins simply saved the show. In the process, the student took the baton from the teacher. It was Robbins's musical theater from then on. As fate would have it, *Forum* was the perfect musical farce, Abbott's original territory.

Abbott directed many musicals after *Forum* but none was successful. The first few—*Fade Out–Fade In, Flora, the Red Menace, Anya, How Now, Dow Jones*—were in the style that had once made him, the style that had carried musicals to their cocky, dominating heyday.

*Eddie Foy, Jr., was the hysterically jealous factory production manager, Hines, and Carol Haney was Gladys, bookkeeper and object of his suspicions, in* The Pajama Game. *This was a delicious and wonderfully funny moment, but the musical seemed jinxed. Sprung to stardom with the show, Haney died at forty, just three days after its tenth anniversary. Others involved with this musical who were to die young within twenty years of its premiere were the co-producer Robert E. Griffith; Jerry Ross, the co-author of the score; the musical director, Hal Hastings; and another of the leading players, Stanley Prager.*

Above: Fiorello! *won a* Pulitzer Prize *for Abbott in 1959, but it was to be his last hit. Brash musical comedies were fast going out of style. Abbott thought he was keeping up with the times by emphasizing dramatic book qualities, but he was too close to see that only minor details were being changed. The trappings of the book show were all around him. Still,* Fiorello! *was as smooth and as entertaining as any musical—and shows that good are always in style.*

Left: *A businessman staked Carol Burnett to a year in New York to break into the theater. She wound up winning stardom as the lead of* Once Upon a Mattress *and then, in accordance with the deal, she staked another aspiring actress to a year. Jane White (center) played the Queen in this musical version of "The Princess and the Pea."*

But these shows failed because the style was then passé. Eventually he was simply offered mediocre shows that hoped to catch the tail end of his waning reputation, and he accepted them because he was so eager to work. *The Education of* H\*Y\*M\*A\*N K\*A\*P\*L\*A\*N, *The Fig Leaves Are Falling*, and *Music Is* were musicals he once would have rejected out of hand. They were all flops.

It was an embarrassing position for a man of such achievement but, though energetically entering his eighties, he had fallen behind the times. His shows looked like revivals. The farcical, melodramatic book musical that he had polished so proudly, so professionally, was being discarded. The practical, workmanlike show that had made his success now seemed old. It is artistry, and only artistry, that can transcend changing taste. Abbott's utilitarianism and inverted snobbery had caught up with him at last. The philistine was nabbed. Broadway was taking to choreographer-directors who created their own show ideas; books were becoming factors of musical staging; dance and concept musicals were emerging as dominant forms; the musical was taking itself seriously. Directors were succeeding with the artistic ambitions that Abbott scorned.

Still, the directors who displaced him and made him obsolete with their experimentation were actually, or indirectly, trained by him: Robbins, Fosse, Prince, Field, and Bennett. Abbott wouldn't regret that. He had always wanted to get on with the show. The show could not have gone on, so far or so fast, if not for him. Every modern director of musicals, whether associated with him or not, owes his career to George Abbott. Broadway musicals just wouldn't have been Broadway musicals without him. In more senses than one, he wrote the book.

**Fade Out—Fade In** *did not endear Carol Burnett to theater people. Business failed and the show closed when Miss Burnett, its drawing card, left because of an illness. Such illnesses often afflict stars who appear in badly reviewed shows. In an almost unprecedented and certainly uncomfortable development, she was sued and lost; she was forced to return to the show and it reopened, but the box office never regained its momentum. None of this hurt Burnett, who had become a major television star. An inspired clown, her career boomed, but she and the theater were never friends again.*

*Show girls are always good for a laugh when ogled by low comics. The routine is basic burlesque and that made it singularly appropriate to* A Funny Thing Happened on the Way to the Forum, *a delirious celebration of low comedy.*

# JEROME ROBBINS

George Abbott's reign as the king of musical theater directors came to an almost ritualistic end the day in 1962 that Jerome Robbins went to Washington, D.C., to help on *A Funny Thing Happened on the Way to the Forum*. It was like the formalization of a succession that had been happening gradually, since Robbins's *West Side Story* five years earlier. Abbott had brought in the hit *Fiorello!*, but it was his only success during this time and would prove his last. The writing was on the wall: *West Side Story* had established dancing as so important to the musical that the future belonged almost exclusively to choreographer-directors, and to the genius among them, Jerome Robbins, in particular.

Robbins came in only to "doctor" *Forum*—to smooth the physical movement and fix the opening number. He replaced that song, a Sondheim ballad called "Love Is in the Air, " with a cheerful production number, "Comedy Tonight." Robbins's intention was simply to tell the audience, at the start, exactly what sort of show this was going to be. He accomplished more than that. He turned a shaky tryout into a solid Broadway success and probably assured Sondheim's subsequent career as a composer. He also established himself as the first star director, one who needed producers less than they needed him.

The personnel of musicals that are in trouble on the road usually cheer up when a celebrated director arrives to fix everything and make dreams of success come true. This was not the case when Robbins came to doctor *Forum*. Zero Mostel was the show's star and Jack Gilford had a featured role. Both had suffered sorely from the McCarthy-era blacklists. A decade earlier, Robbins had named names before the House Un-American Activities Committee. One of those names was Madeline Lee, who is Gilford's wife. It had hardly been forgotten. The situation was tense. Burt Shevelove, who wrote *Forum* with Larry Gelbart and who later became a major director of musicals himself, was delegated to break the news of Robbins's engagement to Mostel. The star's response was sarcastic: "We of the left have no blacklist." A professional, Mostel worked under Robbins not only on *Forum* but again a few years later on *Fiddler on the Roof*. His professionalism, however, did not moderate his hostility. He repeatedly refused to join Robbins in social situations ("I can work with the man but I don't have to eat with him").

Jerome Robbins's Broadway career began auspiciously, as choreographer for *On the Town* in 1944. Written by his friends

*Two of the modern theater's great clowns: Zero Mostel insists that Jack Gilford is "Lovely" in* A Funny Thing Happened on the Way to the Forum, *and Gilford agrees. Gilford, a superb clown in his own right, was one of the few who could hold stage with Mostel and also one of the few Mostel respected enough to allow to do it.*

Leonard Bernstein, Betty Comden, and Adoph Green, it was a stage adaptation of "Fancy Free," a ballet he had choreographed to Bernstein's music earlier that year for the American Ballet Theater. *On the Town* is a conventional musical comedy with exceptional musical values. The likes of Bernstein's score hadn't been heard on Broadway since Gershwin. Here was the full force of a schooled composer applied to the rowdy spirit of the musical theater. Although this was a book show, directed by George Abbott with his typically brisk, farcical touch, *On the Town* set the dance musical on its way.

With this first taste of creative power on Broadway, Robbins was hooked. He was Abbott's regular choreographer for the next fifteen years, working for him on such shows as *Look Ma, I'm Dancin'!*, *High Button Shoes*, and *Call Me Madam*. (He also worked for other directors with *Miss Liberty* and *The King and I*.) Abbott gave him free reign, as if consciously grooming a successor, allowing Robbins all the authority of a director. For example, when Robbins approached composer Jule Styne in 1947 about the *High Button Shoes* dance music, Styne, then a Hollywood songwriter doing his first musical, naturally assumed that the dance pianist would arrange it from his melodies. Robbins insisted that he wanted an original dance score from the composer. "You want ballet music?" Styne answered, "Go ask Bernstein." Robbins icily informed Styne that he expected eight hundred measures of dance music, one hundred measures each on eight original themes. The only music that could be taken from the show's songs would be an introductory melody, to be used as a point of reference. He suggested that he would get this music from Styne if he had to lock the composer in a room until it was done. Styne came through with the famous "Keystone Kops Ballet," and Robbins would ever after draw the best from him. Styne's greatest scores, *Gypsy* and *Funny Girl* (another show Robbins doctored to success), were written under Robbins's command, and so was his fine score for *Bells Are Ringing*.

"Command" is the word. Robbins was never the most beloved man in the theater. An uncompromising perfectionist, he had no time for niceties and no inclination for tact in making demands on those with whom he worked. His sharp tongue regularly reduced performers to tears. But they occasionally had their revenge. During a rehearsal of *Fiddler on the Roof* he had his back to the theater seats as he tongue-lashed the company. Not one actor warned Robbins as he backed toward the lip of the stage and tumbled into the orchestra pit.

George Abbott got Robbins started as a director by giving him a co-credit for the staging of *The Pajama Game* in 1954, but Robbins had already earned himself a reputation as more than a choreographer. When he was staging the counterpoint duet "You're Just In Love" for *Call Me Madam* in 1950, he told Irving Berlin that he trusted the song so much he wasn't going to give it any musical staging at all—none of the special lights, costumes, dance movement, or musical routining that usually support a number. Berlin was aghast but Robbins insisted that nothing distract from the song. Of course, it was a showstopper. Berlin never forgot the deep impression made by the confident young man.

Robbins also directed one of Broadway's several versions of *Peter Pan*, in 1954, but he got his real solo start as a director in 1956 with *Bells Are Ringing*. A conventional musical comedy, it was a hit and a good show. Robbins had his hands full with Judy Holliday, a

magnificent star but one who could neither sing nor dance, yet she wasn't the reason for this musical's modest ambitions. Robbins was still directing in the manner he'd learned from Abbott, compartmentalizing the play, the songs, and the dances. Instead of being a choreographer-director, he was being a choreographer with the musical numbers, a director with the book scenes. But a single year later, his *West Side Story* would become not only the first outright dance musical but the progenitor of the concept musical.

*West Side Story* was the first show to bear a credit that has since become familiar—"conceived, choreographed, and directed" by one person. Its idea, *Romeo and Juliet* transposed to the streets of New York, seems naive today. Planned as a romance between lovers from warring Jewish and Italian communities, it ultimately dealt with Puerto Rican and "American" street gangs. The plot, the characters, and the dialogue are stifled by implied social comment. Musicals, which have only half the normal time to tell the story, are doubly unfit for giving social advice, unless they deal with the subject satirically. *West Side Story*'s liberalism is so ingenuous that the show is embarrassing to revive. However, Robbins's wall-to-wall choreography set a new standard for the musical theater, for not only were his dances extensive and exciting but it seemed as if every step taken by every character during every moment of the show was a dance step: mambos in the gym, stately ballets, and young toughs finger-snapping down the street. Here was a musical that was musical throughout, and not merely when a song or dance was at hand. Its initial success was not as great as many people remember it as being; this was a rare instance when a show's movie version (and not a very good one) established its reputation. Indeed, *West Side Story* wasn't even recognized as the best musical of its season (*The Music Man* won the Tony Award that year). Yet, it is one of the most significant musicals in Broadway history.

*Gypsy* was not the show one would have expected next from

*Robbins was not only the most successful classical choreographer on Broadway, but also the rare one with a sense of dance humor.* Look Ma, I'm Dancin'! *gave him a chance to combine these qualities in a musical comedy about life in a dance company. Its funny lady was one of Broadway's dearest, Nancy Walker, for whom the show was conceived. She played an heiress who subsidizes a ballet company and ultimately dances in it. In the costume fantasy, at top, she poses sexily aloft, wearing a black negligee with a strategically placed heart; above, she argues with a manager (looking on is the show's leading male dancer, Harold Lang).*

*The rumble in* West Side Story. *The "Jets" (the all-purpose "American" gang) and the "Sharks" (the Puerto Ricans) have been looking for trouble and they find it in the shadow of designer Oliver Smith's highway overpass. Rival gang leaders Riff and Bernardo go at each other. The innocent lovers Tony and Maria—Romeo and Juliet—will be victimized by the feuding.*

Robbins. It was a musical play, a book musical with little dancing. Almost the entire *West Side Story* creative team had been reassembled for it—Robbins, Sondheim (lyrics), and Laurents (book). Only Bernstein was missing, having abandoned the musical stage for the concert hall. Jule Styne took his place. Styne was by then a successful composer of engaging scores but, one would have thought, hardly capable of great theater music. For *Gypsy*, Robbins drew from him music that elevated the brashness of vaudeville to scathing archetype. It ranks among Broadway's greatest scores. Perhaps—in terms of the relevance of its material, cohesiveness, and consistency—it is the very greatest of all.

Arthur Laurents's libretto, based on the autobiography of Gypsy Rose Lee, concentrated on her mother, Mama Rose. The casting of Ethel Merman in this role of the ultimate stage mother was pure inspiration. Merman's vocal pyrotechnics and stage magnetism were well established but she was hardly known as an actress. Robbins built the show around her and made her brassiness the cornerstone of the character she was playing. *Gypsy* was to be Merman's greatest success, a show whose cheerful manner built to a savage peak.

The show was not the one Robbins had first envisioned. After *Gypsy* opened on May 21, 1959, he told Laurents, "It's your show. It's a book show," meaning a conventional musical play, which it is. Robbins had hoped that *Gypsy* would further the kind of musical theater that *West Side Story* had initiated. His idea had been to make *Gypsy* a cavalcade of American vaudeville using animal acts, juggler acts, trapeze acts—to make the variety show its concept. Those who worked with Robbins on the show insist that this idea was impractical. Perhaps it was, but a genius should be trusted. He can envision what no one else can see. It was such a need to compromise that finally drove Robbins from the musical theater to the ballet, where the choreographer's power is absolute. Who knows what *Gypsy* might have been? Perhaps a greater musical than it turned out to be. Still, it is a marvelous work with a finale that may well include the single most effective number ever done in a musical. "Rose's Turn" exemplifies the musical theater's greatest possibilities.

Opposite: *Judy Holliday was one of the best-loved stars Broadway ever produced, a wonderful performer. Brainy and endearing, she made her reputation as a dumb-but-wily blonde.* Bells Are Ringing *was her first musical and here she sings its show-stopping "Mu Cha Cha" It was as surefire a number as any musical ever had, managing to lift the audience out of its seats without a whole company of singers and dancers. Miss Holliday was company enough. Her partner is Peter Gennaro, the choreographer-to-be.*

The number is showmanship itself: Mama Rose is having a nervous breakdown. Having made one daughter (June Havoc) a star only to have been abandoned by her, she promptly made the other (Gypsy Rose Lee) an even bigger one. Shunted aside by her too, Mama Rose is now alone onstage. She spits out her frustrations. She'd had a dream ("dream" is the show's recurring motif), she'd dreamt it for June, she'd dreamt it for Gypsy. It was *her* dream and where would they have gotten without it? She'd wanted to live her dream through them. Well now they were stars and where was she? "Out with the garbage"? When would it be *her* turn? *This* is her turn (her chance, and her "turn," or number).

Mama Rose then *does* her turn, a maniacal, stripper's turn, screamed to an empty theater she imagines to be full. And of course it *is* full, for we are there—we are her imaginary audience. Robbins has directed *us* to be in this show, our applause to be Mama Rose's hallucination. With this number's devastating power we rise from our seats, and *still* we are part of Mama Rose's hallucination as she accepts our ghostly standing ovation. We realize this as we applaud and are taken to a still higher plateau. It is as thrilling a moment as there is in all the theater.

Five years later, with *Fiddler on the Roof* in 1964, Robbins reached his peak. He still had not come to grips with the root problem of Broadway musicals—the book that was essentially of the dramatic rather than the musical theater—but he did extend the emphasis on music and dance sequences that had begun with *West Side Story*. Without *Fiddler* there could have been no *Cabaret*, *Company*, *Follies*, or *A Chorus Line*, our modern concept musicals.

*Fiddler on the Roof* was a fabulous success, closing as the longest-running musical in Broadway history (3,242 performances). It proved that art, universality, and popularity could all come of a musical produced on the commercial stage. Robbins's collaborators were new to him. While they were an established creative group, none was prestigious enough to challenge his authority. Joseph Stein drew the show's book from some of Sholom Aleichem's stories, particularly "Tevye and His Daughters." Jerry Bock's score, while limited to "numbers" and not musically ambitious, appreciates traditional Jewish harmonies and prayer-like incantation. Sheldon Harnick's lyrics are especially sensitive. But it was Robbins's depiction of traditional Jewish lore in the Russia of *shtetls* and pogroms that made this show so special. This was hardly a musical play, a slick entertainment. It was Robbins's ode to Jewish history, the Jewish soul, the survival of a people, and it was done as a theatrical version of ballet.

As he had done while doctoring *Forum*, Robbins established the show's concept with its opening number. With curtain's rise at the Imperial Theater the opening night of September 22, 1964, a fiddler was literally on a roof: the roof of a small house on a set that designer Boris Aronson had faithfully and lovingly modeled on the fanciful style of the Jewish Russian painter Marc Chagall. Zero Mostel entered, looked at the fiddler, listened, and spoke: "In our little village of Anatevka you might say every one of us is a fiddler on a roof, trying to scratch out a pleasant, simple tune without breaking our back."

With this, the strings in the orchestra began thumping as Mostel started to sing, to turn, to snap his fingers, to flutter his prayer fringes. The company—the villagers—entered hand-in-hand, first loping and then dancing on a long line—a line that soon covered the

*Robbins's challenge in choreographing* West Side Story *was to find a dance style appropriate to teen-age gangs. Neither ballet nor traditional jazz dancing would do. Robbins took his cue from the finger-snapping crouch that passed for tough and cool on New York's streets. Here (at center), he demonstrates the moves in rehearsal. (At Robbins's right is George Chakiris, who would graduate from the chorus to the role of Bernardo, leader of the Puerto Rican gang, in the* West Side Story *movie.)*

*Opposite: Chita Rivera (left) and Liane Plane explode in a Latin number from* West Side Story. *Among the show's graduates were choreographers Michael Bennett, Patricia Birch, Grover Dale, Lee Theodore, and director Martin Charnin. They all began as gypsies.*

107

*When Zero Mostel began singing the opening number of* Fiddler on the Roof *"Tradition," the first thrilling wave swept over the audience and the show's greatness seemed inevitable. The fat clown had become, incarnate, the spirit of the Jewish people—persecuted, skeptical, joyous, indomitable.*

stage in great, swirling circles. In the center was Mostel, huge and featherlight, singing of "Tradition." For that is the theme and production concept of *Fiddler on the Roof*. This metaphoric history of the Jewish people tells of traditions broken, violated, and changed—and of traditions that had made survival possible. Robbins drew upon the strict rituals of Hasidic Jews for his dances, his musical-dramatic sequences, his stage pictures. And these were inherently theatrical: weddings with strict, ceremonial processes; folk dances; rigid rules of behavior and vivid ways of dress; even persecution that was ritualized by history. Robbins drew upon this fund of lore to create a living picture of old-world Jewish life, presented as a continuum of dance movement. So, this concept, or motif, was a theatrical one as well as an intellectual one.

However, the reason for the success of *Fiddler on the Roof*, as with any show, was not its innovative technique but its heart power. Time and again, as one daughter after another leaves Tevye, as one tradition after another is destroyed, he endures and the show rises to

108

emotional peaks. Mostel projected the traditions, ideas, and feelings that have been the Jewish people's strength through centuries of survival. A man with profound feelings about his Jewishness, he played the role as if it were his personal gift to humanity. In return he was given his greatest personal success, becoming a major star with the show. If hit musicals have anything in common, it is emotional clout. *Fiddler on the Roof* poured that on from the opening "Tradition" through the communal lighting of Sabbath candles in "Sabbath Prayer" to the end, as Tevye abandons his homeland to find a new home in America.

Although Robbins subsequently doctored *Funny Girl* and directed two dramas that failed (Brecht's *Mother Courage* and Maria Irene Fornes's *The Office*), it is *Fiddler on the Roof* that is remembered as his Broadway swan song. Realizing that *Fiddler* and *West Side Story* had been but the beginnings of a new type of musical theater, he sought the privacy of a studio to develop it. With a $300,000 grant from the National Endowment for the Arts, he began his American Theater Laboratory. It was a project that lasted two years and generated no productions. Except for a musical adaptation of Brecht's *The Exception and the Rule* that never materialized, Robbins has not been associated with the musical theater since. He joined the New York City Ballet, presumably to be George Balanchine's heir as its artistic director. As he had been groomed to follow George Abbott, so Robbins left Broadway with trained successors to carry the torch: Harold Prince and Bob Fosse.

Yet the Robbins legend has haunted Broadway. Virtually every new musical was submitted to him, which he encouraged by claiming that he would do the right show if it came along. This has only sustained his awesome reputation. Every Broadway director and choreographer either idolizes him or competes with his myth even though musicals have since gone beyond what he did. Perhaps Robbins misses the excitement of a musical's date with a Broadway opening night. Perhaps he became satisfied with the abstract, leisurely, uncommercial, and authoritarian advantages of the classical ballet. There is no way of knowing whether he could have continued as Broadway's regal director-choreographer. But his amazing run of successes is on record; his achievements remain and his reputation is secure. The musical theater could not have progressed without his trailblazing genius. From a working choreographer to a myth, Jerome Robbins has remained the man who brought dance and drama together, and thus led Broadway musicals to greatness.

*Some felt that* Fiddler on the Roof *was a cynical attempt to cater to Broadway's Jewish audience. What Robbins did, in this masterwork, was to make the rituals and lore of Jewish life, such as this Hasidic wedding, universally meaningful.*

109

# BOB FOSSE

When the choreographer-directors succeeded performers and composers as the dominant figures in the Broadway musical theater, Bob Fosse emerged as one of these new kinds of stars. Coming into New York with *Dancin'* in 1978, Fosse had either choreographed or directed ten musicals on Broadway and *every one of them had been a hit.* This record, unparalleled among his contemporaries, was surpassed only by George Abbott.

Some choreographers are strictly dance people. Not all of them can direct, though nearly all of them have tried to. Supervising an entire production, working on a musical's book, and staging actors in dramatic scenes obviously demands more than just a talent for choreography. Like Jerome Robbins, Fosse was introduced by Abbott to the techniques of directing musicals. Directing three of the first shows choreographed by Fosse (*Pajama Game, Damn Yankees,* and *New Girl in Town*), Abbott showed the young man how to whittle a script down to its basic events and keep the story moving; how to assort, vary, and build the musical numbers to first- and second-act peaks; how to direct book sequences; when to make use of dancing and when not to. Most of all, Abbott taught Fosse the basic facts of show business life: that if a number isn't working, it must be dropped no matter how "good" it is, for the audience knows better; that art is for bohemians; that the only good show is a hit show.

For all of Bob Fosse's Broadway success, he's never had a giant hit on the scale of Robbins's *Fiddler on the Roof*, Champion's *Hello, Dolly!*, or Bennett's *A Chorus Line*. Yet he is the man who's wanted when any musical is in trouble on the road because, like his mentor Abbott, at that point he concentrates only on bringing in a winner. That is why he is the most dependable of directors in an under-the-gun situation, but it is also why he's never had one of those giant hits. The giant hit usually has an element of greatness to it, and a show cannot be great when commercial success is its only goal.

Although Robbins and Prince had served their apprenticeships under Abbott too, Fosse seemed more influenced by the old master. He avoided the idea of art, convinced that flimflam, tricks and gimmicks, the old *razzle-dazzle* (as he put it in *Chicago*) comprise showmanship even among the most ambitious musicals. Because of his modest horizons he was reluctant to follow the trend toward concept musicals, dance musicals, or any musicals that aimed for more than entertainment. Like Abbott, Fosse actually prided himself on commercialism. So, until *Pippin*, his shows were second-generation musical comedies.

*Fosse rehearses his longtime star, friend, onetime wife, and performing alter-ego, Gwen Verdon, for* New Girl in Town. *The locked ankles, the backward lean, and the pelvic thrust are Fosse trademarks. Offstage, so is the cigarette in Fosse's mouth. For the photographer, Verdon mocks him with her own cigarette.*

While he is as competitive as anyone in show business, Fosse is essentially a modest man. Having begun in Chicago as a teenage dancer in vaudeville and burlesque, and having continued dancing as a stage gypsy, he fancies himself "only a hoofer," a song and dance man. He is vaguely ill at ease in his role as an eminent director. Like most dancers he prefers to express himself onstage.

Bob Fosse's dance style is drawn from the jazz dancing of Jack Cole rather than the classical choreography of Robbins, who sponsored Fosse in the first place (recommending him to Abbott for *The Pajama Game*). Cole, who did the dances for *Kismet* and *Man of La Mancha* among other shows, invented the kind of choreography that characterized Broadway throughout the forties and fifties. Cole-style dancing is acrobatic and angular, using small groups of dancers rather than a large company; it is closer to the glittering nightclub floor show than to the ballet stage. It is called "jazz dancing" because Cole preferred setting his work to big band jazz music rather than to the Broadway imitations of classical ballet scores that were popular in his time. However, the steps that he set to this dance band music were drawn from exotic, ethnic dances—African, Cuban, East Indian, Spanish. We have come to find such choreography vulgar, especially since Cole was inclined toward flashy costumes, but it established the Broadway dance vernacular, and it had a brass as unique as the sound and feel of a pit band. Most Broadway dancers consider Cole their spiritual father.

Fosse found his own way of using Jack Cole's dance language with his first show, *The Pajama Game*, and his first showstopper, "Steam Heat." Three dancers, two boys and a girl, appeared in Charlie Chaplin tramp costumes. They moved in unison to staccato, syncopated rhythms in angular jerks—they popped their elbows and pumped their derbies up and down above their heads; they turned their toes inward; they knocked their knees and sometimes danced on them. The number was uncommon for its intimacy; it was eccentric, understated, and refreshing. Fosse put a "Steam Heat" type of dance in almost every show he did. In *Damn Yankees*, the show that made Gwen Verdon a star, it was "Who's Got the Pain?" In *Bells Are Ringing* it was "Mu Cha Cha." (Fosse was so pleased with one of his dancer's improvisations for this number that he trusted him to choreograph much of it. The dancer was Peter Gennaro, later to become one of Broadway's classiest choreographers.)

Fosse's basic dance is the pelvic bump, doubtless recalled from his adolescence as a dancer in burlesque shows. Also, the marked sexuality in his shows may well have been influenced by burlesque. The women dancers he chooses are statuesque, with fabulous, sexy bodies, and are costumed and treated to celebrate their physical, sexual grandeur. Most Broadway choreographers are gay. Fosse's dances are plainly and refreshingly heterosexual.

*New Girl in Town*, an adaptation of Eugene O'Neill's *Anna Christie*, was the last show Fosse did strictly as a choreographer. It was also his final association with Abbott, and it was an unpleasant experience. According to Abbott's autobiography, *Mister Abbott*, "the number which [Fosse and Verdon] held dearest was a dream ballet showing life in a house of prostitution. . . . The sequence was just plain dirty." This exemplifies the conflicts that can arise when a theater piece is created by committee. Abbott shows tended toward the puritanical, Fosse's toward the sensual. It is not surprising that Abbott would consider Fosse's easiness with sexuality to be "just

The Pajama Game *was Fosse's first Broadway choreographing job, and this picnic dance (featuring Carol Haney) shows that his style was not yet defined. Yet even in this standard dance number, Fosse showed a budding inclination toward smaller groupings and turned-out, Chaplinesque, flat-footed steps.*

*Period costumes cannot disguise this trio from* New Girl in Town *(with Gwen Verdon in the center) as Fosse's creation. Though not the usual derby-hatted, black-suited, white-gloved threesome, the cocked hats, slightly bent knees, and parallel arms betray his trademark. Fosse sticks with something as long as it works.*

plain dirty." Nor is it hard to understand the frustration that Fosse, or any choreographer, would feel in having to cope with and be overruled by a director with a different set of values and tastes. This is why Fosse prepared, after *New Girl in Town*, to direct as well as choreograph the shows he worked on.

His career as a director is divided. The first half was concentrated on such second-generation musical comedies as *Redhead*, *How to Succeed in Business Without Really Trying*, and *Sweet Charity*. In the second half he finally turned to progressive musicals like *Pippin*, *Chicago*, and *Dancin'*. Between them, he directed the movie version of *Cabaret* and contact with that early concept musical of Harold Prince's made the difference between the halves of Fosse's career.

*Redhead* (1959) was so much a vehicle for Verdon (she and Fosse were married a year later) that it was even named for her. She was, by then, one of the biggest and best-loved dancing stars in Broadway history. Fosse's choice of *Redhead*, although it was a perfectly appealing show with a catchy score by Albert Hague and Dorothy Fields, revealed Fosse's ties to Abbott and the musical comedy of the past. It is a thriller set in a wax museum, but the story is stretched to include elements of English music hall entertainment. Such a contrivance is typical of the paste-up school of musical-book writing represented by Abbott. Fosse's direction was similarly old-fashioned. He revealed his inexperience by skipping from still one more "Steam Heat" type of dance ("The Uncle Sam Rag") to another dream ballet. Fosse got away with it because he made the musical work. It ran for 452 performances.

An episode during the tryout of his next show, *How to Succeed in Business Without Really Trying*, exemplifies Fosse's show-making approach. Frank Loesser, a composer idolized on Broadway, was the most influential person involved with the production. Included in his score was a bouncy little song called "A Secretary Is Not a Toy," but it was not going over. The producers and Abe Burrows, the co-director, asked Fosse if he could help the song through musical staging. Fosse locked himself into a studio and rehearsed for days with the singers and dancers. Nobody was allowed to watch. When he was through, Fosse nervously called in the producers and, even more nervously, Mr. Loesser. If he didn't like the number, Fosse said, please don't shout, please don't scream, just see the whole thing through. Then, Fosse promised, he'd just as quietly abandon it.

He told the singers and dancers to go ahead. Loesser had written the song to a skipping rhythm. Fosse turned it into a syncopated soft-shoe number. When the dancers were finished, there was dead silence as everyone waited apprehensively for Loesser's fury. "Terrific," he said. Fosse's number stopped the show every night of its lengthy run. The number was so successful Fosse copied it for *Little Me* the next year (1962) when he was in trouble with the second act's opening: it was "Real Live Girl." It too became a showstopper. This sort of success has made Fosse cynical about artistic pretensions. He knows about manipulating audiences with irrelevant, distracting, and even imitative flash. He thinks that honoring such greasepaint practicality as "art" would be a lot of baloney.

*Little Me* had more going for it than just that second-act opening number. Though we still call the musical theater "musical comedy," we are no longer accustomed to comic musicals—those that are actually funny. Humor is not usually Fosse's strength, but *Little Me* is one of the funniest of all musicals. With Cy Feuer, his co-director on

*The high kicks in* Redhead *were unusual for Fosse. He is the most contemporary of choreographers and the old-fashioned loose-limbed, relaxed movements of high kicks are out of keeping with Fosse's usual tight, tense formations and movements.*

*The show is* Redhead, *the star is Gwen Verdon (center), and the derbies are classic Fosse. He is original among Broadway choreographers in using abstract costumes to add an extra pictorial dimension to his dances. Though this may isolate the dance from the rest of the show, the effect is striking.*

Above, and at right: *These are book-end dances by Fosse, "Rich Kids' Rag" from* Little Me *and "Rich Man's Frug" from* Sweet Charity. *Again featuring Fosse's knock-knees, angular movements, and thrust chins, the two dance numbers are Broadway classics.*

the show, Fosse deserves considerable credit for making this show so polished, so energetic, and just plain funny. Its "Rich Kids' Rag" is a long, inventive, and charming dance for which Fosse designed a counterpart— "Rich Man's Frug"—in *Sweet Charity*.

*Sweet Charity* (again starring Verdon) is an adaptation of Federico Fellini's film *The Nights of Cabiria*. The story is about a vulnerable, victimized prostitute, but bowing to Broadway morality, Fosse made her a taxi dancer (dance hall hostess). That the Fellini movie was not a particularly musical choice revealed Abbott's continuing influence over Fosse. Holes had to be pried open in the story for songs to be stuck into. Moving its setting from Italy to New York only made it characterless. Still, *Sweet Charity* showed Fosse stretching. For one thing, it had been his idea from the start; he even began writing the libretto, though he ultimately needed help from Neil Simon. For another thing, he now had the confidence and craft to bring any show to a high polish. Finally, *Sweet Charity* showed Fosse opening up his dance imagination, working with larger groups and

functioning more as a director who choreographed than as a choreographer trying to direct. Time and again in this show, Fosse musically staged a whole song instead of waiting till the end of the singing before going to the dance. "Big Spender," "There's Gotta Be Something Better Than This," and "I'm a Brass Band" were all done this way. The dances were also longer, more muscular, and more ambitious. Still, *Sweet Charity* was more or less a standard musical. Fosse's real growth was to begin, ironically, with the movie version of *Sweet Charity* that nearly did in his career. For the next five years, because of this box office dud, he was "dead" in show business. Cy Feuer, who had produced *Little Me*, may well have saved Fosse's floundering career by asking him, in the midst of this dry spell, to direct the film version of *Cabaret*.

The *Cabaret* movie had no "Steam Heat" eccentric dances, no "Real Live Girl" soft-shoe numbers. Cynics could say that Fosse found no way to fit them into an expressionistic work about prewar Berlin, but when those trademarks were not to be seen in *Pippin* either, Fosse's rebirth was complete. He had survived his exile to return bigger and better than he had ever been. The tremendously successful *Cabaret* movie had done him two important favors—it got him back on top and it put him in touch with concept musicals.

*Pippin* marked his return to Broadway. The show didn't give Fosse much to work with. The score was by Stephen Schwartz, perhaps the luckiest composer in Broadway history (he wrote three mediocre scores for three mediocre shows that all became hits—*Godspell, Pippin,* and *The Magic Show*). *Pippin*'s book, by Roger O. Hirson, told a false-naive fairy tale about Pippin, the son of Charlemagne. The book's main concern is Pippin's quest for the meaning of life. Fosse responded to such philosophical questions by throwing the show's authors out of rehearsals. He made *Pippin* into one long production number. Though only the first act of Fosse's *Pippin* really holds together, this production consolidated his new-found reputation. For the 1972–73 season, he won a Tony Award for *Pippin*, an Academy Award for *Cabaret*, and an Emmy Award for a Liza Minnelli television special. Being the first director to win all three prizes made Fosse the rare musicals director who was a movie success as well.

Fosse returned to Broadway in 1975 for *Chicago*. One can only guess whether the decision to tell *Chicago*'s story through a production idea rather than naturalistically came from Fosse or John Kander and Fred Ebb (who also wrote the *Cabaret* score). What matters most is that Fosse staged the show and could never again go back to the straightforward musical comedies of his past.

The *Chicago* production concept is a vaudeville show. It tells the story of Roxie Hart, who murders a lover, manages to get an acquittal at her trial, and then capitalizes on her notoriety by becoming a performer on the variety stage. This story is told through broad versions of vaudeville acts. Each act—a ventriloquist, a battered clown, a female impersonator, and so on—is devised to work *as* an act while furthering the plot at the same time (the ventriloquist is Roxy's "mouthpiece" lawyer, the clown is her husband, and so on).

*Chicago* is without any heart, more impressive than thrilling. Nevertheless, it was a fabulous accomplishment, a spectacular exhibition of staging skills. It also displayed Fosse's grudging willingness to grow. With this show, Fosse acknowledged his ability to go beyond musical comedy.

*Chicago capitalized on an ironic contrast between an upbeat vaudeville style and a cynical content. Gwen Verdon (right) and Chita Rivera were no longer ingenues, and were deliberately costumed to look like underdressed, older chorines. Both of them superb and impeccably professional performers, Rivera and Verdon ignored vanity to achieve power.*

*With his success in directing the movie version of* Cabaret, *Fosse grew infatuated with the degenerate, decadent, grotesque look and brought it to* Chicago. *He had always shown unusual interest in costumes and pictorial qualities, so the powerful imagery here was not new for him. But the* Cabaret *look influenced a new turn in his dances—a turn away from conventional gracefulness, away from small groups doing cute steps, away from unison dancing.*

Chicago's rehearsals had been postponed as Fosse underwent heart surgery. When he recovered, he was anxious to keep working, as if working meant living. Months before Chicago ended its two-year run in 1977, he went into rehearsal with a group of dancers with no fixed project in mind. The situation was comparable to the workshop in which Michael Bennett had created A Chorus Line. Operating without deadline pressures was a new way of doing musicals. Fosse had months for rehearsals instead of the standard six weeks, and worked as casually as was possible for him. Yet, like Bennett rather than Robbins in a workshop situation, he had no patience for research in the abstract; work could only be justified by a production. His idea was to do an all-dance musical that had neither book nor scenery, yet was a theatrical piece rather than a ballet program. He wanted to work with contemporary pop and classical music instead of "Broadway" music. This show, which eventually became Dancin', faced Fosse up to weaknesses of his own as well as to the limits of the Broadway musical itself. Without a script and without a story, this show had to find something else to organize it, give it form, and provide a stimulating opening, a carrying theme, and a satisfying conclusion. He found a choreographic motif in the idea of "dancin'"—that is, informal dances such as tap, soft shoe, and the song and dance act. But he used little singing in Dancin', and singing had always been the very heart of Broadway musicals. With little

dialogue, what was to make *Dancin'* a musical, as Fosse promised, rather than a dance program?

Fosse knew he was in trouble with the show in Boston. Some dances were vulgar; others were simply bad and Fosse cut them mercilessly. It was an important point in his career. Having become powerful and celebrated by working solely for commercial success, with *Dancin'* Fosse was at last aiming to win the respect that Robbins, Prince, and Bennett had earned for their artistic achievements. Yet when it came to crisis, his background and instincts led him to George Abbott's principles: fix, remake, satisfy the audience, come in with a winner. Having a show without structure, he bound it with speed—no blackouts, no time for the audience to think. He packed three acts into two hours, with no pause in the relentless energy and musical volume. He planned every number to be a showstopper. Fosse got away with this, but *Dancin'* was still a dance program and not a musical: it had neither form nor continuity.

So, *Dancin'* was Fosse's eleventh hit in a row and further proof that he could whip almost any material into commercial shape. But having set out to establish himself as a choreographer on the ballet level, he only proved himself, once more, the ultimate, practical show maker. Does being an artist matter? For many on Broadway, Fosse is the most reliable musicals director of the lot.

*Here is the big "Percussion" number in* Dancin' *Fosse's dances have always been essentially abstract even though they were in musicals with stories.* Dancin', *strangely enough, was a musical without any story and yet this was a program dance—a dance about drums.*

123

*Watching auditions for* South Pacific *is a distinguished group of theater professionals: Director, Associate Producer, and co-librettist Joshua Logan slouches at left; behind him is Richard Rodgers, Oscar Hammerstein II looking over his shoulder; in the foreground is Casting Director John Fearnley; behind Rodgers are Assistant Casting Director Shirley Rich and Producer Leland Hayward.*

# THE DIRECTORS' ERA

In *Getting to Know Him*, a biography of Oscar Hammerstein II, Hugh Fordin describes how Rodgers and Hammerstein maneuvered Josh Logan into waiving his right to royalties as *South Pacific*'s co-author. While Logan was out of town, Rodgers and Hammerstein's lawyer cornered Logan's lawyer with a contract, giving him *two hours* to sign. The threat was naked: If he didn't waive the book royalties, Logan wouldn't direct the show. The lawyer signed the contract.

If perhaps in extreme, this unpleasant behavior exemplified the imbalanced power structure of the 1949 musical theater. Songwriters and stars had the clout. Things did not remain that way for long. By 1957, *West Side Story* ushered in the era of the director. There had been well-known directors before Jerome Robbins was given the unprecedented credit for having "conceived, choreographed, and directed" *West Side Story*. George S. Kaufman, Moss Hart, Abe Burrows, and George Abbott were all successful, experienced, active, and reputable directors of musicals. They remained, however, mere hirelings, staging materials that had already been created. They were secondary to the composers and performers. But it was Robbins who emerged most prominently among the creators of *West Side Story*, and never after would major directors be pushed around as Logan had been. Following Robbins's example, they started becoming co-owners of their shows. Indeed, directors came to develop such influence that *they* called the shots on royalties. Contrary to Logan's experience, it became common practice to give the director a share of the librettist's royalties even when he hadn't written a word of the book. The justification is that he invariably suggests dialogue and even creates scenes. Of course, that is the director's job, but a hit Broadway musical is too involved with too much money for most people to be generous. The minimum royalty for a composer, lyricist, or librettist is 2 percent of a production's total receipts (the "gross"). The average, sold-out musical takes in about $200,000 each week. Two percent of that is $4,000 a week for the New York company alone. (Touring companies, foreign productions, and ultimately summer stock yield still other royalties.) Not satisfied with their own royalties, some directors demand a share not only of the author's but even of the composer's and lyricist's royalties, contending, rather greedily, that they collaborate on *every* aspect of a show. If the director's name is big enough, his demands are met.

In Robbins's wake came Bob Fosse, Harold Prince, Gower Champion, and Michael Bennett. They were the musical's new prodigals. Shows would henceforth be known as Fosse or Champion or

Opposite: *This scene from* Cabaret's *bizarre Kit Kat Klub shows Joel Grey (also seen above) as the androgynous master of ceremonies. Broadway had never seen anything like the visual metaphors for decadence that Harold Prince daringly presented on a stage accustomed to pretty pictures.*

*In directing* Cabaret, *Prince effectively mixed different levels of realism: the expressionistic with the conventional. Opposite, below: A character from the show's naturalistic story— Fräulein Schneider, played by Lotte Lenya —dances against the background of the Kit Kat Klub, a garish and grotesque place that symbolized the decadence of the times. The contrast makes the scene.*

Prince musicals and often for good reason: No longer merely directing ready-made materials, these directors were actively reshaping scripts and songs and even initiating projects themselves. There was a recognizable stamp to their shows. Directors were being accepted as those most responsible for what finally takes place onstage.

Of these new star directors, Harold Prince was the only one who wasn't also a choreographer, tribute enough to his success in a choreographer-dominated field. A tense, confident, opinionated, and educated man, he practically manufactured himself into a director. He had leaped from being George Abbott's stage manager to being his producer, co-presenting almost every musical Abbott directed between 1954 and 1962. A mere twenty-six when he teamed up with Robert E. Griffith and Frederick Brisson to produce *The Pajama Game* in 1954, Prince had the youthful vigor and the concomitant malleability that appealed to Abbott. The old master gave Griffith and Prince their first hit and young Prince was promptly labeled Broadway's whiz kid. By 1957, he had co-produced three more musicals, all hits: *Damn Yankees*, *New Girl in Town*, and *West Side Story*.

Griffith's death in 1961 apparently had a maturing effect on Prince. Light commercial musicals no longer appealed to him. He was not interested in stars or their vehicles. He produced *A Funny Thing Happened on the Way to the Forum*, hardly a traditional musical comedy. He presented the trailblazing *Fiddler on the Roof*. He was then committed to being a director, but, no fool, first tried himself out on shows that others produced, *A Family Affair* in 1962 and *She Loves Me* in 1963.

*She Loves Me* concentrated on story, mood, style, and song. For here was an intimate, elegant show without elaborate shifts of scenery or a large chorus. Instead, it presented a small cast in an exquisite perfume shop that revolved as if a jewel on display. The show was perhaps *too* stylish for its time.

Jerome Robbins's *Fiddler on the Roof* was one of the last musicals Prince presented on behalf of another director, but it gave his subsequent directing focus and purpose. When Robbins abandoned the theater, Prince assumed responsibility for refining the concept musical. Plainly, he saw himself as Robbins's successor.

It was *Cabaret*, in 1966, that established him as a director. Here, he was actually creating a show—imagining a theater beast and giving it life. The script was only an excuse for the living picture to be heaved upon the stage. As never before, Prince demonstrated his sense of the "stage show." He raised the curtain on a huge mirror which reflected the audience in distortion to make the point that America, like prewar Germany, had the potential for fascism and degeneracy. Whatever the philosophy behind the mirror (American racism, according to Prince), it created a striking theatrical effect. Though half of *Cabaret* was a conventional book musical, Prince thrived on the sequences set in the German nightclub, where he made garish stage pictures with lighting and costumes and makeup. Prince regularly came up with such painterly devices. He conceived effects such as a "curtain of light" pouring down on the front of the stage so that only the downstage actors could be seen, with everything behind them blacked out. Such creative theatricality is neither choreography nor orthodox direction of book scenes. It is staging—the stuff of theater.

With *Zorba* (1968), Prince attempted to move on from *Cabaret*, but the show was only a Greek *Fiddler on the Roof*. Prince was still

learning his craft, and the concept musical was still in an evolutionary stage. There were fundamental questions to be dealt with, primarily what to do about the libretto if the musical play was to be replaced with a more fluid and less playlike scheme for providing story and structure. Prince's book-sense was the advantage he had over his choreographer colleagues. He was better equipped to deal with book problems and book problems are the musical theater's main problems. The problems went a long way toward solution in 1970, when Prince began a collaboration with Stephen Sondheim that produced the most significant musicals of the seventies. The team's imprint came to guarantee ambition, artistry, and seriousness of purpose. With the Sondheim shows, Prince refined the idea of the concept musical.

Harold Prince's direction of *Company* blended music with dialogue and dance and even scenery as had never before been done in the musical theater. Boris Aronson's chromium and glass structures and skeleton elevators gave Prince a picture through which to set the style, mood, and point of the show. No musical had ever looked like this one, so abstract and self-contained and cool. Sets have moved vertically before, but only in the sense of scenery being flown down from above the stage. Here, Prince also set his human traffic moving vertically on the elevators, giving the feel of life in New York's chilly skyscrapers. Doubtless, few directors could have conceived of a musical made from George Furth's related playlets about marriage. Prince's literary imagination gave him the edge.

Prince's production of Follies *was inspired by the photograph above: Gloria Swanson standing in the rubble of the demolished Roxy Theater, a New York movie palace. Building a stage work from this image, Prince created a musical about youth, decay, age, and memory.*

Opposite: *In* Follies, *echoes of the past— "ghosts"—were played by six-foot-tall show girls on pedestal shoes that made them still taller. Prince had them stalk the stage, wandering through the action to give the show an eerie, out-of-time feeling. Designer Florence Klotz, one of Broadway's most gifted, created fabulous costumes in what was one of the most spectacular-looking shows in the history of musicals.*

In terms of sheer visual power, *Follies* of the next year topped everything Prince had done before. Towering Follies girls of the past stalked his stage, white-faced and ghostly, haunting the present. Scaffolding loomed from the bowels of the Winter Garden's stage and Aronson even designed the theater's proscenium arch to make it look half crumbled.

Prince spent an extravagant (for 1971) sum on fabulous costumes designed by Florence Klotz, bringing the *Follies* "nut" to an unmanageable $80,000. A weekly nut is Broadway jargon for a musical's running cost, the sum of salaries, rents, and royalties that must be paid each week to operate a show. For a musical to be financially viable, its potential income when sold-out must exceed that nut by a comfortable margin. In the past, Prince had been a prudent spender. As producer he had kept his directing self in check. *Company,* for example, had been budgeted to "break even" (or meet its weekly nut) when playing at a mere sixty percent of capacity. On the other hand, the maximum potential gross at the Winter Garden for *Follies* was just over $100,000 weekly. It needed to play at eighty percent of capacity *just to break even.*

When he did *Follies,* Prince seemed unable to separate his producing responsibilities from his directing ones. He felt that the show deserved its expense and that his well-rewarded investors owed him the right to an indulgence. Had he been producing *Follies* for a different director, Prince would surely have felt otherwise and, in the long run, would have done better by the show. Although *Follies* was magnificent, its loss of $685,000 (despite a year's run) eroded Prince's investors' confidence. For his next musical, Prince had to take an unprecedented (for him) step and go looking for backers where once his word had been all that was necessary to raise production money. And, as he wrote in his published notebooks, *Contradictions,* "if this one didn't pay off, I would be back doing auditions."

So his next show, *A Little Night Music* (1973), was, as Prince admits, "about having a hit." It was as close to actually *going commercial* as he could get. The show was based on Ingmar Bergman's film *Smiles of a Summer Night.* It was a musical with real style, but it had a spurious, imitative feeling, as if trying too hard to be sophisticated. Bergman's wry and urbane qualities were too European to translate convincingly to the Broadway stage. Moreover, though *A Little Night Music* was much more accessible than *Follies* or *Company,* the story's details were too complex to present clearly, and Prince didn't work as successfully with his librettist (Hugh Wheeler) this time. Nevertheless, *A Little Night Music* was the most financially successful of the Sondheim-Prince collaborations. Prince could raise money again, which meant he wouldn't have to compromise to get a show produced.

He took a break from Broadway in 1974, working with Brooklyn's Chelsea Theater Center to successfully remake Leonard Bernstein's *Candide. Candide* reflected an arty influence in its use of arena staging and its emphasis on Shakespearean bawdiness, but ultimately it suffered more mundane problems when Prince decided to be its producer for a Broadway engagement. Arena-style staging so limited his theater's seating capacity that, despite 740 performances, the production lost money and Prince was back in trouble with his investors.

*Pacific Overtures* then stretched his backers' patience to the breaking point. This 1976 musical marked the peak of the Sondheim-Prince collaborations, but it also took the team into an artistic

*Freed from the conventional means of story telling,* Follies' *conceptual approach permitted the young and old embodiments of characters to appear onstage at the same time. Among the "old" stars in this scene are Yvonne de Carlo at the far right and, in the red dress, Alexis Smith, who found a new career in musicals as a result of her brilliant performance.*

hothouse. Mass audiences just wouldn't buy the show because it lacked the singular quality they demanded of all musicals: emotional power. This had been a noteworthy lack in all the Sondheim-Prince collaborations, but never before had there been such an atmosphere of cold artifice. *Pacific Overtures* had no show business to it although, ironically, Prince's intention was to demonstrate the West's corruption of the East by making Kabuki theater into the stuff of a Broadway musical.

In his supervision of the Hugh Wheeler–John Weidman script, Prince advanced the revolutionizing of libretto structure beyond the point he reached with *Company*. But *Pacific Overtures* never had a chance. The only sort of Oriental musical that Broadway audiences would buy is the very Caucasian *King and I* or *Flower Drum Song* sort. Prince's prestigious production was a million-dollar disaster. Thereafter, he had to find other producers to raise the money for his shows. Perhaps they would provide a more realistic influence. Perhaps they would not restrict his artistic freedom.

Harold Prince personifies the dilemma of an artist operating in a commercial marketplace. Can the creator survive when his decisions are dependent on consumer acceptance? An artist must follow his inspirations, but on Broadway's stages, shows must pay their own way. As Prince himself wrote, "*Company* . . . paid off [repaid its investors] and shows a profit. And that is what the commercial theater must ask of itself."

Sondheim and Prince so resented the success of vulgar musicals over their own that they seemed to perversely court the artistic projects most likely to fail commercially. This attitude took on aspects of martyrdom. But their musicals are almost all landmarks and both men are so inspired one could only hope their new need of other producers' faith would have positive results.

In 1978, Prince directed the first musical he hadn't personally produced since *Baker Street* in 1965, and his first non-Sondheim show since *Zorba*. This was *On the Twentieth Century*. Prince developed it into a comic opera in the style of *Candide*. Once more, he proved himself peerless with book work. Preparing the show with its lyricists-librettists, Betty Comden and Adolph Green, he helped them toward a stylization they'd never before achieved. He kept their touch light. He staged the show as if to prove that since he had to do a book musical, he would show how it ought to be done. He also revealed a sense of humor in directing physical comedy as well as in supervising the wit in the script. (If there had been any laughs in the shows Prince did with Sondheim, they were dry, even bitter.) Prince didn't make *On the Twentieth Century* a conventional musical comedy. His sense of musical theater was too refined for that. One scene in it was even on the *Follies* level: an actress trying to decide between doing a mannered comedy or a religious spectacle. Prince staged her imagined merging of the two as a marvelously mad scene with monks and biblical figures among a cocktail party's guests. He encouraged the composer (Cy Coleman) and lyricists to write a long, complicated, manic musical sequence—virtually a mini-opera— called "Babette." This was an example of how much gifted professionals can do when greater demands are made on them. It was for such collaborative influence, expertise, and creativity that Prince became the most important musicals director of his time, a seminal figure. In many ways, the musical theater's continuing progress was in his hands.

As the choreographer of *Company* and co-director of *Follies*,

Michael Bennett was the heir Prince produced to continue the line of directors that had begun with Abbott. With a single show, *A Chorus Line,* Bennett was catapulted to fame and power. This was because by the mid-seventies, the musical theater had become a place where a modest success could run two or three seasons and an outright smash was an industry. When *A Chorus Line* opened in 1975 to wild enthusiasm, Bennett was plunged into a one-show, multimillion-dollar career. Within weeks of its Broadway opening, he was rehearsing three touring companies simultaneously. Big business? In a single week, various productions of the show were grossing over $600,000!

The business of *A Chorus Line* occupied Bennett for two years, during which he did little but oversee it. Such success is not artistically fruitful. It is also disproportionate to actual accomplishment. After all, this show was Bennett's only success as a director and he was already being ranked with Fosse, Prince, Champion, and even the legendary Robbins. Yet, there was no denying his ability or the artistic achievement that *A Chorus Line* represented.

Bennett is about as industrious, self-disciplined, and ambitious a director as the musical theater has had. His career has seemed almost calculated for success. A chorus boy to begin with, he pushed himself into choreography, at first doing flops and finally having a hit with 1968's *Promises, Promises.* Though that was the only hit to Bennett's credit, Prince noted his work. If success is a matter of recognizing opportunities and capitalizing on them, Bennett made no mistakes. After *Company* he insisted on co-director credit for *Follies.* When *Seesaw* was in trouble on the road, he took over out of town and brought the ailing 1973 musical into New York in respectable shape, winning a reputation as a money director (one who functions under pressure). Having learned from Prince the importance of a musical's book, and determined to understand playwriting and actors as well as dancing and dancers, he turned from musicals to plays, directing several of them on Broadway. So Bennett, whose background had been restricted to Broadway dancing, conscientiously and systematically educated himself to become as sharp and canny a play director as there was in New York. Then, instead of proceeding with his career in the orthodox fashion, reading scripts and considering offers, he found a way of emulating Prince's artistic freedom without actually becoming a producer. He convinced Joseph Papp to let him use the New York Shakespeare Festival's facilities for a musical theater workshop. This gave him a show in which, as producer, he owned a sizable share, and six months of rehearsal time to develop it instead of the usual six weeks. The result was *A Chorus Line,* which had a brief engagement at Papp's downtown Newman Theater before moving to Broadway for a record-shattering run. No other director in the history of Broadway musicals succeeded so purposefully, so quickly, or so flamboyantly.

While all of this attests to Bennett's single-minded drive, it must not detract from the tremendous accomplishment that *A Chorus Line* was. The show achieved what the Sondheim-Prince musicals were unable to—vast popular success as well as artistic integrity—and without a doubt the achievement was Bennett's.

*A Chorus Line* is the Broadway musical in a mythic state. It opens in a blacked-out theater—without an overture, without a curtain—to a company of dancers being drilled by a choreographer. Suddenly, trumpets begin to blare and the full flush of the Broadway musical sweeps over the audience. There have been opening numbers so devastating that shows have been unable to top them. Here was one risking that and more, for it proclaimed that the audience wasn't merely at a musical. It was at *the* musical. *All* musicals.

Bennett wanted the show to celebrate Broadway's "gypsies"—those itinerant dancers who go from one show to another; who dance unrecognized in chorus after chorus; who practice and study and achieve their skills while seeking stardom or at least the speaking parts that for most will never come. He saw in all this a metaphor for "everyone who has ever marched in step." This metaphor was not entirely thought out or clearly presented in the production, but it hardly mattered; *A Chorus Line* was expertly orchestrated as a stage work and provided tremendous emotional rewards. On May 21, 1975, when it opened at the Newman, the show was already established as a legend. At the climactic curtain calls that night, with the company finally in full costume, the entire audience rose to its feet and cheered for the duration of the number. I have never seen such an occurrence at any other opening night. This was an ovation for history's sake, a cheer on behalf of all musical theater. The sense of community—between the audience and the actors and the occasion—was overwhelming.

*Based on the life of couturiere Chanel, Coco proved less a musical than a fashion show. It succeeded because of the spectacular presence of Katharine Hepburn. Michael Bennett's striking choreography rose above the surrounding mediocrity.*

A Chorus Line *for real: Michael Bennett rehearses dancers for* Promises, Promises.

Ballroom *was the musical Michael Bennett finally did after his colossal success*
A Chorus Line—*directing, choreographing, and even producing it. Bennett gave
the show spectacular looks, but ballroom dancing has its limitations and surprisingly,
this was a conventional book musical. As Bennett himself conceded,* A Chorus Line
*was an impossible act to follow and* Ballroom *ran but three and a half months,
becoming Broadway's first two-million-dollar flop.*

Promises, Promises, *of 1968, was Michael Bennett's first hit as a choreographer.
Composer Burt Bacharach's tricky, offbeat rhythms were fun to dance to, and Bennett
set this number, "Turkey Lurkey Time," to discotheque steps new in the theater. Like
Bennett, these dancers went on to other successes: Baayork Lee (left) would be featured
in* A Chorus Line; *Donna McKechnie (center) would be the lead dancer in*
Company *and star in* A Chorus Line; *and Margo Sappington (hidden on the
right) would choreograph the international quasi-pornographic success*
Oh, Calcutta!

135

Bennett had calculated the effect. He is aware of the "emotional rush" that can sweep over a musical's audience in a way that the dramatic theater never quite achieves. He manipulated *A Chorus Line* to generate such waves of emotion. Here was the director puppeteering not just on his stage but out over the audience. We come to the theater wishing to be manipulated in just this way. Michael Bennett became a star director on the basis of managing this just once, but who had done it so fabulously before? There was no doubt he would do it again, although the pressure for him to do it in his very next show—*Ballroom* of 1978—was fearsome.

Gower Champion was the only one of the star directors emerging in the sixties who was not a descendant of the George Abbott line. First a Broadway dancer, he'd gone on to stage such forties revues as *Small Wonder* and *Lend an Ear*. But Champion made his name in Hollywood, as a performer in film musicals. He seemed movie people rather than show people, and his early work reflected that.

The production that established Champion as a Broadway choreographer-director was *Bye, Bye, Birdie* in 1960. It was a solid example of the simpleminded but energetic, muscular kind of musical comedy that was popular as the sixties got under way. Champion followed the period's practice of directing the book scenes as if they were part of a straight play, only turning his work musical for the songs and dances. Many of the devices he created for the show were cute in a Hollywood sense rather than Broadway's, but, to cite the theater's ultimate rationalization, they worked.

Champion had another success a year later with *Carnival*, but the show that made him a star was the tremendous hit of 1964, *Hello,*

Overleaf: *A Chorus Line quadrupled.*

*Dolly!* Here was one of the best-directed musicals in Broadway history. There was not a move in it that Champion did not choreograph, not a moment when he lost track of the elegant style he'd set for it. Although *West Side Story* is remembered as *the* dance musical, *Hello, Dolly!* was just as thoroughly choreographed. Champion not only created many exhilarating dances but even during scenes, or with a ballad concluding, he'd have two or three dancers move cross-stage. This use of choreography as background was novel and ingenious; it created for the show a fabric of waltzes and cakewalks against which its primary colors were set.

Champion's hot streak of hits cooled after *I Do! I Do!* This was a stunningly staged musical that was more appreciated for its stars —Mary Martin and Robert Preston—than for Champion's work. *I Do! I Do!* offered obvious challenges, being a two-character show based on Jan de Hartog's play *The Fourposter.* Champion managed to give it full Broadway size as well as a special charm by denying the story's naturalism. He regularly reminded the audience that it was watching actors in performance (Martin and Preston would apply makeup onstage). A striking example of this conceit was the opening of the second act: With the playing of the entr'acte overture, the lights suddenly went up behind the stage cyclorama (a high curved cloth stretched the width of the stage). Behind this, where we never expected to see them, were the orchestra and conductor. The stage picture was dramatic, glamourous, and exciting. Such brainstorms are what the theater lives for and they showed Champion expanding. *I Do! I Do!* is a warm, handsome, and whimsical musical, expertly assembled, and made for any pair of star players. That is why it continues to be popular in annual summer productions across the country. Champion didn't receive fair praise for it.

*The Happy Time* in 1968 began his downslide. Champion had become powerful enough to be choosy but he wasn't proving wise in choosing. He didn't seem to have the literary instinct for good scripts. Composers claimed he wasn't even interested in their scores. *The Happy Time* had been a fairly successful play about a photographer returning to his home in Canada. There was nothing basically musical about it, and the musical version never came alive.

Champion then had a string of flops. *Prettybelle,* with a Jule Styne score and Angela Lansbury as star, closed during its out-of-town tryout. *Rockabye Hamlet* made it to opening night, but not much longer. *Sugar* was that bewildering, seventies breed of failure, the one that runs a year on Broadway and is still not considered a success. The 1973 revival of *Irene* was even more exasperating. Broadway nostalgia was booming; *No, No, Nanette* had been a great success in revival. Of all people, John Gielgud was signed to stage this old American musical. Here was a superb classical actor but an only occasional director whose British repertory background had not the slightest connection with Broadway musicals. His being engaged was traditional theatrical madness. It was inevitable that he would be replaced somewhere along *Irene*'s road to Broadway, and that it would be an expensive replacement. For when a show is in trouble, the replacement director knows of the crisis and can exact a stiff price. Then the producer has to pay royalties to two directors for as long as the show runs, which can place an intolerable burden on its running cost. Gielgud was ultimately replaced by Champion, who brought *Irene* to Broadway not a good show but certainly a hit. It played 604 performances and grossed millions, but its operating expenses were so great it could not return a penny to its investors.

Bye, Bye, Birdie *was the first book musical directed by Gower Champion, shown here with its stars, Chita Rivera and Dick Van Dyke. Champion had previously directed only revues:* Small Wonder, Lend an Ear, *and* Three for Tonight. *The great success of the energetic and immensely likable show,* Birdie, *established Champion as a choreographer-director who could stage dramatic scenes and supervise the overall construction of a show.*

*Gower Champion had a problem staging "The Telephone Hour" number in* Bye, Bye, Birdie—*how to show a whole townful of kids on their telephones. His now legendary solution was this beehive set. Theatrical and practical, it established physical separation without losing the shoulder-to-shoulder volume and group presence of a chorus. The number became a showstopper.*

*Relaxing during rehearsals for* I Do! I Do! *are stars Robert Preston and Mary Martin, Director Gower Champion (right) and the show's producer, David Merrick. Negotiating his contract with Merrick, Preston promised to make no superstar demands. "All I want," he said, "is what Mary gets."*

I Do! I Do! *(below) needed to carry a big Broadway stage with only two characters. Champion managed to give the audience the sense of a full-size musical by capitalizing on his larger-than-life stars and by "choreographing" Oliver Smith's airy, stylized scenery so that it soared the height and width of the stage.*

As a producer of musicals, David Merrick was the most prolific in the history of Broadway. His name became as well known as any of the stars, composers, or directors he hired. He made himself famous, not for ego's sake but because he knew the value of publicity. Merrick became the man people loved to hate, but as long as they lined up at the box office, he had no objections.

Merrick was the last of Broadway's flamboyant producers. Some of his promotional schemes have taken their place in theater lore. When his Subways Are for Sleeping opened to devastating pans, he found seven laymen who had the same names as the drama critics and ran an advertisement quoting from their "rave reviews." It made several early newspaper editions before being spotted for a fraud.

When Anna Maria Alberghetti took sick leave from Carnival, Merrick aired his skepticism of her illness. When she returned to the show, he had an actor impersonate a psychologist who supposedly would verify her honesty were she to complain again. Merrick also hired a Staten Island cowboy club to roar up and down Forty-fifth Street for the sake of Destry Rides Again, and he erected a statue of a belly dancer in Central Park to promote Fanny.

Fanny, in 1954, was Merrick's first show. During the next twenty-two years he produced twenty-five musicals. With one of them, a good show called Oliver, Merrick virtually outwitted the New York critics by touring it at length before its New York premiere. With its songs already popular hits by the time of the opening night, it was almost pan-proof—but got good reviews anyhow. Another of his innovations was replacing Carol Channing, once she'd left Hello, Dolly!, with a series of well-known stars—Ginger Rogers, Betty Grable, Martha Raye, Pearl Bailey, and finally Ethel Merman, for whom the show had originally been designed. Hello, Dolly! may well have been the most deftly prolonged success in Broadway history, running an astounding 2,844 performances on successive bursts of publicity.

Merrick's most active years were from 1958 through 1966, during which he produced seventeen shows, including hits Gypsy, Irma la Douce, Stop the World—I Want to Get Off, Carnival, I Do! I Do!, and Promises, Promises. His taste wasn't artistic, his aspirations weren't artistic, and as a result he produced few artistic musicals. He inclined to book musical comedies, slickly produced, and his theory seemed to be that if you fired often enough, something would hit the target. He respected professionalism and tended to work with proven regulars of the musical stage. Though his feuds were legendary, he repeatedly worked with director Gower Champion and composers Harold Rome, Jerry Herman, Bob Merrill, and Jule Styne. As Carol Channing said, "I'll never work for him again until he offers me another great show."

With the arrival of the seventies, Merrick lost his touch and suffered a devastating series of flops. Three expensive musicals closed during their pre-Broadway tryouts—Mata Hari in Washington, D.C., The Baker's Wife in Los Angeles, and Breakfast at Tiffany's in the midst of its New York previews. Mack and Mabel failed on Broadway. He produced the successful revival of Very Good Eddie in 1975, but the show was essentially a transfer from The Goodspeed Opera House in Connecticut. Merrick turned to movie producing, perhaps realizing that the Broadway he'd enjoyed no longer existed. It was impossible for any man to single-handedly raise the money for a full-scale musical; impossible to produce more than one show every few years; impossible to treat the musical theater on the personal level that had been such profitable fun for so many years. With his departure, the era of brassy Broadway shows as well as of brassy Broadway producers had more or less ended.

*Although choreographer-directors are known for their dances, when they are called in to "doctor" a show in trouble on the road, they seldom have time for choreography. Gower Champion came in and indeed saved the elaborate 1973 revival of* Irene *(above) from disaster. But its dances were by the original choreographer, one of Broadway's best, Peter Gennaro. This number, led by Debbie Reynolds, is typical of Gennaro's airy elegance.*

*Champion took over many shows that were in trouble during tryouts. He reshaped* Irene *into a hit. In 1977 he made Kander and Ebb's* The Act *respectable. He had less success the next year with Adams and Strouse's* A Broadway Musical. *The show closed on opening night and down the drain with it went this spectacular dance (right) that Champion staged—an affectionate look at the black shows of the thirties called "Hot Chocolates."*

In 1977, John Kander and Fred Ebb's *The Act* ran into problems on the road. Problems had been on the horizon right along for here was one musical whose star, Liza Minnelli, had all the clout. She was a surefire box office attraction and it was assumed that whatever the quality of the show, she would guarantee business (this was typical of the merchandising approach that was beginning to appear in the Broadway theater of the time). Minnelli was given her choice of director, which is tantamount to theatrical suicide since it puts the star's wishes ahead of the show's needs. She demanded Martin Scorcese, a filmmaker who had never worked on the stage, let alone on anything as complex and peculiar as a Broadway musical. Ultimately Minnelli *allowed* Champion to take over the show and bring it to Broadway in respectable condition, but only so long as Scorcese was still billed as director. The theater is not as far from its madcap roots as it likes to think.

Champion, still the professional, pulled *The Act* through, but he claimed to have lost interest in the routine of show making, and in choreography generally. Doubtless his series of disappointments—*Sugar, Mack and Mabel, Rockabye Hamlet*—had much to do with this. Failed shows are devastating to theater makers. The chilly critical response to *The Act* surely didn't make Champion feel enthusiastic about new projects. Within the year he stepped in as director for *A Broadway Musical.* It closed on opening night. Yet, even then, he began planning a stage version of the classic movie musical *42nd Street.*

Ron Field was another director who had let Broadway's ups and downs get to him. Having revived *On the Town* in 1971, plainly

*Lauren Bacall had never danced or sung on a Broadway stage. For* Applause, *Director Ron Field (left) showed her what she was capable of and how to do it. He masterfully delivered her to stardom. A hard-working woman with brains and elegance, Bacall never denied him his credit.*

hoping to succeed to Robbins's mantle by redoing his show, Field had fled to California in the wake of its failure. He spent his time staging nightclub acts and television specials, licking his wounds and waiting to be offered the show to take him back to Broadway. The show would be *King of Hearts* in 1978 and it would fail.

Field's New York reputation as a choreographer-director had been based on one show, but that show had been *Applause* (1970)—a solid hit whose success had obviously been Field's doing. *Applause* did not have an especially good book or score and its star, Lauren Bacall, was not a major theater attraction when the show opened. Ron Field used sheer craftsmanship to fashion the show's mediocre materials into sleek entertainment. He proved to be a thoroughbred professional, directing at his best when under pressure.

There were other director-choreographers active going into the seventies. Michael Kidd had been one of the first of the breed with a career dating back to the forties, when he'd done the dances for *Finian's Rainbow.* He had the choreography for such major hits as *Guys and Dolls* and *Can-Can* to his credit. But his vigorous theme-oriented work (lasso dances, whip dances, jackhammer dances) was associated with the brassy musicals that Broadway had outgrown, and his reputation as a director had been clouded by a series of unsuccessful, old-fashioned book musicals. Joe Layton had a similar

*Michael Kidd's "Quadrille" (below) from* Can-Can *is danced in a courtroom where a judge must decide if it's obscene. Second from left and in the sequence at right is Gwen Verdon, on her way to stardom.* Below: *The show's billed star, Lilo, confronts Verdon and Hans Conreid, who played the second male lead. A better part, spectacular dances, and her own tremendous talent all gave Verdon the chance to steal the show from Lilo. Steal it she did.*

*Michael Kidd stages the choreography for* Destry Rides Again. *Kidd had been one of the first choreographer-directors and, in the fifties, was one of the busiest.*

*Andy Griffith, in the checkered suit, and Dolores Gray, in the slit skirt, fight it out in a production scene of* Destry Rides Again, *with Scott Brady as the rather exuberant referee. Exuberance was considered necessary to any musical staging at the time (1959). Gray's stage presence and voice led to expectations of her becoming Merman's successor but the brassy type went out of style.*

*The show is* Mame, *directed by Gene Saks, the star is Angela Lansbury (center) making her big Broadway splash, and the dance is by Onna White, one of Broadway's classiest choreographers.*

association, though in his case it was ironic since he'd been but sixteen when he danced in *Oklahoma!* A ten-year streak of flops nearly did him in, though *Drat! The Cat!,* which he directed and choreographed in 1965, had a fresh and quirky fun about it. Fresh and quirky musicals have always had a tough time of it on Broadway.

The musical theater's new emphasis on director-choreographers still left room for nonchoreographing directors like Gene Saks, Burt Shevelove, and Gerald Freedman. Saks was the rare director who could move easily between the worlds of plays and musicals, and had great musical successes with *Mame* and *I Love My Wife.* Shevelove's big hit was the revival of *No, No, Nanette,* and his staging of the 1972 revival of *A Funny Thing Happened on the Way to the Forum* threatened to surpass the original in wit and stylishness. But, without question, the era belonged to the choreographer-directors, and there were gifted others waiting for the major hit to establish them—Donald McKayle, Grover Dale, Billy Wilson, George Faison, Tommy Tune. There was still hope that Herbert Ross would return from a successful career in film directing to the musical stage he'd started on.

The seventies was not merely an era for the choreographer-director but for the person able to conceive shows whole. The director had become the musical's maker.

*Those involved with* Drat! The Cat! *in 1965 should have learned from the previous year's* Anyone Can Whistle *that offbeat musicals are risky. Focused on a bumbling cop's romance with a millionairess/cat burglar, the show was directed by Joe Layton, who was never better; stars Lesley Ann Warren and Elliot Gould were charming; the Milton Schaefer-Ira Wallach score was witty. But musicals cannot succeed on appeal to special or too-educated tastes.*

149

ALVIN
MIKE NICHOLS
Annie
A New Musical
WINNER OF 7 1977 TONY AWARDS
IPANEMA DISCOTHEQUE

# RUNNING A SHOW THROUGH-ANNIE

When the theater is spoken of as "illusion," it is not in any philosophical or mystical sense. As the houselights go down and the curtain rises, we make an unconscious adjustment: We forget that we are in a darkened auditorium; we hardly notice that the stage is much brighter than an ordinary room. We believe the story as it begins; we pretend the actors are really the characters they are playing. This much we give to the show we are about to see because we want to be entertained. In the familiar phrase, we extend a "willingness to suspend disbelief." The show must then take us the rest of the way by sustaining the illusion. How does it do that?

If asked, most theatergoers would have a general notion of what it takes to present a drama. Few, however, realize what is necessary to present a full-scale musical, eight performances a week. Audiences are serenely ignorant of the people, the planning, the coordination, and the details necessary to give a performance.

It is a breathtakingly complex operation that demands precise synchronization both on and backstage.

Let's follow a show through a performance and see just what is necessary. The musical we're going to observe is Annie, a show that opened to a small advance sale at the Alvin Theater on April 21, 1977, and went on to be a huge hit. I've chosen Annie because it is a complicated production that uses all the technical resources of the musical theater. With rising costs, some musicals have tried to cut corners by using one set and by keeping the cast small and the show simple. Being a big Broadway musical, Annie is old-fashioned. In backstage parlance, it is a show with a "heavy book," a technically complex production.

There are twenty-three actors who appear at one time or another, as one character or another, in Annie. There are also three "swing" actors—a male, a female, and a child who can play (or "cover") any role that isn't assigned to an understudy. The "swing" actors appear only when someone is ill. They do not have parts of their own. They cover the uncovered, filling in the last role as everyone moves up a notch. Even Sandy, the dog in Annie, has a standby (named Arf).

Then there are four stage managers—Janet Beroza, the supervisory production stage manager; Jack Timmers, the stage manager who actually pilots the show; and two assistant stage managers. There are also twelve dressers to sort, clean, and change costumes. A wardrobe supervisor is in charge of them.

Annie has a stagehand staff of thirty-three and that includes carpenters, electricians, fly men, and a sound man. The "fly men" are the stagehands who control the scenery that "flies" or drops from the "fly floor" high above the stage. There are also "sliders," stagehands who push sets in and pull them out, manually or on one or two treadmills. Other set changes are mechanized, using "winches"—cables that pull scenery on and off.

Down in the orchestra pit there are eighteen musicians and their musical director (conductor), Peter Howard. Standing by, again in case of illness, is an assistant musical director.

All of this makes for an Annie production staff of ninety-six people. And two dogs. This does not include ushers or ticket takers or the house (theater) manager. The production people meet at the Alvin Theater before every performance and then run through a split-second, two-and-a-half-hour routine that will look to the audience as if everything began at curtain time and involved only twenty-three actors onstage.

The ritual of an evening performance of Annie begins at seven o'clock, an hour before curtain time. The physical Annie is literally upside down. The set for the finale, the Warbucks mansion decorated for Christmas, is onstage. The house "prop" (properties) man is vacuuming the stage, cleaning up the "snow" that has lain there since the company took its curtain calls the night before. The props in the wings are those that were last removed from the stage. The first-act props are buried behind them and the sets are scattered, some leaning up against walls, others in the flies. Most Broadway theaters are cramped backstage. They were not built for complex, modern musicals, which have to be shoehorned into them. The Alvin Theater is particularly small.

At seven o'clock, the prop men begin to switch scenery and props from where they end up to where they start. Every piece must be placed exactly where a particular stagehand will expect to find it during the pressure of performance. (There had been but a day and a half before previews for the director to figure all this out!) The placement of every piece becomes routine but it must be checked at each performance. Should one step in this "preset" ritual be overlooked, the entire performance can be thrown out of whack. What, indeed, would happen were Miss Hannigan's desk to slide out without its chair? Or without the radio on it (she has to turn it on at one point)? Or without the pack of cigarettes and lighter (she smokes)?

Also at seven o'clock, the sound man is testing the amplification system; the production electricians are doing a light check. They aren't checking only for burned-out bulbs and frayed wiring. The "gels" (gelatin filters) that tint the lights can also burn out. A burned-out blue gel, for instance, will cast an amber light at the center, not very appropriate in a moonlight scene.

Miss Beroza, the production stage manager, is running through the "preset checklist," an organizational plan not unlike the checklist a pilot uses in preparing for takeoff. None of it can be trusted to memory.

At 7:30, a half hour before curtain, the entire Annie cast except for Raymond Thorne, the actor playing President Franklin Roosevelt, is required to be in the theater. Because Roosevelt doesn't appear until the second act, Thorne can arrive forty-five minutes after show time. But three of the four leading actors usually arrive at seven: Reid Shelton, who plays Daddy Warbucks; Dorothy Loudon, who plays Miss Hannigan, the mistress of the Municipal Orphanage; and Sandy Faison, who plays Warbucks's secretary. Shelton likes to relax before a show; Loudon takes her time putting on her costume, makeup, and wig. Faison vocalizes, preparing her voice. Andrea McArdle, the show's original Little Orphan Annie, is a relaxed youngster who strolls into the theater close to curtain time and plays at her dressing room pinball machine for the last few minutes. (McArdle had become the show's star but her stay was limited. She began playing the eleven-year-old Annie when she herself was fourteen; soon she became too old for the role and was replaced in March, 1978.)

The entire crew of stagehands is also due at 7:30. Only then can the production stage manager rehearse understudies on the set, which, according

152

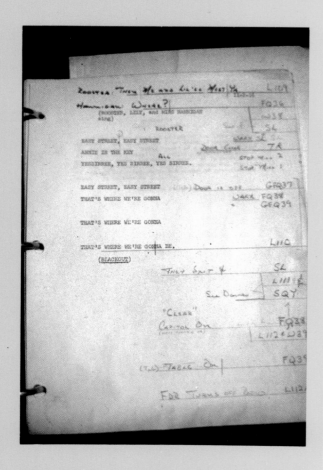

154

to union regulations, requires the presence of a stagehand. Sometimes, scenes have to be restaged, their dialogue rearranged, even the set changed. All of this rearrangement must wait until the half hour before curtain time. It is done as the audience is filing into the auditorium.

Jack Timmers is the stage manager who runs Annie. He is indeed a pilot. He is also the commander, the navigator, and the troubleshooter. He is in charge of the entire backstage army and controls everything short of the performers. During shows, they are in the hands of God and the conductor.

A musical's stage manager has a stand-up desk in the "wings" (just offstage). On the desk is the most important prop in the production—the "prompt book." In this working script is marked every single cue for running the show—every light cue, sound cue, winch cue. Annie has 135 light cues, 42 winch cues, 40 fly cues. Working from the prompt book, the production stage manager controls every physical move and change. Before he gives the go-ahead—which tells the person responsible when to move a prop or switch on a spotlight—he gives an alert, or warning signal. All of these cues are marked down in the prompt book precisely, even between two words of dialogue. There is a system for cuing everyone. The cues may be vocal (the stage manager wears a headset with a microphone) or visual (turning on a light for the alert, turning it off at "go"). There are also physical cues such as the tapping of the rope man's shoulder at the exact moment for raising the curtain at the end of the overture.

Above the stage manager's desk and facing him at eye level are a series of switches. These control the light bulbs that cue fly men, light-board operators, winch operators, and the sound man. One of these buttons is labeled "panic" and it is neither a joke nor the actual panic button. There are so many switches around it that it could be accidentally pressed. It is a reminder that there is a real panic button, located on a shelf above the stage manager's desk. When pressed, it instantly cuts off the electricity backstage. Even scenery dropping from the flies would stop in midair. This panic button exists in case of any accident or dangerous situation, such as a foot caught in a treadmill. That actually happened to Miss Loudon during the first out-of-town performance, but luckily, she managed to rescue her toe without stopping the performance.

From Timmers's desk, most of the performance is hidden by a "tab" curtain, which rises to let scenery slide through and then drops so that the audience will not be distracted by backstage light. But if the light can be blocked, the noise can't. It is difficult to believe that the clanging, banging, and clonking of the moving scenery can't be heard by the audience. Especially noisy scene changes are covered by musical underscoring but sometimes that can't be managed. Reid Shelton's big second-act ballad, "Something Was Missing," is sung in the midst of a massive "move" (scene change) and Shelton, an otherwise gentle man, has a running quarrel with the stagehands about the noise behind him.

Because of the tab curtain the stage manager can only see part of the show he is running. He sees the rest on a television monitor. A camera fixed to the front center of the balcony transmits this picture to the stage manager and also to the light men. The light boards that control the profusion of stage lights are set on a platform ten feet high above the stage manager's desk, and the light men there can see the results of their work only on another television monitor.

As the minutes clock down to curtain, the preset routine speeds up. Now 7:45, Timmers is running his finger down the prompt book checklist. The opening scenery has now been put onstage, the actors are in costume. Miss Beroza is giving "notes" (criticism) to the company, based on the previous performance. The dance captain is also giving notes on musical numbers. A musical's dance captain is usually the female swing dancer, but since all the

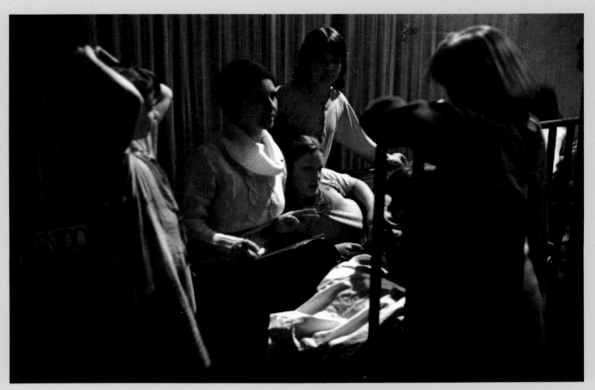

dancers in Annie *are children, the captain is never in the show. She is responsible for keeping all the musical staging clean. So the maintenance of a show, as far as performers are concerned, is divided among the production stage manager, the dance captain, and the musical director.*

*At two minutes to curtain time, one of the assistant stage managers announces, "Places, please, for Act One." Soon, Timmers is in radio contact with the house manager out front, "holding" (delaying) the curtain if there are blocks of unoccupied seats down front, where latecomers would distract the performers. Now the actors are ready, backstage is ready, and the audience is ready. Getting a go-ahead from the house manager, Timmers whispers into his microphone, "May I have the house to half, please?" That is an alert to the electrician. With Timmers's whispered "Go," the auditorium lights dim half- way to blackout. Timmers asks for "curtain warmers," the lights focused on the bottom of the curtain so it won't look forbidding. He alerts Howard, the conductor, for the overture and then whispers, "Go." The overture begins. The house darkens. Miss Beroza is still onstage, whispering last-minute instructions to an understudy. There has been no announcement of a re- placement. Actors Equity (the actors' union) requires two of three specified ways to inform an audience that an understudy is performing: an insert in the program, a sign in the lobby, or an announcement over the public-address system. Like most productions, Annie avoids the last alternative. Nobody wants a groaning audience to demoralize the company.*

*As the overture comes to an end, Timmers taps the rope man, and the curtain rises on the opening scene of Annie, in the Municipal Orphanage. The moment is as exciting as anything in the theater—the tap on the shoulder, the pull on the rope, the soar of the curtain, and the transformation of the actors behind it from mere mortals into actors performing for an audience of 1,300 people.*

*Annie's first act will run about one hour and fifteen minutes. From one performance to the next, the running time will not vary by more than two minutes. Timmers is relaxed at his desk now, though his eyes seldom stray from the prompt book. As soon as one cue is given, he turns the script's pages to the next one. He paces nervously between the desk and the tab curtain. An orphan exits into the wings and cries to him that she's forgotten the lyrics of her song. He calmly recites them to her, but two steps from Timmers, you'd hardly know*

that a show was in progress. Clusters of stagehands are in conversation, even with visitors. The show out onstage can hardly be heard except for the trumpets. Actors are out there singing but nobody is watching from back here.

There are two musical numbers in Annie's opening scene, "Maybe" and "It's a Hard Knock Life." Suddenly, the scene is over and Timmers must supervise the show's first big "move." The orphanage windows are flown. The columns are flown. The beds and the door unit start to travel offstage on the treadmills. As the door unit reaches center stage on its way off, it is just in front of the bridge painted on a traveler at the rear. As they coincide, stagehands behind the set begin sliding the bridge off on its tracks, in the same direction as the door. This is all designed as a montage of horizontal and vertical movement all over the stage. The audience is never given a chance to watch any one piece of scenery completing its move to exit because that goes beyond the point of interest. As soon as one unit or flat or slide establishes the direction it is going in, another begins to move, and then another. With the orphanage door unit approaching the wings, the traveling brownstones begin to glide in on their tracks, from both sides of the stage. These brownstones are only eighteen feet high but David Mitchell, Annie's gifted set designer, devised them in accurate perspective from the audience's point of view. They are flat sets that will be the next scene's background. So, one set is being removed from the stage (or "struck") while the next setting is being introduced. This process is accompanied by lighting changes and musical underscoring. It is an elaborate scenic choreography, so effective that directors often successfully use it to instigate applause at the end of a number.

After its first big move, Annie is rolling. Little Orphan Annie has fled the orphanage, adopted the dog Sandy, sung "Tomorrow," and been taken in by a Depression community. The "Hooverville" set is onstage and the company is stepping into its number. Timmers sings along, under his breath, at the stage manager's desk.

But meanwhile he is preparing another major change: Some scenes later, Annie will visit the Warbucks mansion and then go out with the millionaire for a stroll uptown. This is the show's "N.Y.C." number and it involves not only an elaborate Times Square set but a crowd of chorus members. Among the show's many complex scenes, it is the most complicated because it requires maximum activity, not only from the backstage people but the actors as well. You see, though "N.Y.C." shows *many New Yorkers* onstage, Annie doesn't have so large a chorus. The days of big choruses disappeared with inflation. In order to make it look as if there are many pedestrians onstage during this number, the director has his company saunter into the wings and then change costumes and wigs to reappear on the other side as different people. But at the Alvin Theater, the costume, wig, and dressing rooms are in the basement. So, as "N.Y.C." progresses, actors are cheerful, songful, choreographic, and casual as they stroll offstage only to abruptly bolt down a steep spiral staircase, tear into the basement, grab new wigs from the table where they'd been set out, change (or be changed) into the next costume, and then roar up the stairs on the other side to emerge onstage, once more cheerful, songful, choreographic, and casual. The audience has no idea of the breakneck behind-the-scenes activity. It should have no idea.

The performance flows along with no problems so far. Another big move takes the action back to the orphanage, and Loudon launches into "Easy Street," dancing along with Robert Fitch, who plays her villainous brother, and Barbara Erwin, as his wife. The number is a showstopper, as always. Performing, selling herself, giving to the audience, working the room, Loudon seems to be all the performers in stage history. Timmers loves the audience response. But he knows that an audience is human too. It always responds to "Easy Street" but the response is different from one performance to the next. If the applause is disappointing, the company's morale can be affected. If the number draws an especially long ovation, it can slow the show down and affect the cast's timing. The stage manager must deal with either alternative.

With the intermission, the stage fills as the theater empties. At fourteen minutes, Annie's intermission is one minute shorter than the Broadway usual. This is a long show and nobody wants to make it longer. Each one of the fourteen minutes is necessary since one major set has to be replaced with another, but nobody wants to keep the audience out one minute longer than necessary because it can lose interest and become restless. In short, the audience is considered another aspect of the production and, to the extent that it can be, it too is controlled.

Everyone is busy backstage while the audience is having its intermission break. The stagehands are striking the Warbucks mansion and setting up the thirties radio station that opens the second act. Actors and assistant stage managers cluster in small groups onstage, ironing out minor problems.

Soon, the house manager advises Timmers that the "front" (the audience's side of the stage) is ready for the second act. An assistant stage manager tells him, "We are ready onstage," meaning the setting is in place and the actors, properly costumed, are in their places. Timmers starts the second-act ritual. "Stand by houselights . . . warning house, warning [curtain] warmers. . . . May I have the house to half. . . . Warmers, go," and with that Howard gives the downbeat for the entr'acte.

The second half of Annie is much lighter, in terms of backstage activity, than the first. Musicals' second acts are almost always shorter than the first. Annie's runs fifty-eight minutes, as compared with an hour and fifteen minutes for the first act. Also there are only six scenes to the first act's eight and the last three are all in the Warbucks mansion, meaning no changes of scenery except for the raising of a flat and the hauling in of a Christmas tree.

The second act of Annie has one of the show's few total blackouts. It is used not to cover a change of scenery but for artistic purposes. This particular

scene deals with President Roosevelt's cabinet and it is more vaudevillian and less naturalistic than the rest of the show—Roosevelt is treated in a comic way and even leads his cabinet in song. The blackout, by putting a "button" on the scene to end it conclusively, emphasizes the nature of the scene as a vaudeville sketch, which keeps it from being presidentially disrespectful.

The second act also leaves time for everyone backstage to relax, with back-to-back scenes and songs for Annie and Warbucks. The audience's mood is relaxed too; it knows by now that it is enjoying Annie and besides, the show is developing its sentimental side.

The show at last moves into its finale and the audience response is warm. Annie is not great or significant; it is an old-fashioned book show built on the theater's corniest devices—children, Christmas, even a dog—but to use the key word in the Broadway musical theater, it works. The audience has gotten its money's worth. The curtain plummets down and then soars up again as the company takes its bows. The actors' faces are lit up, not merely by the lights but by their response to the audience and the applause. Timmers begins his final cues. "Bring it home," he tells the rope man at his side and the man drops the curtain for the last time. "Houselights, please." The traditional "walkout music" begins as the audience starts up the aisles. They whistle Annie's hit song, "Tomorrow." The show is done.

At least it is done for twenty hours. At seven o'clock the next day, the preset ritual for the evening performance will begin all over again.

# COMPOSERS: THE GIANTS

# JEROME KERN

Jerome David Kern was the father, the teacher, the master—the king of American theater composers. They are all in debt to him and they all admitted it. It was Kern who took operetta music through an American door and into the twentieth century, Kern who invented the show song. Is it really possible that he wrote "They Didn't Believe Me" in *1914?*

From the early twenties until 1945, when he collapsed of a fatal cerebral hemorrhage on a New York sidewalk at the age of sixty, Jerome Kern created the foundation on which Broadway show music has been built. He never seemed fully convinced that high theater music should not be in the operetta style. His songs prove otherwise. He came upon an American energy, an American freedom, an American expressiveness, an American directness. His best music—so fresh, so true, so straight —was rooted in that Americanism.

It was as.if our musical theater had been waiting for a song to match its stage sense. Once the two met, history could be made.

Drawn from thirty-six shows, the catalogue of Kern theater songs is prodigious and beloved. It ranges from the early "Till the Clouds Roll By" through the *Show Boat* score to the final lilting melodies ("She Didn't Say Yes," "I've Told Every Little Star") and exquisite ballads ("Smoke Gets in Your Eyes," "The Touch of Your Hand").

Kern did not have a steady lyricist. In the first half of his career, P. G. Wodehouse was his most frequent collaborator. He never had a regular partner afterward, although he wrote several shows with Anne Caldwell, Oscar Hammerstein II, and Otto Harbach. On his last five shows, his partners alternated between Hammerstein and Harbach, as if he were even then wavering between the operetta tradition of the past that Harbach was tied to and the musical play of the future, to which Hammerstein was looking. If Kern and Hammerstein had considered a steady partnership, their 1939 failure, *Very Warm for May,* would have put an end to the notion. Hammerstein went on to team up with Richard Rodgers. Curiously, those two were the producers of what was to have been Kern's last show, *Annie Oakley,* with lyrics by Dorothy Fields. When Kern died, the project was turned over to Irving Berlin. It became *Annie Get Your Gun.*

Too bad that Kern never worked with the likes of Lorenz Hart or Ira Gershwin. He wrote frequently with Dorothy Fields, but only for movies. Because he was unwisely arrogant toward lyrics—he was not inclined to change even a note for their sake—Kern might well have had trouble working with any confident and strong-willed lyricist.

A trained musician, Kern studied piano, theory, and harmony at the New York College of Music and under private tutors in Germany. Despite this training, he wrote his songs in the elementary lead-sheet form of melody plus basic chords. Only once—in 1942, three years before his death—did he try his hand at concert music, with "Mark Twain: A Portrait for Orchestra." It isn't much.

Kern began his theatrical career by interpolating songs into scores written by others ("They Didn't Believe Me" was contributed to *The Girl from Utah*). An aloof man not usually given to humor, Kern once joked that interpolating songs was such a common practice that a producer could go to the rear of a theater to congratulate a composer on a show's opening-night success and find a whole crowd of songwriters saying thanks. Well, he was an aloof man, not usually given to humor.

In 1917, though, he had no fewer than five musicals entirely his own—*Have a Heart, Love o' Mike, Leave It to Jane, Miss 1917,* and *Oh, Boy!* All but *Love o' Mike* were written to lyrics by P. G. Wodehouse. *Oh, Boy!* was one of the legendary "Princess shows." These were a series presented at the Princess Theater, a midtown house with the size and feel of latter-day off-Broadway. Kern wrote four Princess musicals, the best remembered being *Very Good Eddie* and *Oh, Lady! Lady!* As a group, these intimate musicals are less celebrated for their staying power than for having once and for all eliminated the ornate trappings of operetta from Broadway musicals. Here was the birth of musical comedy.

The following year, Kern again came up with five shows. Prodigious as this output was, it was matched by other composers. Musicals had caught on with the public in a very big way. By the twenties, as many as two dozen were being produced in a season. Productions were intimate and uncomplicated. Even for the times, costs were low. Audiences were easily satisfied, expecting little more than gaiety. A libretto was considered only an excuse for a mindless entertainment—songs, dances, comedians, and pretty girls.

*A twenty-one-year-old Vivienne Segal looks glum in the chorus of Kern's 1918 Princess Theater musical* Oh, Lady! Lady! *She would later hit her stride as the star of* I Married an Angel *and* Pal Joey.

Kern was now hitting his musical stride. The tentativeness he had shown in his early work was replaced by confidence and self-assertion. He and the Broadway musical had arrived. His 1920 *Sally* included "Look for the Silver Lining," the kind of perfect melody that comes entirely to mind with the mere mention of the title. Apparently a companion piece to his earlier "Till the Clouds Roll By" from *Oh, Boy!*, it is one of those songs whose lyrics (by B. G. DeSylva) seem to exactly catch the mood of the melody. Where would "You'll Never Walk Alone" be without "Look for the Silver Lining"? But the inspiration is not only in the words; the *melody* gives us a lift.

In our enchantment with music, we tend to take melody for granted. Melody is one of the most indescribable, unanalyzable elements in all art. Even when enriched by harmony and rhythm, melody is the essence of song. Kern was a knowing musician and his music could be ingenious: uncommonly long or short, daring in its surprises. "All the Things You Are" is a virtuoso construction of breathtaking modulations, considered by many theater composers to be the finest American song ever written. Burton Lane says he leaped from his seat when he first heard it in *Very Warm for May*. Technique can enrich a song and make it fascinating. Melody, however, is the magic. If Kern did not possess a genius for melody, his music would be of only academic interest. It was not his musicianship that made him great but his songfulness. For sheer melody he simply had no superior.

Having as much as invented stage ballads with "They Didn't Believe Me," he proceeded to develop production numbers. If his ballads might be considered pop music of a decidedly higher class, "Who?" (*Sunny,* 1925) couldn't be considered pop music at all. Here was a song made for the stage—for a chorus to sing and dancers to dance. Kern had been working his way up to such "numbers" with the title song for *Leave It to Jane,* for example, but it was not until "Who?" with its breathless excitement—the held notes stretched over an unrushing rhythm—that he perfected the type. This was the Broadway-to-be.

The sad fact of Kern's career, however, is that the musical theater was not ready to match his music with stagecraft. Though his songs are awesome, they can be sung only out of context; the shows themselves, with their foolish books, are better forgotten. *Very Good Eddie* was given a Broadway revival in 1976, but its modest success was based on nostalgia rather than respect.

*Show Boat* is his only show that will be regularly revived. It must stand alone representing him in performance, but, fortunately, the score was his best. It is as if Kern realized that at last he had gotten his hands on a property worthy of his musical and theatrical ideas.

His partner on *Show Boat* was, of course, Oscar Hammerstein II, who wrote the book and lyrics. Hammerstein's libretto is based on Edna Ferber's novel, and its main plot deals with the ongoing romantic problems of Magnolia Hawks and Gaylord Ravenal. Since Magnolia becomes a stage star in the story, and because a show boat figures as a prominent setting, there are ample opportunities for show-within-a-show numbers.

Today, *Show Boat*'s story seems melodramatic and gauche. To understand its significance as a libretto for the musical theater, we must put it in historical perspective. *Show Boat* opened in 1927. The standard musical fare on Broadway had been musical extravaganzas, revues, and the operettas of Victor Herbert, Rudolf Friml, and

Marilyn Miller, the tiny dancing superstar, went from revues to a series of musical comedies with girls' names—Sally *(1920),* Sunny *(1925), and* Rosalie *(1928).* **Above:** *Here she is as Kern's* Sally, *where she got to introduce his gorgeous "Look for the Silver Lining" (lyric by B. G. DeSylva).* **Left:** *A somewhat unlikely lover in this scene from* Sally *is the low comic Leon Errol, best known to habitués of television's Late Late Show. The object of his ardor is the achingly beautiful Miss Miller.*

Sigmund Romberg. The operetta was characterized by an exotic locale, a fairy-tale story, and stock characters. They all thrived side by side with the new American shows of the twenties—mostly featherbrained musical comedies with wide-eyed ingenues and earnest young men.

*Show Boat,* on the other hand, deals with adult and not always happily ended romance. Hammerstein's lyrics refer to the story and so are sung in character. This forced the composer to consider the particular story when writing his songs, for melody had to match character and suit what a particular character was thinking or feeling at any given moment. *Such lyrics also forced the audience to keep the story in mind while enjoying the musical numbers.* This was the first step toward integrating songs with story in a musical. It was a singular contribution to the development of Broadway musicals.

*Show Boat* does smack of operetta, but how could it not? Breaks with the past are never made overnight. Hammerstein, after all, had collaborated on *Rose Marie* and *The Desert Song.* Kern had developed his light, "American" approach to show songs with the intimate Princess Theater musicals. *Show Boat* is a big period piece. Naturally, it tugged him back to the more grandiose music of operetta. So, Hammerstein and Kern pulled each other toward the past while at the same time pushing each other ahead to the future. Their show's opening number, a traditional strolling chorus to introduce the setting ("See the show boat"), hearkens back to Victor Herbert. Other songs in the score also spring from operetta: the declamatory

Above: *Norma Hawks was Magnolia and Howard Marsh played Gaylord in this, the original 1927 production of* Show Boat. *The greeting card scenery and elaborate costumes suggest how close the show was to operetta. Yet, its serious approach to script, lyrics, and music cut the ties with the past forever and sent Broadway's musical theater on its way to being a uniquely American stage genre.*

Opposite: *A show within a show—an old-fashioned melodrama in the theater on the Show Boat—was an ambitious device for the musical theater of its day. Here, Charles Winninger plays Cap'n Andy, fiddling the accompaniment to the stage play while the attention of the real audience turns to an assassin in the balcony.*

Overleaf: *A revival of* Show Boat *at Lincoln Center in 1966 starred David Wayne as Cap'n Andy, Barbara Cook as Magnolia, and Stephen Douglass as Ravenal; William Warfield was Joe and Constance Towers played Julie.*

167

"You Are Love," the foursquare "At the Fair," and the very Nelson Eddy–Jeanette MacDonald "Why Do I Love You?"

But this score also includes the most marvelous of the American Kern: the exquisite "Make Believe," the touching "Bill," the gliding easygoing, unmistakable Kern of "Life Upon the Wicked Stage." The bluesy "Can't Help Lovin' That Man" is a rare example of Kern being influenced (by Gershwin) but it is and deserves to be a classic. Its double-time production reprise even manages to be ingratiating while treating blacks as hand-clapping darkies. And as for "Ol' Man River," while not sung as often as it once was because of its racial stereotyping, it is still a giant among American songs. Though it is an art song it doesn't sound stuffy because its subject, unlike romance, is big enough to justify musical oratory.

That *Show Boat* was created in 1927 is astounding. It is the only musical from the period that can bear consideration in a modern context.

Kern never developed the musical play beyond this point. Perhaps he was too close to see what possibilities it invited, perhaps he was still song-conscious when theater-consciousness was the order of the day. Although he had discovered the need to tailor songs to character and situation for the stage, he never really committed himself to it. For all the integration of *Show Boat*'s music and story, Kern was a composer interested mainly in his songs. *Sweet Adeline,* which he wrote with Hammerstein in 1929, was a step back to musical comedy. Others were to surpass the steps these partners had taken.

In 1931, for example, the Gershwins had already written outright theater music for *Of Thee I Sing* while Kern was still doing

*Several wonderful Kern songs came from the 1931 success* The Cat and the Fiddle; *(left and above) among them, "She Didn't Say Yes" and "The Night Was Made for Love." Kern's score framed Otto Harbach's story of a competitive romance between a composer of operettas (played by Georges Metaxa at the piano) and another who writes popular songs (Odette Myrtil on violin). Throughout the thirties there were many such battles between the popular and fine arts, endless competitions between ballet dancers and chorines, symphony orchestras and jazz bands.*

*Kern's last shows talked about being modern instead of trying to just be it. Here is a scene from* Music in the Air, *written in 1932 with Oscar Hammerstein. The gentleman on his feet is a slender Walter Slezak. The other quarreling lovers in this musical about operetta are, from the left, Natalie Hall, Katherine Carnington, and Tullio Carminati.*

172

isolated songs for *The Cat and the Fiddle*—still wavering between operetta and Broadway. This show's "The Night Was Made for Love" is reminiscent of Friml's "Indian Love Call."

*The Cat and the Fiddle,* a musical about the making and unmaking of an operetta, was unusual in showing the competition between new and old theater music but is hardly of a whole as is *Of Thee I Sing.* It had a decent run of a year or so, like the subsequent *Music in the Air* (1932) and *Roberta* (1933), but none of the shows was theatrically notable. They included marvelous songs, it goes without saying, but more than good songs were already expected of musicals.

While Kern was in so many ways a daring composer, his choice of book material tended toward the journeyman. Though a literate, urbane man, he lacked an instinct for the theatrical, and is posthumously paying the price. Among the early Broadway musical giants, only those with a sense of theatricality left shows that had a chance for endurance while those who concentrated mainly on their songs did not: Rodgers rather than Berlin, Gershwin rather than Porter.

Yet none of them, perhaps, would have become what they became without Kern. He is the father figure. He came first and he comes first.

*The elegant fashion parade above, from* Roberta, *was designed by co-choreographers John Lonergan and José Limon, who would later become an important force in modern dance. Among Kern's songs for the show were four exquisite ballads: "Lovely to Look At," "The Touch of Your Hand," "You're Devastating," and most memorable, "Smoke Gets in Your Eyes."*

Opposite: *Kern's* Roberta *featured Sydney Greenstreet (standing at far right), George Murphy (seated at far left with his back to the audience) and Bob Hope (seated at center). One would become a cult movie actor, another a film dancer and United States senator, and the last would become, well, Bob Hope. As for Roberta, it would become forgotten for its romance between an American football hero and a Russian princess. But, ah, the Kern songs.*

# RICHARD RODGERS

Richard Rodgers is the grand master of Broadway theater music. He wrote more than forty musicals, *almost all of them hits.* He had two separate careers, one in partnership with Lorenz Hart until 1942, the other with Oscar Hammerstein II until 1960, and either collaboration would have assured his historical position. His *Oklahoma!* was the first legitimate musical to play a thousand performances, and he wrote the music for three other shows to reach that milestone: *South Pacific, The King and I,* and *The Sound of Music.* No other composer can match the number of Rodgers show songs that outlived their productions to become standards.

Richard Rodgers was the only one of the giants to bridge the first half-century of the musical theater's existence and to write for all the different kinds of shows—the revues of the twenties, the musical comedies of the thirties, and the musical plays that followed. Kern died without capitalizing on the innovations of his *Show Boat.* Gershwin was cut down in his youth. Neither Porter nor Berlin was one for stage adventure. If he finally became a theater conservative, Richard Rodgers was responsible for so much progress, over so long a time, that his place in stage history is doubly secured—as a master writer of theater songs and as an activist in the musical's development.

Seldom has a composer's style been so affected by his lyricist. The Rodgers who wrote with Oscar Hammerstein II is practically a different man from the one who wrote with Lorenz Hart. Rodgers's music was light and bittersweet with Hart, serious and milky with Hammerstein; sophisticated with Hart, sincere with Hammerstein; romantic with Hart, ardent with Hammerstein; popular with Hart, theatrical with Hammerstein.

Was Rodgers a musical schizophrenic or was he merely adaptable? Probably both. He generally wrote his music *before* Hart wrote the lyrics but *after* Hammerstein wrote his. From this, one might infer that his music with Hart was that of a professional composer, writing tunes and leaving it to the lyricist to set specific thoughts to them; that with Hammerstein, on the other hand, he tried to match his music to the lyricist's meanings, feelings, form, and theatrical purposes.

The kind of music that resulted in each situation was perhaps predictable: Rodgers's work done with Hart seems generally relaxed and more purely musical than that done with Hammerstein, which sometimes sounds contrived, as if he were restraining melodic freedom to fit Hammerstein's thoughts as well as meters. A prewritten

*Richard Rodgers (left) with Irving Berlin. When we hear the songs written by these men—or any of the giants—we dissolve. Songs can't be better. Are they playing Rodgers's song? Berlin's? Porter's or Gershwin's or Kern's? When we hear any of them, we think he is the greatest songwriter of all time.*

lyric limits not only the composer's musical invention but his music's mood as well. Hammerstein's tendency to coyness was reflected in the occasional Rodgers's melody that has an insincere ring to it. Rodgers's best songs unquestionably were written with Hart.

But his best theater music was written with Hammerstein. Hart was a man for set pieces—songs that can stand on their own—and perhaps the best lyricist America ever produced. Hammerstein was a man of the theater and his lyrics were meant not to stand alone as poems but to further a plot. So, with him Rodgers tended to write songs that referred to a particular show, music to be dramatically presented rather than merely sung.

The shows that Rodgers wrote with Hart are not as significant or as revivable as those he wrote with Hammerstein. First of all, they came earlier, when little was demanded of a musical comedy. Though the team claimed to be ambitious, the importance of *Show Boat, Of Thee I Sing,* and *Porgy and Bess* apparently eluded them. They seem to have been satisfied with the musical comedy form. Working at a time when performers and songwriters were stars, they couldn't keep themselves from writing hit tunes. As a result, they wrote many hit shows but few memorable ones. *Pal Joey* is their lone classic. *The Boys from Syracuse* can still play, if its cardboard construction and corny jokes are overlooked. Otherwise, the team must be remembered not for its shows but for its songs. Even with George Balanchine as their choreographer, for *On Your Toes, Babes in Arms, I Married an Angel,* and *The Boys from Syracuse,* their works were not ambitious, and, despite the inclusion of a full-length ballet, "Slaughter on Tenth Avenue," in *On Your Toes,* none grasped the potential of dance musicals.

The Rodgers and Hart collaboration began in earnest when the composer, then eighteen years old, and the lyricist, twenty-five, wrote the songs for *Poor Little Ritz Girl* in 1920. Rodgers was a New Yorker who from adolescence had idolized Jerome Kern. He was so theatrically precocious that he wrote *Poor Little Ritz Girl* while a student at Columbia, and that college was chosen because of its annual undergraduate musical, the Varsity Show. Rodgers had no formal musical training at Columbia, but he later took classes in harmony and theory at the Juilliard School of Music (then called the Institute of Musical Art). By his own admission his "piano playing would never be more than adequate." As stage composers go, Rodgers was better trained than most, but not really a schooled musician. Melodic instinct and musical integrity made his success but he never shared Gershwin's fascination with the harmonic and rhythmic intricacies of music and he never aspired to orchestrating.

Hart, a descendant of the German poet Heinrich Heine, was also a New Yorker. He had been something of an intellectual prodigy, in love with the theater and obsessed with rhyming. A tiny man, destined to be plagued by emotional problems, he lived for his words and was employed as a play translator when he first met Rodgers. Though Hart had long since quit Columbia, the two worked on Varsity Shows together, one of which led directly to *Poor Little Ritz Girl.* When it opened on Broadway, half their score had been replaced with songs by others, which was not at all unusual at the time.

*Poor Little Ritz Girl* was a flop, as was *The Melody Man* of 1924. Their first hit show was the 1925 revue *The Garrick Gaieties,* with its marvelous "Manhattan." Their subsequent history is astonishing: only one failure, the 1928 *Chee-Chee,* whose subject matter—the

The legendary "Slaughter on Tenth Avenue" from On Your Toes *was one of the first ballets to be used in a musical. Choreographed by George Balanchine for Ray Bolger and Tamara Geva, its music was written by Rodgers himself.*

*Though one of the theater's best-loved dancing stars, Ray Bolger did not make the successful transition to stardom in movies as Gene Kelly and Fred Astaire did. His vaudevillian, "eccentric" dancing style was essentially humorous and less suited to a movie's romantic lead than Astaire's sophistication or Kelly's acrobatics. Here (and overleaf), in Rodgers's* On Your Toes, *Bolger demonstrates the airy filigrees that were his specialty.*

castration of a Grand Eunuch—was less than inspired. Everything else they did was successful, and with those shows came a glittering array of songs. Rodgers and Hart were to create their own special American musical language, a deliciousness of melody tempered by lyrics of wit and honesty. They also had their more pretentious moments. The early *A Connecticut Yankee* (1927) included the pompous "My Heart Stood Still." It resembled Kern at his stuffiest, but Kern was, after all, Rodgers's idol. However, the show also included the lilting "Thou Swell," which was pure Rodgers and Hart. "Thou Swell" is a "charm song," as was "Manhattan" before it. As defined by conductor Lehman Engel in his book *The Making of a Musical,* "Charm songs are...songs with steady rhythmic accompaniments and an optimistic feeling (optimistic lyrics), with a steadier sense of movement than one finds in most ballads."

Rodgers and Hart may well have invented the charm song. Certainly, they perfected it. Such numbers, almost as often as comic songs, tend to be musical throwaways. Composers traditionally hoard their melodies for the ballads because these were the songs that sold records and sheet music. Rodgers had such a gift for melody that he could afford to spend a good tune on a light number.

The team worked almost exclusively for the theater. They spent most of the early thirties in Hollywood, but they weren't happy there. The movie musicals of the time were not musicals, they were romantic comedies with musical numbers. Unmotivated songs were

*Romantic leads, in the original 1927 cast of* A Connecticut Yankee, *were these two stars-to-be, Constance Carpenter and William Gaxton. If you got to introduce both "Thou Swell" and "My Heart Stood Still," you'd become a star, too.*

*Robert Chisholm played King Arthur, helped by Vivienne Segal and Dick Foran in the 1943 revival of* A Connecticut Yankee *(left). One new song had been written for this production, the last by Rodgers and Hart—"To Keep My Love Alive." The night after Hart died, during the show's run, Miss Segal—who had adored the lyricist but rejected his marriage proposal—forgot her lines. She stopped in mid-song, told the audience, "I'm so sorry," walked offstage, checked the lyric, reentered, and sang it. She received a standing ovation and later said that the audience "must have realized what I was going through."*

apparently difficult for Rodgers and Hart to write. Successful as they had been before they left for Hollywood, it was upon their return that the team hit its stride, as if relieved to be home and on the stage. The 1935 *Jumbo,* a mammoth circus spectacle, included "The Most Beautiful Girl in the World" and "My Romance." *On Your Toes* (1936) had "Glad to Be Unhappy" and "There's a Small Hotel." There were two Rodgers and Hart musicals in 1937—*Babes in Arms* and *I'd Rather Be Right.*

*Babes in Arms* had a choice Rodgers and Hart score, practically a primer for every type of show song. Its ballad is "Where or When," a brooding mood piece of exquisite melody. Its charm song is "The Lady Is a Tramp," a wry list song. The show had the perfect comedy song in "I Wish I Were in Love Again." But if you want to talk of quintessential Rodgers and Hart you need go no further than "My Funny Valentine."

One requisite of a great songwriter may be the composing of a masterpiece—one song of which it could be said, had the composer written no other, it would have been enough. "My Funny Valentine" is such a song. Its music seems inseparable from its lyrics, the partnership between them perfect. It is pure melody, so inevitable that it cannot be performed in any way other than as it was written. There is nothing musically unusual about the song. It is a straight-forward, thirty-two-bar tune in the standard AABA form (four eight-bar sections consisting of the main theme, repeat of main theme, release with a different theme, and main theme). Though it may be one of many fine examples of such a song, none is better. It will be sung forever.

*For Rodgers's music to "Johnny One-Note" in* Babes in Arms, *Lorenz Hart came up with the line, "Got in Aida/Indeed a great chance to be brave." This inspired choreographer George Balanchine to do an Egyptian ballet. Such brainstorms are what made the thirties the thirties. That's Duke McHale and Mitzi Green at center.*

Opposite: *In his autobiography, Rodgers describes the 1937* I'd Rather Be Right *as an unhappy experience and blames George M. Cohan (on the podium) who came out of retirement to play President Franklin D. Roosevelt. While crediting the celebrated star's performance, Rodgers says Cohan hated Roosevelt so much that he ad-libbed abusive alterations to Hart's lyrics and treated the famous song-writing team with "thinly veiled, patronizing contempt."*

181

Both *I Married an Angel* and *The Boys from Syracuse* were 1938 successes, *Angel* an ordinary show and *Syracuse* an unusual one because it was based on Shakespeare's *A Comedy of Errors*. The creators of musical comedies have always taken their comedy lightly; unfortunately, *The Boys from Syracuse*, despite its literary source, is no exception.

Its librettist, George Abbott, was one of the most influential men in the history of musical theater, but he tended to be an anti-intellectual snob and shared with Rodgers and Hart a practical theater-making attitude. Shakespeare, for Abbott, was strictly *material*. Still, it is the Shakespearean source that makes *The Boys from Syracuse* enjoyable beyond its era; it is what Abbott did to it that prevents it from being a classic musical comedy. Abbott merely reduced the play to a breakneck farce, snipping scenes from it and placing them between songs. *Syracuse* has some songs typical of Rodgers and Hart in peak form —a melancholy ballad in "The Shortest Day of the Year," another one of their charm songs in "Sing for Your Supper," and one of the composer's most beautiful waltzes in "Falling in Love with Love." Nobody could write waltzes like Richard Rodgers and every stage composer has tried to write waltzes like Rodgers. He managed to maintain the sweep of the dance while replacing European bravura with an American freshness.

*Pal Joey* (1940) has a not entirely deserved reputation as a landmark musical. Its distinction is in *tone*. Though it has the look of a musical comedy, it is cynical and its central romance is an opportunistic one. The show is based on a series of stories in letter form that John O'Hara had written for *The New Yorker*. The title character is a punk master of ceremonies, working in seedy nightclubs, willing to do anything to get ahead. He was hardly the usual type of leading man. The match he meets is a society woman with a taste for slumming.

Directing his fifth (and last) Rodgers and Hart show, and col-

*Eddie Albert has enjoyed one of the most enduring careers in American show business, a stage and film star for over forty years. In* The Boys from Syracuse *(here with Muriel Angelus) he got to introduce "This Can't Be Love."*

Opposite: *Jimmy Savo clowns through the ritualistic opening—"The Masks"—of* The Boys from Syracuse, *which featured one of the finest of all Rodgers and Hart scores.*

Below: The Boys from Syracuse *had costumes by Irene Sharaff, sets by Jo Mielziner, and a libretto based on* A Comedy of Errors. *"If it's good enough for Shakespeare," Hart was quoted as saying, "it's good enough for us."*

laborating with O'Hara on the book, Abbott inevitably made it in his own mold—swift-paced and wisecracking. This has dated *Pal Joey*. Though the show can still work, one must overlook much about it.

Of all the Rodgers and Hart shows, *Pal Joey* has the best-integrated score. The songs are consistent with each other as well as with the book. Of course, the show has marvelous individual songs: "I Could Write a Book" and "Bewitched, Bothered, and Bewildered" and "Take Him" and so on. They all work for the show's purposes, except for "Zip," an irrelevant satire of Gypsy Rose Lee, which ought to be dropped from any revival.

*Pal Joey* has been frequently revived. It is accepted as a classic. This is less because of total quality than because it has such unique character.

Although Rodgers and Hart wrote several more shows, including their longest-running, *By Jupiter* (1942), *Pal Joey* marked the peak of their partnership. Hart by then had become hopelessly trapped in alcoholism and despair. In 1943, Rodgers found a new partner.

Oscar Hammerstein II proved to be much more than a new collaborator. His partnership gave Rodgers a second career—a career even more successful than the first, and certainly less troublesome. Hammerstein was steady and dependable while Hart had been erratic and careless. Hammerstein's seriousness about his work was appealing. Although Hart had co-written the books for *On Your Toes, Babes in Arms,* and *I Married an Angel,* Hammerstein was a playwright and had far-reaching ambitions for the musical theater. Rodgers's music shed its old skin and assumed a new character.

The Rodgers and Hammerstein collaboration began with the fabulously successful *Oklahoma!* in 1943. Hammerstein had been largely responsible for originating the musical play in writing the book and lyrics for *Show Boat.* Sixteen years and many flops later, he established the musical play definitely and successfully with *Oklahoma!* Others continued to write musical comedies, but that form dominated Broadway no longer.

It's difficult to believe that the Rodgers who wrote *Oklahoma!* was the same man responsible for the Rodgers and Hart catalogue. *Pal Joey* was young and tough while *Oklahoma!* was mellow and

*Gene Kelly (left) leaped to stardom in* Pal Joey. *Van Johnson had a small speaking part but stepped out of the chorus to dance with June Havoc (above).*

*Johnson and Havoc rehearse "The Flower Garden of My Heart," in which chorus girls "water" chorus boys lying on their backs. Frank Loesser had much the same fun satirizing nightclub dance routines for* Guys and Dolls *ten years later.*

"Pore Jud Is Dead," from Oklahoma! Audiences laughed along with the virtuous Curly (Alfred Drake, right) at his needling and ultimate punishment of the villain Jud, played by Howard da Silva. Jud was so evil he hung girly pictures in his shack.

In changing partners from Hart to Hammerstein, Rodgers found an utterly new musical style for himself and an enthralling one at that. Oklahoma!'s "The Surrey with the Fringe on Top" is a creamy show song unlike anything he'd written before. Alfred Drake and Joan Roberts, in the surrey, are the romantic leads; Lee Dixon and Celeste Holm formed a secondary comic romance. This foursome formula was carried over to musical plays from musical comedy.

sunny. The Kern whom Rodgers idolized, especially the Kern inclined to art songs, robust and openhearted, now influenced his music more directly. Hammerstein had worked with Kern for so long that his lyrics prompted the same kind of straightforward music. Rodgers's "People Will Say We're in Love" is very reminiscent of Kern's "Why Do I Love You?" and "Make Believe." They are all in the operetta style, all ways of saying "I love you." Much in Oklahoma! has the same operetta feel.

Oklahoma! had the nerve to open with a slow song ("Oh, What a Beautiful Mornin'") when musicals were expected to begin with rousing production numbers; it included a ballet dealing with the heroine's dreams; it even had a villain. Jud Fry is a heavy whose bad character is indicated by the pinup pictures in his shanty. That's Hammerstein's morals for you. Such prudishness marred the Rodgers and Hammerstein collaboration. Yet there's no denying the significance of this show, or its grandness. If Porgy and Bess, Show Boat, and Of Thee I Sing hadn't settled the issue, Oklahoma! finally established the musical theater as a stage form to be reckoned with. Though none of its numbers, not even the hits, have more than nostalgic value when considered as individual songs, the score as a

*Rodgers and Hammerstein engaged Agnes de Mille as choreographer for Oklahoma! precisely because they wanted ballet rather than Broadway jazz dancing. Within a few seasons, almost every new musical had a ballet in it. None matched de Mille's classics.*

188

whole is one of our theater's great ones. It is music fitted to a story, music for the stage, all of a piece, and I love it.

*Oklahoma!* can be accused of a certain simplemindedness—after all, the show's crucial concern is whether Jud or Curly will take Laurey to a box social—but it also is a downright thrilling Broadway musical. It has marvelous and showmanly numbers: a fine charm song in "Kansas City," two first-rate comic songs (the kind Hammerstein wrote best) in "All er Nothin'" and "I Cain't Say No," and another perfect Rodgers waltz in "Out of My Dreams," which is the show's one melody reminiscent of the Rodgers of Rodgers and Hart. It brings back his special knack for the melancholy.

*Oklahoma!* made permanent a giant step taken by our musical theater. It also allied Rodgers with a man who took the musical theater seriously. It prepared Rodgers for composing a considerably more sophisticated and important score for *Carousel.*

*Carousel,* which opened in 1945, was the second in the mighty Rodgers and Hammerstein quartet—the musicals that established the team as a national institution (the others are *South Pacific* and *The King and I*). Like *Oklahoma!* it deals with a rural, white Protestant America. This was an image with which the country had long identified itself, an image that sustained America through the Second World War—the image of a clean-living, morally authoritarian, agricultural country. Just what Rodgers and Hammerstein had to do with that America is hard to understand since they were big-city, Jewish boys. Contrary to the old writing rule, *nothing* they wrote had anything to do with their background.

*Oklahoma!* was based on Lynn Riggs's play *Green Grow the Lilacs.* *Carousel* transported Ferenc Molnár's *Liliom* from Budapest in 1919 to New England in the late 1800s. It is the story of the romance between Billy Bigelow, a ne'er-do-well, and Julie Jordan, a nice girl. Billy is killed in a robbery and goes to heaven, leaving Julie a lifelong widow who rears their daughter on a sea of sentiment. A starkeeper in heaven gives Billy just one day to return to earth, see his daughter, and make amends.

Although its story is soppy, *Carousel* has a magnificent score, the most ambitious and successful Rodgers ever wrote. It opens not with an overture but with a dance-pantomime set to "The Carousel Waltz" which, among Rodgers's great waltzes, is the greatest of all. This is orchestral music and the best argument I can think of for composers to write their own dance scores. Rodgers's waltz has an openness of construction unfettered by the demands of lyrics; it has a duration sufficient for a scene; it has a wealth of melodic invention and development, enriched by throat-catching harmonies and swept along by its marvelous calliope sound. It is a piece of music that need not apologize to the concert hall. In fact it was *written* for the concert hall—as a concert piece for Paul Whiteman's jazz band—and not for *Carousel* at all. Whiteman never performed it.

*Carousel* is the most musically venturesome of all the Rodgers and Hammerstein shows. The body of its score is musical scene writing. Following the "Carousel Waltz" prologue, the show plunges into the intertwined "You're a Queer One, Julie Jordan" and "Mr. Snow." That leads to "If I Loved You," which runs nearly ten minutes! Most people know this only as an ardent ballad in the Kern manner with still another Hammerstein lyric dealing with "Make Believe," but—and Hammerstein deserves much credit for this— these *Carousel* numbers are mini-operas that cover great swatches of book. "If I Loved You" is an entire courtship, and "You're a Queer

*The original leads in* Carousel—*John Raitt and Jan Clayton.*

Opposite, top: Carousel *opens with a ballet-pantomime prologue rather than an overture. The music for it is "The Carousel Waltz." As orchestrated by the gifted Don Walker, it has the irresistible charm, sound, and beat of a calliope and is among our theater's most glorious music.*

Opposite, below: Carousel *offered something new in musical theater in showing the ne'er-do-well with a heart of gold, Billy Bigelow, dead onstage; he has killed himself while committing a robbery. Later, he returns briefly from Heaven to comfort his fatherless child with "You'll Never Walk Alone." Thoroughly corny and thoroughly moving.*

One" contrasts Julie's introversion with her friend's exuberance in "Mr. Snow." For "If I Loved You," the verse, which usually introduces a song, is routined into the middle of the song. It is so fully developed and exploited that it becomes a theater device, not merely leading back into the main theme, but revealing the inconsistency, hesitation, and character of Bigelow. In short, these numbers accomplish in musical terms what would otherwise have to be done through textual exposition.

As for the rest of the *Carousel* score, it includes two magnificent production numbers: "June Is Bustin' Out All Over" and yet another great waltz, "This Was a Real Nice Clambake." Neither is musically ordinary, neither a standard production number. The show also has the touching "What's the Use of Wond'rin'," with a lyric that promises the gorgeous "Something Wonderful" to come in *The King and I.*

And of course there is "Soliloquy," a number of unprecedented length. One may well smirk at the idea of a song sung by a hero alone onstage, dealing sentimentally and superficially with the hopes and fears of an expectant father. But the theatrical idea is more important than the lyric's lack of grace. And as for the music, only Kern could have come up with so continuous a flow of melody, as of course he had done with "Ol' Man River." Whatever "Soliloquy" may owe to that song, and however much Rodgers is indebted to Hammerstein's theatrical idea, this is a stunning number, a solo of pioneering duration (seven minutes). It is that rare creature, a showstopper that is pensive rather than exuberant.

Rodgers may have matched the melodic constancy of *Carousel* elsewhere, and may have written more delicious songs with Hart, but in terms of theater music, this show is his crowning achievement.

The difference between artists and scientists is that scientists are logical. Rodgers and Hammerstein had discovered something with *Carousel* and promptly looked for progress in another direction. They had the future of musical theater laid out before them. *Carousel* had established the notion of long musical sequences that were braided with drama. This was a change in *form,* which is where stage progress is made. Yet, in trying to be adventurous with their next show, they managed to avoid the very door they had opened.

Produced in 1947, *Allegro* was the first Rodgers and Hammerstein musical that wasn't an adaptation. It was cast from the same "experimental" mold as Thornton Wilder's *Our Town.* Indeed, the two works have much in common: a bare stage for an avant-garde look, a theme celebrating small-town America, and moral platitudes. *Allegro* is about the life of a doctor who is faced with a choice between a society practice and work with the poor; it deals with life in capital letters; it even, heaven help it, has a Greek chorus.

The team should have realized how much more had been attempted by *Carousel.* Yet the Rodgers and Hammerstein imprimatur was already such that *Allegro* could run for 315 performances and the collaborators' success so great that Rodgers would consider so respectable an engagement "disappointing."

The most important thing about *Allegro* was that it stimulated them to erase the failure with another hit in the *Oklahoma-Carousel* class. I say that without sarcasm. The urge to make a hit is the very adrenaline of Broadway musicals. Rodgers and Hammerstein got that hit in 1949, the kind of hit that sets New York on its ear: *South Pacific.*

*South Pacific* is among the least important of the monster hits.

The show was conventional; it wore liberalism on its sleeve; it established the Rodgers and Hammerstein institutional quality; it marked the beginning of a musical drama formula as repetitious as that of the old musical comedies. Broadway was back to ballads, comedy turns, charm songs, and production numbers.

Such *musical plays* proved more play than musical. Despite all the talk of the Rodgers and Hammerstein integration of songs and story, musical plays in general and *South Pacific* in particular were not integrated where it counted. The lyrics may well have related to the plots but the distinction between book and musical elements was as great as ever. The story still stopped for songs; there was no unified musical structure. Such musical plays were abbreviated naturalistic plays in the fast-fading style of Clifford Odets, Lillian Hellman, Sidney Kingsley, and Arthur Miller. Their story elements, dotted along with cues for songs, had no connection in mood with their musical moments. This was drama with songs, not musical theater.

For *South Pacific,* Hammerstein collaborated with the director, Joshua Logan, in drawing a libretto from three stories in James

*The finale of* Allegro: *Dr. Joe Taylor, the hero (John Battles, clenching his fists) realizes—while his dead mother (Annamary Dickey in the apron) beams—that by becoming a rich and famous society doctor, by gosh, he hasn't accomplished anything at all. He is going back home to be a small town doctor.*

Set against the background of World War II, South Pacific *was about a romance between two utterly different people—Ensign Nellie Forbush (Mary Martin) from Arkansas and the French planter, Emile de Becque (Ezio Pinza). Though there was some concern that Pinza's operatic basso might overwhelm Martin, the contrast actually helped the show, underlining the differences in the characters' backgrounds.*

*The comic relief in* South Pacific *was provided by Myron McCormick (right center and below), who played Luther Billis, the wheeling and dealing Seabee.* South Pacific's *moment of glory was 1,925 performances long. It was a fabulous success, the kind that could make New York dizzy with hit fever.*

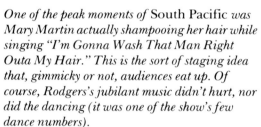

*One of the peak moments of* South Pacific *was Mary Martin actually shampooing her hair while singing "I'm Gonna Wash That Man Right Outa My Hair." This is the sort of staging idea that, gimmicky or not, audiences eat up. Of course, Rodgers's jubilant music didn't hurt, nor did the dancing (it was one of the show's few dance numbers).*

Michener's *Tales of the South Pacific.* Two romances are interwoven, one about an average American nurse and an aristocratic French planter, the other about a naval officer and a native. What made *South Pacific* the first of the blockbuster musicals was the combination of Rodgers and Hammerstein with two oddly mated stars, Mary Martin and Ezio Pinza. Pinza was the reigning bass of the Metropolitan Opera, and in 1949 the prestige of opera was so awesome and the respectability of musical theater so tentative that the meeting of grand opera and Broadway musicals was an occurrence of immense occasion, not to mention a commercial brainstorm.

Rodgers catered to Pinza's operatic background with "Some Enchanted Evening" and "This Nearly Was Mine." His songs for Martin were similarly tailored: "I'm Gonna Wash That Man Right Outa My Hair," "Honey Bun," and "Cockeyed Optimist." They suited her buoyancy and freshness. This individual customizing did not lead to a wholeness of score, and ultimately, *South Pacific* is but a series of spot songs and special material. It shows no real musical character. Still, it is a moving show and certainly was successful, second only to *Oklahoma!* in the length of its run. Now, however, it is all but forgotten and practically unrevivable. Musicals about current events are particularly prone to dating but the main reasons for *South Pacific*'s transience are its conventional, period construction; the summer-camp quality inevitable in any military musical; the show's lack of dancing; and the unrelieved mellowness of Rodgers's score.

Many of its faults were corrected in the 1951 *The King and I,* the team's most loved and best show. Had the production techniques and book writing of musicals been more sophisticated at the time, this show surely would be a classic in every way. As it is, it holds up very well in revival. Its story is absorbing and moving. It has relevance to universal issues of leadership, human frailty, the contrast between Eastern and Western civilizations, parenthood, and male-female relations. Its Siamese setting is rich in musical implications.

194

Rodgers grasped these implications as he had never managed elsewhere, in the process writing songs of aching beauty and charm.

*The King and I* does suffer from shorthand playwriting, arbitrary song placements, awkward scene-changing cues, and a thin second-act plot. Some of these flaws were surely due to its director, John van Druten, who was inexperienced with musicals. Van Druten was best known as a successful but lightweight playwright. A musical is particularly susceptible to the direction, not only in its staging but in its actual creation. At the outset, the music and book that are begun with are at best blueprints, to be revised and remade during rehearsals and tryouts. Van Druten's inexperience hurt *The King and I*. With a weak director, Hammerstein could resist changes in his book and lyrics; Rodgers could demand that songs remain.

Gertrude Lawrence starred in the original production of *The King and I* and making a musical of Margaret Landon's novel *Anna and the King of Siam* had been her idea. Her first choice for its composer was Cole Porter. It is curious to imagine *The King and I* with a Porter score and one smiles at the possibilities (Yul Brynner singing "Anything Goes"?). But it is impossible to imagine the show without the music it was finally given, and that is the best test of a fulfilled project.

Yul Brynner, playing the King, proved the show's real discovery. Others have played the role. Alfred Drake and Rex Harrison were actually offered the part first. Brynner owned it.

There is much to love in Rodgers's score for this show. "Something Wonderful" is a perfect example of a dramatic song: It tells a great deal about both the King and the head wife who sings it. "The March of the Siamese Children" is an orchestral piece of marvelous emotional effect (and, to Van Druten's credit, he and not Robbins staged it so beautifully). It is exactly what Rodgers means when he speaks of writing exotic but not alien music. "Shall I Tell You What I Think of You?" is a soliloquy in the *Carousel* tradition and anticipates Rex Harrison's talk-singing in *My Fair Lady*. However, *The King and I* also has its share of extraneous songs, particularly the ballads "We Kiss in a Shadow" and "Hello, Young Lovers."

Without detracting from Rodgers's achievement in writing *The King and I*, at least some credit for it must be given to Robert Russell Bennett, the orchestrator who worked for so many years with Rodgers, and with Kern as well. Bennett spent a career in their shadows. He gave the music of Kern and Rodgers a fullness the composers alone did not always provide. Rodgers wrote more detailed arrangements than did Kern, three-stave arrangements rather than lead sheets. But detailed as Rodgers's notation was, he would not deny Bennett's great contributions to the final sound of his music. A first-class musician, Bennett has been one of the theater's most influential orchestrators.

With *The King and I*, the best work of Rodgers and Hammerstein was done. They had shows of varying success in *Me and Juliet* (1953, 358 performances), *Pipe Dream* (1955, 246 performances), and *Flower Drum Song* (1958, 600 performances), but these lacked the impact of their previous shows. The team had become the theatrical General Motors. Hammerstein's folksiness was overdone. Success made Rodgers's composing complacent. His late style is staid and respectable. It is not music for the stage's irreverent, anarchic spirit; certainly not music to dance to, and Broadway was fast becoming a place of dance musicals. Rodgers and Hammerstein became victims of their own legend. *The Sound of Music*, their last show and a

*Flower Drum Song was set in San Francisco's Chinatown. The romance between Larry Blyden's character and Pat Suzuki's was complicated by his arranged engagement to another. It was typical of the era's show business that hardly anyone in this Rodgers and Hammerstein musical was Chinese. The rare intelligent performer, Blyden doted on Broadway's clowns, finding parts in musicals with Bert Lahr (Foxy) and Phil Silvers, whose revival of A Funny Thing Happened on the Way to the Forum Blyden also produced.*

great success, was a work almost entirely devoid of artistic merit.

Because it was the last Rodgers and Hammerstein musical and because it was ultimately the most successful, *The Sound of Music* is significant in any accounting of their career. Despite lukewarm reviews, the show was a great success on Broadway (1,443 performances) and a stupendous hit as a movie. Musicals usually do not translate well to film because their spirit is essentially *live*. It was perhaps predictable that *The Sound of Music* would be an exception. It had no theater spirit for Hollywood to destroy, though it did have some lovely songs in "Sixteen Going on Seventeen" and "My Favorite Things," the ultimate list song.

The show was the last of Rodgers and Hammerstein. The lyricist took ill during the pre-Broadway tour and died some months after the New York opening. "Edelweiss" was their final song. The bond of the two men, as a team and as friends, can be felt in this beautiful melody's tenderness and intimacy, the lovely lyrics. Hammerstein at last wrote with uncontrived simplicity. Fittingly, the music was a simple Rodgers waltz.

Rodgers was stunned by the loss. It showed in the turn his career took afterward. He was a man who had worked with but two lyricists over a forty-year career. Though relatively young at fifty-eight, he was in no mood to go looking for another collaborator.

Yet, he insisted, the sweetest sounds he'd ever heard were still inside his head, or so his song in *No Strings* said, as if announcing that he had no intention of quitting. *No Strings* was a successful 1962

Opposite: *Based on the real story of Maria von Trapp,* The Sound of Music *had bankable sentiment. In the scene at left, Mary Martin prepares for her marriage in the abbey where she once was a novitiate. The abbess, opera singer Patricia Neway, takes the opportunity to sing "Climb Every Mountain," that year's "You'll Never Walk Alone."*

*In his later shows,* The Sound of Music *particularly, Hammerstein's lyrics made naïveté positively revolting. Here, Mary Martin sings the music lesson "Do Re Mi."*

production (580 performances). Rodgers wrote his own, perfectly presentable lyrics for the show. It was a mildly adventurous musical whose title was based on the story as well as on the absence of stringed instruments in the orchestra. The show's novelty was in the placement of its musicians backstage and occasionally onstage (a device used fifteen years later in *I Love My Wife*). Otherwise, it was a production of only passing interest, notable at the time for an interracial romance that was never to be, as period liberalism dictated.

It was apparent that the composer's heart had gone out of his work. Richard Rodgers was by then a corporation and it was his business side that seemed to be the piano.

The post-Hammerstein musicals of Richard Rodgers proved to be a letdown after such a previously successful career. He had been celebrated with Hart and personally satisfied with Hammerstein. He was disinclined, after so many steady years, to look for still another permanent partner. Yet he was eager to keep composing and by no means just for the money. He was already the wealthiest composer who ever lived. Rodgers was by nature a worker, and looked upon retirement as death. As the preeminent American stage composer, he was bound to be sought after by lyricists who were either in awe of him or anxious to use him to further their own careers. After a lifetime of success, he was also in the habit of writing major shows, Broadway events, and so he looked to grand subjects and famous stars rather than for exciting, original ideas. The combination of these factors led Rodgers to a series of routine musicals—*Do I Hear a Waltz?* (1965), *Two by Two* (1970), and *Rex* (1976). His *I Remember Mama* flopped in 1979, and he died at year's end.

Of course, nothing can detract from the astonishing body of work he left behind. The songs that Rodgers wrote with Hart are ones America will sing forever. This is *music*. The shows he wrote with Hammerstein were the ones that gave the musical theater respectability. For sixteen years this team ruled Broadway, its names more important to the theatergoing public than the stars or the name of the show. No other authors in the musical theater's history inspired such trust or could insure a run as Rodgers and Hammerstein could. Whether justified or not, they stood for stage quality—they were not merely songwriters but the Broadway musical theater itself.

In light of that, Rodgers's prior career with Lorenz Hart is all the more amazing. Overall, the man created a staggering body of work. Two separate careers. There is nobody—*nobody*—who has contributed as much to the musical theater as he.

Top: *For his first collaborator after Hammerstein's death, Rodgers chose his former lyricist's protégé, Stephen Sondheim. Do I Hear a Waltz? was not a happy experience for either of them and seemed a heartless, manufactured show. The stars were Sergio Franchi and Elizabeth Allen (right, center).*

Above: *Danny Kaye starred in Rodgers's 1970* Two by Two, *a musical version of Clifford Odets's* The Flowering Peach. *The original play retold the Old Testament story of Noah in Yiddish terms. The Rodgers version was as Jewish as apple pie.*

Opposite: *Diahann Carroll's glamour inspired Rodgers's* No Strings, *and he asked playwright Samuel Taylor to base a libretto on "a chic black woman—not a symbol of her race but a believable human being." Miss Carroll's leading man was Richard Kiley.*

# COLE PORTER

Among America's musical giants, Cole Porter was unique: He did not emulate Kern; he was not as productive as Rodgers; he had no pressing musical or theatrical ambitions, unlike Gershwin; he wasn't inclined to Berlin's simplicity.

Porter was Porter and nobody's songs are more recognizable. His catalogue does not reveal an awesome number of standards, but his big songs are among the most famous of all, and not just because of their dashing melodies. His lyrics are as responsible for his enduring reputation as his music, and why shouldn't they be? They are as bright and delicious and dextrous as any ever written.

Without them, his place in history might not be so assured. He wrote marvelous songs, but he did not have the melodic gifts or the versatility of his towering colleagues. Perhaps his musicianship, which was greater than theirs, allowed him to do more with the talent he had. For Porter's songs are ingenious rather than inspired, smart rather than warm or emotional. They are dramatic, subtle, and moody.

It is the combination of words and music that makes Porter great. For though he wasn't the only one to write both, nor even the first (there was Berlin before him), nobody ever did it with such virtuosity and verve. There is an obvious advantage in being a composer-lyricist. It makes for a unity that can only be approached by a team. When one man writes both words and music, they agree. They rise from one soul and come closest to expressing the composer's heart in words. That is certainly true of Irving Berlin's work and it is true of the work of some other composer-lyricists. Cole Porter's best music was so original and so idiosyncratic that it's hard to imagine anyone else setting lyrics to it; in fact, it sometimes seems the other way around: that he was the only one who could possibly have created the right *music* for his lyrics. As but one example, consider the song "Anything Goes." Who but the author of the lyrics would have given such musical exclamation points to the key words "mad," "bad," "white," "night," "gent," and "cent"?

> The world has gone mad today
> And good's bad today,
> And black's white today,
> And day's night today,
> When most guys today
> That women prize today,
> Are just silly gigolos...  (*Anything Goes*)

Porter received so much publicity that as well as he was known for smart songs, he was just as celebrated for living the storybook life of an international sophisticate. Severely crippled in a 1937 riding accident, he suffered excruciating pain until his death in 1964. Here, then, is the irony: the glittering prince of New York, in white tie and tails, who cannot attend an opening night unassisted (it is the premiere of Noel Coward's revue Set to Music *on January 18, 1939*).

*Porter's* Red, Hot, and Blue *was the last chance audiences had to see Bob Hope on Broadway and his big song was "It's De-Lovely," more or less a follow-up to "Anything Goes." Excluding him in this routine are Ethel Merman and Jimmy Durante, playing a parolee called "Policy" Pinkle.*

Not only do six successive lines end with "today," which the music emphasizes with repeated notes, but it is only on the *rhymes* that the melody changes, moving up the scale chromatically until the music is finally resolved.

Only a composer with a lyricist's heart would have been so sensitive to the rhymes and the intentions of this word pattern. Porter was so pyrotechnical a wordsmith with so special a sensibility that, when it comes to both words and music, he is in a class by himself. There have been lyricists as brittle—W. S. Gilbert before him, Lorenz Hart and Ira Gershwin in his time, and Stephen Sondheim later—but nobody else has ever been able to so perfectly mate the razzle-dazzle of sophisticated lyric writing with consonant music.

Porter is best loved for his exotic ballads and the witty lyrics of his charm songs. He always meant words and music to serve each other and alternated between them as he wrote: He came up first with the title, then wrote the music and finally the lyrics. The exotic songs are a genre of Porter's invention, songs almost born to be performed by dance teams in nightclubs. There is a story, perhaps apocryphal, that Porter complained to George Gershwin about not having enough hits. Gershwin advised him, so the story goes, to "write Jewish," which Porter took to mean writing Middle Eastern, in minor keys. And so the beguines began. Whether the story is true or not, the formula became Porter's signature and made him. "Just One of Those Things," "I've Got You Under My Skin," "I Get a Kick Out of You," "I Concentrate on You"—they are characterized by long melodic lines in those minor keys, set to tropical rhythms. What is more closely linked to our fond notions of thirties suavity? When we think of Cole Porter, we think of them.

His charm songs include the most celebrated of all list songs, "You're the Top." It begins by comparing a lover with the Colosseum and the Louvre Museum and then runs a race among topped comparatives and unexpected metaphors. The lyrics for "You're the Top" are positively ingenious. Even so, the best parts are the two introductory verses. The second and less familiar is the one I'd rather quote in full:

> Your words poetic are not pathetic,
> On the other hand, boy you shine
> And I can feel after every line,
> A thrill divine
> Down my spine
>
> Now gifted humans like Vincent Youmans
> Might think that your song is bad,
> But for a person who's just rehearsin',
> Well I gotta say this my lad     (*Anything Goes*)

Not a list number but on the same order as "You're the Top" as a charm song is "It's De-Lovely" (from *Red, Hot, and Blue*). This number succeeded because of the lyric's device: "delovely" and "delightful" and "delicious," "delirious" and "delectable" and finally "delimit." It's an Ira Gershwin sort of trick, something like " 'S Wonderful" of nine years earlier. But there is a fine rhythm and an irresistible melody to "It's De-Lovely." Again, as in "You're the Top," the melody of the release ("You can tell at a glance/What a swell night this is for romance") is catchier than the main tune, and the interior rhyme—"tell" and "swell"—aids the effect. In general, a

song's chorus speaks personally and expresses feelings directly, while verses tend toward humor and releases generalize. Perhaps this is why Porter, who was so emotionally covert, was prone to do more relaxed work with verses and releases. As a person more inclined to wit than sentiment, he also unsurprisingly wrote freer music and lyrics for his sly charm songs than for his ballads.

Cole Porter was born in 1891 in Peru, Indiana, the son of a gentleman farmer and a doting mother. Educated at private schools and Yale, he went to Harvard Law School under pressure from his grandfather, a lumber millionaire. Porter had been musical since childhood. While at Yale, he wrote theatricals and cheer songs, the "Yale Bulldog Song," as everyone knows, among them. He ultimately convinced his grandfather to let him transfer from law school to the Harvard department of music. It was there that he received the kind of musical training so rare among Broadway composers, and he later supplemented it by studying in Paris under Vincent d'Indy. This complete and luxurious education was typical of the Porter style.

Unlike Kern, Rodgers, Berlin, and Gershwin, Porter was not a Jewish New Yorker. Perhaps this is why he didn't try as hard as the others to be American and write American-sounding music. At a time when so many Jews were recent immigrants, "Americanism" was often an important matter to them. To Porter, a Midwestern WASP, Europe was no reminder of a déclassé past but a place to visit

*As in Rodgers's* I'd Rather Be Right *and Gershwin's* Of Thee I Sing, *the White House provided a setting for* Red, Hot, and Blue. *The show's political-comical libretto had everything that makes thirties musical comedies impossible to revive. Even the characters' names. Here is Merman, playing "Nails" O'Reilly Duquesne. Porter's songs were wonderful. In addition to her duet in "It's De-Lovely," Merman got to sing "Down in the Depths on the 90th Floor," and the super "Ridin' High."*

posh hotels and resorts. This might be the reason the other composers tended to do shows set in America while Porter's were as often as not set on the Continent.

His way of life was almost as celebrated as his work. Porter lived splendidly, in town, in the country, and finally at the Waldorf Towers. He mingled with society rather than show people and traveled constantly, luxuriously. All this was well publicized. Although the fashionable life he led was beyond the reach of the general public, he did not become a target of resentment, not even during the Depression. For he was living out everyone's fantasies, and he made his glamourous society life available for everyone to share by putting it into his songs.

In a peculiar way, wealth and the high life were obstacles for him to overcome. He had to prove himself no mere dilettante. He had to surpass celebrity to be given the due his songs merited. We should have such problems, perhaps, but Porter had them.

Ultimately, he had much graver problems. In 1937, at the peak of his success, he was thrown from a horse. His legs crushed, he underwent countless operations, finally an amputation, and remained crippled and physically agonized until his death in 1964. The irony was overwhelming, for Porter's personal and career image had been of a man heaven touched. His was supposed to be a life of elation and dancing, of good looks and dash, of perfect luck. The image gave way to a ghastly reality: the man in white tie and tails being carried into the theater on opening night.

Cole Porter wrote twenty-three shows but only his 1948 masterpiece, *Kiss Me, Kate*, is memorable. Though his songs are theatrical, most are isolated numbers, not part of score units or related to particular musicals. Almost all his great songs were written in the early thirties. Though his musicals continued to be successful into the forties, few great songs came from them. His career ebbed and it wasn't until *Kiss Me, Kate* that he resurfaced. How much the curve of this career relates to his disastrous accident in 1937 is a matter of psychological speculation.

Porter wrote songs for revues and several unsuccessful shows—and a ballet score, "Within the Quota," his first and last attempt at orchestral music—before he established himself and his special brand of sophistication with *Fifty Million Frenchmen* in 1929. The string of hits that followed included *The New Yorkers, The Gay Divorce*, and the 1934 *Anything Goes*, with its fabulous score: the title song plus "I Get a Kick Out of You," "You're the Top," "All Through the Night," and "Blow, Gabriel, Blow."

A shipboard musical not unlike many shows of the twenties, *Anything Goes* has the feel of one of Jerome Kern's Princess Theater musicals, probably because it was first written by Kern's collaborators on most of those musicals, Guy Bolton and P.G. Wodehouse. The revised script by Russel Crouse and Howard Lindsay is credited with saving the show, but *Anything Goes* still cannot be revived except as a period piece. These shows of Porter's golden years served mainly to solidify the popularity of musical comedy. Although they broke no new ground, each contributed to the tradition and the establishment of musicals as a stage genre. This was an important function of the workaday production. If every musical were a trailblazer, there would be no body of shows to satisfy the public on the belly level. Bread-and-butter shows bind techniques and refine innovations. Such shows have also been the source of the magnificent collection of theater songs that are our national treasure.

*Victor Moore, a fugitive posing as a minister, tries to explain things in Porter's* **Anything Goes**. *William Gaxton is the manly hero and at his side is an unusually demure Ethel Merman.*

*The story that librettists Howard Lindsay and Russel Crouse cooked up for* Anything Goes *provided for–follow this–a gospel number sung by a former evangelist turned nightclub owner, Reno Sweeney (played by Merman). All this took place during a transatlantic crossing on a luxury liner as the captain decides to entertain his passengers. Above, Reno Sweeney prepares, aided by the spurious Reverend Dr. Moon (Moore) and the handsome Billy Crocker (Gaxton). Watch the ship's trumpeter on the balcony. For the number (left) turns out to be "Blow, Gabriel, Blow."*

Of course, we remember only the best songs from the usual dozen in a musical. Most of Porter's stage songs (as most of Kern's and Rodgers's and Gershwin's and Berlin's) courted oblivion. But those that have lasted are jewels. His *Jubilee*, for example, may be a musical best forgotten but not its songs "Begin the Beguine," "Just One of Those Things," and "Why Shouldn't I?" "Begin the Beguine" is Porter's most famous song, noted, among other things, for its extraordinary length—108 measures as compared to the usual 32. It is a wonderful song even if it does have just one "Oh yes, let them begin the beguine" too many. But to my mind, the archetypal Porter song is "Just One of Those Things." This song doesn't have an expansive melody either, but musical containment works in its favor because the lyric is about *emotional* containment. The words are rueful and ironic, but one senses that the character singing the song is truly brokenhearted, which establishes a tension within the song. This is an ideal example of a matched mentality in lyrics and music, and what is truer to the Porter style than being debonair in pain? "Here's hoping we meet now and then." The high note on "hoping" reflects the marvelously corny dash in the lyric, a cape flung over the shoulder and out into the night. It's too much. "Just One of Those Things" is pure Porter. Still, of these three *Jubilee* songs, it seems to me that "Why Shouldn't I?" is the impeccable one. It *sings* more than most Porter, up and down the scale. It develops its main theme right away, without going on about it. It has a middle part or release that can stand on its own, a little melodic surprise with a catch in its throat ("You'll be kissed and then you'll be kissed

207

*For* Jubilee *in 1935, the imaginative Tony De Marco choreographed Porter's "Begin the Beguine." Movable panels shaped like tropical leaves set off the singer, June Knight (above); removed (opposite), they reveal the interior of the Café Martinique.*

again"). The lyric is simple and doesn't try to prove anything, always a sign with Porter that he knew he was on to a good melody. This is a beautiful song.

There were only six years in this, Porter's most fertile period, from *Fifty Million Frenchmen* to the 1935 *Jubilee.* By then, most of his great ballads had been written. He began to concentrate on the charm, novelty , and patter songs. Writing lyrics at this time seemed to stimulate him more than composing. Perhaps words always had come more easily. Perhaps he was spurred by the competition of Noel Coward in the same vernacular. In any case, he remained successful and was at the peak of his popularity on the autumn day in 1937 that he was pinned beneath that flailing horse.

He has been quoted as saying that while awaiting rescue he worked on "At Long Last Love," for *You Never Know.* His debonair response to pain, now real, physical pain, is touching. "Just One of Those Things" indeed. He probably never felt physically comfortable again, or very cheerful for very long, and yet his career continued to thrive. In the next seven years he had six hit shows, five of which ran over four hundred performances.

How does the quality of his post-accident work compare with what went before? The 1938 *Leave It to Me* included "My Heart Belongs to Daddy" and "Get Out of Town." He wound up the thirties with "But in the Morning, No," "Friendship," and "Well, Did You Evah?" for *DuBarry Was a Lady.* Nobody could say the scores for *You Never Know, Leave It to Me,* and *DuBarry* were noticeably different from what a painless Porter might have written. But his career was riding on momentum and soon skidded.

Ethel Merman, who had electrified *Anything Goes,* was the star of

*Panama Hattie,* but her presence could not mask the thinness of the score. Porter got Danny Kaye to leave *Lady in the Dark* in the middle of its run for the lead in *Let's Face It,* but aside from giving Kaye special material in "Farming" and "Let's Not Talk About Love," he wrote no memorable songs.

*Something for the Boys* (1943) was Merman's fifth Porter musical, and again she was given no classic songs. The show was no more than a passing hit. So the composer's downhill slide went: *Mexican Hayride* was a forgettable success, and the shows that followed were not even hits. *Seven Lively Arts,* a pretentious and arty revue, failed. *Around the World in Eighty Days*—with a book by Orson Welles—was an outright disaster. If Porter had not been crushed along with his legs, had time passed his style by? By 1948 the composer was virtually a has-been. When along came *Kiss Me, Kate,* his greatest and most memorable success.

There had been no anticipating it. Not from a Porter who had seemed written out, whose name alone no longer guaranteed financing. It was the start of a second career that seemed to have no connection with his previous work. In the past, Porter had taken a blithe attitude toward his shows, often handing in his songs and then disappearing. By the late forties, musicals had grown more demanding of composers. Not only did a show's songs have to relate to stories but its music was expected to play a larger role in general. The composer was expected to work with the show. With his career skidding, Porter could no longer afford to be so cavalier, especially since he had not been handing in hit songs. Perhaps this is one reason why he provided *Kiss Me, Kate* with more music than he'd ever given a show before. It is also one of the greatest of all musical

Opposite: *Porter's* DuBarry Was a Lady *featured a zany nightclub scene in which Merman (she's the one without the fruit basket on her head) sang "Katie Went to Haiti" and Bert Lahr (below) dreamed he was Louis XIV. The million-dollar legs he is examining are, of course, Betty Grable's. She got her start on Broadway singing "Well, Did You Evah?" (which Porter later used in the movie* High Society). *Lahr and Merman introduced Porter's "Friendship."*

Panama Hattie, *of 1940, was one of Porter's biggest hits despite an ordinary score and a silly Herbert Fields-Buddy DeSylva story about a Canal Zone bar girl in love with a rich Philadelphia kid. Everybody was in it: Merman, of course (shown here with one of the theater's great straight men, Arthur Treacher), and also Betty Hutton, James Dunn, Rags Ragland, and Pat Harrington. Theater quiz: In the chorus line below are future movie stars June Allyson, Betsy Blair, and Vera-Ellen. Who wrote the show's lyrics?*

theater scores. It plays as if it had been written in running order, the overture first and then every song in sequence. No show music is ever written sequentially and yet all the great scores have this inevitability about them.

The show is based on Shakespeare's *The Taming of the Shrew.* It was adapted by Bella and Samuel Spewack, a pair of commercial comedy writers who had previously worked with Porter on *Leave It to Me.* They used a backstage story device: The stars of a musical *Shrew* are, like the Shakespearean characters Kate and Petruchio they are playing, a couple of squabbling but inseparable lovers. There are other parallels with *Shrew* but the *Kate* book is hardly a work of literary ingenuity. It was enjoyable in its time but it bears the stigmata of everyday forties musicals—melodrama and farce in the Abbott manner (although he was not the show's director), episodic construction, cursory song cues, superficial dramatics, wisecrack humor, and a shorthand story. There are few dances, and the songs are so separated from the story that there is no sense of musicality when the book is in progress. Because of these flaws, *Kiss Me, Kate* will always be marked as an old musical. Yet the Spewacks' script gave Porter something he'd never had before: a *musical milieu.* I cannot too strongly emphasize its importance to a composer. A milieu can inspire a score and provide a unifying style. Good songs can be written without it, but they are prone to wander off in unrelated directions, a series of numbers rather than a *score.*

Porter's music for *Kiss Me, Kate* could only be for *Kiss Me, Kate,* it is that consistent in tone, and it is amazing. There is nothing in his past to suggest a talent for so self-contained a score, so refined in its theatricality, so inventive and melodic and exuberant. It is positively *healthy.* Its success owes much to the show's Shakespearean/Eliza-

*The play-within-a-play of* Kiss Me, Kate *is a musical version of* The Taming of The Shrew, *and it begins with "We Open in Venice." Patricia Morison and Alfred Drake (left) play Kate and Petruchio, while Lisa Kirk and Harold Lang (right) are Bianca and Lucentio. Between performances, they maintain the same relationships—and squabbles—as Shakespeare's characters. Opposite: Petruchio begins to soften his shrew with the beguine "Were Thine That Special Face."*

Right: *Kate remains obdurate in the face of Petruchio's wooing and sings the lusty "I Hate Men." Below: In their offstage personas, Fred Graham, the actor, and Lilli Vanessi, his ex-wife, bicker a while, but then reminisce about earlier and happier days in the mock-Viennese "Wunderbar."*

*Near the end of* Kiss Me, Kate *the two mobsters who have been pursuing Fred Graham to collect an overdue gambling debt announce that because their boss has been rubbed out the debt is cancelled. Moreover, they have got the smell of the greasepaint. Hence, Porter's delightful "Brush Up Your Shakespeare." Funny gangsters were a speciality of forties musicals, but none had better lyrics to sing than Porter's.*

bethan/Italian setting, which gave Porter a head start, a tone, a style, a mood, a floor for his work.

Another reason why the score of *Kiss Me, Kate* is so marvelous and enduring is that at last Porter did not try to write hits and instead aimed for musical integration. Generally speaking, the better a score is as theater, the fewer of its songs can be singled out. "So in Love," a lovely song with a long and flowing melodic line, was one of the few songs in *Kiss Me, Kate* whose lyrics made sense outside the story. That is why it became a popular hit. Most of the other songs were too well fitted into the show to be sung outside it. "Were Thine That Special Face" is the kind of beguine that Porter's career thrived on— one of his best—but with a lyric in Elizabethan English it had small chance of becoming a hit. Most of the *Kate* score was similarly handicapped in the commercial sense. "Why Can't You Behave?," a fine bluesy melody, makes no sense apart from the story. Both "We Open in Venice" and "Tom, Dick and Harry" have a madrigal feel to them. They are real theater songs and are eminently performable, finer and of a higher caliber than most stage pieces and certainly most pop tunes of their era. But it is difficult to imagine them being sung out of context. Both "I've Come to Wive It Wealthily in Padua" and "Where Is the Life That Late I Led?" are inspired by lines in Shakespeare's text, and "I Am Ashamed That Women Are So Simple" is almost entirely taken from *The Taming of the Shrew*. All these songs celebrate the common bond between the showmanship of Shakespeare and that of the Broadway musical theater. Are not both drawn from the same bloodline? It is a line richer, more rewarding, and certainly more consequential than song popularity charts. Though he was not particularly culture-conscious or literary, the bright and quick-witted Porter delighted in collaborating with Shakespeare as one man of the theater to another.

Porter never again reached this artistic level, though he tried two years later with *Out of This World*. It had some good songs— especially a rare Porter waltz, "Where, Oh Where"—but *Out of This World* was not successful.

His 1953 *Can-Can* began the final phase of the Porter career. Situated in the composer's beloved Paris, it had just enough story and scenery to look like the musical plays then fashionable. Despite lukewarm reviews, the show gave him his second longest run (892 performances). The book by Abe Burrows is an original story. Set late in the nineteenth century and presumably based on fact, it is about the birth of the controversial and racy can-can dance at a café operated by the leading lady. Not only does the story have her save the day by romancing a judge, it even manages to come up with a Garden of Eden ballet for the second act. It was in this ballet that Gwen Verdon made her Broadway splash. Verdon went on to stardom, but she was by no means all that *Can-Can* had to offer. Its score has never been given its due. "It's All Right with Me" is a wonderful Porter ballad with the sort of ironic lyric he wrote best ("It's not her face but such a charming face/That it's all right with me"). "Never Give Anything Away" has a neat rhythmic catch to its music and a French flavor in the lyric. The French titles of "C'est Magnifique" and "Allez-vous-en" seem pretentious, especially since the rest of the lyrics are in English, but the melodies are lovely. One explanation for the good score is, again, the presence of a musical milieu. The show is set in the Montmartre of Toulouse-Lautrec's posters and, being about dancers and dancing, it has a basic musicality tied to a unique place and period with its own kind of music. Perhaps Porter's

*Charlotte Greenwood built an entire career on high-kicking. Here, she sits it out as Greek goddess Juno in Porter's* Out of This World, *a variation on the Amphitryon myth. The unsuccessful show had its share of Porter gold but it takes hit shows to make hit songs and many of the titles are familiar only to the cognoscenti: "Where, Oh Where," "Nobody's Chasing Me," and "Use Your Imagination." Ironically, the show's best-known song, "From This Moment On," was cut during out-of-town tryouts, yet survived on its own.*

score wasn't all *that* French—"I Love Paris" is musically *Russian*—but then Porter tended to write his songs and pay little attention to the rest of the show.

Just as *Can-Can* was musically different from *Kiss Me, Kate,* so the composer's next project, *Silk Stockings,* was again different. These final Porter shows have nothing in common with each other, nor their music with his past. The critics were kind to *Silk Stockings,* which was a musicalization of *Ninotchka* and yet another Porter show set in Paris. It ran a respectable 477 performances. Some of the songs in this show ("Stereophonic Sound," "As on Through the Seasons We Sail," "The Red Blues," "Siberia") are not only musically cheap but lyrically silly. Their manner couldn't have been further from the once stylish Porter.

*Silk Stockings* was Cole Porter's last show. He went on to write several television specials and film scores , including the marvelous *High Society,* but his career had all but ended. He died in 1964, finally relieved of an irony he had been enduring for twenty-eight years: fulfilling an image of devil-may-care while in constant pain. He left behind not merely a body of idiosyncratic songs but a name that has come to represent a special period and attitude in American history. "Cole Porter" means American theater of the thirties and at its most sophisticated and, well, *swank.* He was not only a master of style and stylishness but placed his own imprint on everything he did. Respected by the other great Broadway composers and able to communicate to the mass public on a sophisticated level, he was indeed unique.

*Don Ameche played a Hollywood talent agent romancing a Soviet cultural commissar (Hildegarde Neff). The song was "Paris Loves Lovers," the show was the 1955* Silk Stockings, *an adaptation of the popular Garbo film* Ninotchka *and Porter's last Broadway musical.*

# GEORGE GERSHWIN

George Gershwin is the greatest theater composer Broadway has produced. Kern and Rodgers might have been purer melodists. Berlin was certainly more versatile a songwriter. No composer ever reflected an era as perfectly as Porter did the thirties. But Gershwin was as much a man of the theater as of music. It was his music's energy, its animal and sexual force, that spawned the unique exhilaration we identify with the musical theater. Gershwin exemplified the kind of music we think of as "Broadway." In short, he was a stage natural, and, as Leonard Bernstein has said, "one of the true authentic geniuses American music has produced."

George Gershwin's name on a theater marquee still creates an excitement in the air; the sound of his music in an orchestra pit still sends a shiver down the spine. Though a "songwriter" and proud of it, he took song writing beyond its customary limitations. By the time he was through he had graduated from hit tunes to show songs to concert pieces, past musical comedy to opera. Yet after all that, he could still compose as simple and exquisite a song as "Love Walked In." For Gershwin never fell out of love with his American musical roots. That is why all his music sounds like Gershwin, energetic and alive, whether it is a pop song or a concerto.

His death in 1937 of a brain tumor just before his thirty-ninth birthday broke the country's heart and it still hurts. With it the thirties ended prematurely and forever, but just think of his legacy: twenty-four shows in seventeen years, not to mention the concert works!

Gershwin's life has been fully, if not clearly chronicled. According to various sources, in 1898 he was born Jacob Gershwine to Morris and Rose Gershovitz and grew up as Jacob Gershvin. Well, it doesn't matter. Though not a child prodigy or educated beyond piano lessons, he demonstrated musical talent as a boy. At fifteen, he was in the grubby world of music publishing, plugging songs to get them performed. While selling other people's songs, Gershwin (as he called himself almost immediately) kept writing his own. Within a few years, some of them were published. But he was disgusted with the banality of popular songs, even the ones he was writing himself. Then he heard his first Kern and was convinced: Good songs could be written, but only in the theater. Pop music had to appeal on too low a level. He got his theatrical start in the traditional way—one of his songs was interpolated into Sigmund Romberg's *The Passing Show of 1916*. Soon Gershwin was working with his idolized Kern as a rehearsal pianist.

*Al Jolson was a star and Gershwin a nobody when the singer heard the composer's "Swanee" (lyrics by Irving Caesar) and had it interpolated into* Sinbad *in 1918. The song became Gershwin's first hit and, though a great career lay ahead, no song of his ever surpassed its commercial success.*

La, La, Lucille, in 1919, was Gershwin's first complete Broadway score but its mild success didn't establish him and he went back to interpolating songs and trying to knock out pop tunes. He became, at last, strictly Broadway when taken on as the composer for *George White's Scandals,* the series of revues that had thirteen editions between 1919 and 1939. The revue—a series of sketches and musical numbers—was the dominant form of musical theater in the twenties. It was stifled by musical comedy, much to our loss. Gershwin wrote five *Scandals* scores, working with several lyricists of whom only B. G. ("Buddy") DeSylva would make a name for himself. Gershwin had already begun collaborating with his brother, but Ira Gershwin so feared being accused of using family connections that he wrote these lyrics under the pseudonym "Arthur Francis" (Arthur and Frances were the first names of the other Gershwins, a brother and a sister).

In 1922, George Gershwin wrote his first songs in the style that would ever after characterize his music. These were collaborations with DeSylva; one, "Do It Again," interpolated into *The French Doll,* which otherwise had a score by one A. E. Thomas; the other, "I'll Build a Stairway to Paradise" for the *Scandals.* "Do It Again" is much the better song, an insinuating melody built on an ABAB pattern (first theme, second theme, first, second); the thirty-two bar AABA structure had not yet become the standard.

The 1922 *Scandals* contained something more portentous for Gershwin than "I'll Build a Stairway to Paradise." It included his first attempt at opera, a one-act piece then called *Blue Monday Blues.* (It was renamed *135th Street* when revised several years later.) Written in a week and performed by whites in blackface, it was damned by most of the critics and withdrawn after the opening night performance. Its libretto, by DeSylva, is clumsy, racially offensive, and melodramatic, but its music promises the *Porgy and Bess* to come thirteen years later. Nobody seemed to realize how unusual it was for a twenty-four-year-old Broadway composer to be writing a mini-opera for a revue.

Gershwin certainly did not think it was unusual. He never would view his theater music and concert music as different in kind. He was serious about both and wrote both from the start, seeing them simply as different forms to put his music into. Composing, to him, was virtuoso exercise. He never played a song twice the same way. Not only did he play the piano for fun—he played it perpetually and he played it spectacularly well. His extemporaneous improvisations on his own songs are legendary for their ingenuity and complexity. For him, playing the piano was as much an athletic as an aesthetic activity, and he was a serious athlete. It is not hard to see the rhythm and muscle of his music as an expression of that athleticism, and Gershwin spoke of this connection more than once.

After writing several scores for the *Scandals,* Gershwin was unmistakably on his way, but he didn't hit his stride until he teamed up with his brother on a full-time basis. One can argue for or against the importance of the right lyricist to a composer, the right lyric to a song. Composers are better known than lyricists. When we say "Gershwin" we think of George, not Ira. Our impulse is to credit the melody for a song's specialness. Yet, there are many cases in which the lyric makes the song. (Rodgers and Hart's "Blue Moon" was given three different sets of lyrics until the fourth established it.) There are also instances in which lyricists challenge and inspire the composer. Would Gershwin have been equally successful with

*Composers loved to write for Fred Astaire because his voice, though thin and reedy, had the easy style of his dancing. Astaire also gave composers the chance to write songs about dancing. For this show,* Lady, Be Good! *in 1924, Gershwin gave him "Fascinating Rhythm."*

Girl Crazy *starred Ginger Rogers (left) as the postmistress of a small Arizona town who falls in love with a playboy sent out West by his father to keep him away from gambling and girls. Predictably, the wastrel (played by Allen Kearns) sets up a nightclub and surrounds himself with ladies (below). Gershwin provided many memorable songs: "I Got Rhythm," "Bidin' My Time," "But Not for Me," and "Embraceable You."*

another lyricist? Perhaps, and perhaps his musical maturity simply coincided with the start of the partnership. Unquestionably, the team had a special chemistry.

It is no coincidence that George Gershwin's best theater songs began flowing when he turned from revues to musical comedies. Revues presented a series of isolated turns, which encouraged the pop song in a composer, while musical comedies, silly as they were, provided a story in which to set a song and demanded a bigger "feel" in a song. "Fascinating Rhythm" from *Lady, Be Good!* is typical of the fun Gershwin had with music, and the show was typical of the ensuing series of musical comedies that were to establish George and Ira Gershwin between 1924 and 1929. *Tip-Toes, Oh, Kay, Funny Face,* and *Girl Crazy* cannot be revived unless their foolish books are rewritten, but their songs form the basis of Gershwin's enduring popularity. These songs were quick to engage the public: "Someone to Watch over Me" (sung to a doll by Gertrude Lawrence in *Oh, Kay*); the exquisite "He Loves and She Loves" (*Funny Face*), with its swimming and voluptous harmonies; the bluesy "How Long Has This Been Going On?" (*Rosalie*); and the marvelous score for *Girl Crazy.* The overture itself is exciting, as overtures ought to be. They and the walkout music lie at the heart of Broadway musicals. The *Girl Crazy* overture spoons the audience right into the show. It can only be topped by a curtain soaring up on an opening number, but it's topped by more than that: "Embraceable You," "I Got Rhythm"—which introduced Ethel Merman—"Bidin' My Time," "But Not for Me," and the unfortunately titled "Broncho Busters," a thrilling orchestral number that anticipates Jule Styne's "Don't Rain on My Parade." (When asked to count the odd time of "Broncho Busters," Styne listened and then smiled. "It's simple," he said. "Its time is Broadway.") Yet such great songs were not exploited by the pit bands and the orchestrations of the period. Those who did the work were not always careful about realizing Gershwin's detailed piano arrangements and at the time orchestrating styles were primitive anyhow. Only by studying the scores or actually sitting down at the piano can one grasp the unpredictable turns of Gershwin's musical mind and appreciate the harmonic ingenuity and the rhythmic invention of his composing.

Gershwin differs from his great colleagues in that he quickly tired of musical comedy. Unlike the others, he could not be content writing successful scores for frivolous shows. He needed greater stage challenges. Six years with musical comedy were enough. His last musicals before *Porgy and Bess,* his final work, were three political satires—*Strike Up the Band, Of Thee I Sing,* and *Let 'Em Eat Cake.* Each of them takes a step away from light-headed entertainments toward a new kind of musical. The last of them, *Let 'Em Eat Cake,* is the strangest of *all* Gershwin shows.

A crusty theatrical pragmatist, George S. Kaufman hardly seemed the one to be writing political satire. Kaufman's experience had been as a sketch writer, particularly for the Marx Brothers. Yet, for the 1927 *Strike Up the Band,* he wrote a book that was half musical comedy, half comic opera, mocking American patriotism and economic imperialism. Those were times of America first. This show actually had the United States warring with Switzerland over the Swiss-cheese market and even banning Swiss books as anti-American. Even though Gershwin was at the height of his personal popularity, audiences were so offended by *Strike Up the Band* that it closed after several weeks on the road. Three years later, with its book

toned down by Morrie Ryskind—still another Marx Brothers writer—the show was remounted. This time it reached Broadway and had a respectable run of six months, exemplifying the principle of "the New York show": More than miles separate a tryout city from Broadway.

In contrast, *Of Thee I Sing* breezed through its tryout and had a spectacularly successful Broadway opening. Its run was the longest (441 performances) of any Gershwin show. It had the adult spirit and brightness of *Strike Up the Band* but not the venom. The book, co-written by Kaufman and Ryskind, is about a pair of politically manipulated candidates—John P. Wintergreen and Alexander Throttlebottom—running and winning a presidential campaign on a platform of "love." The vice-president is a meek, fumbling, adorable man who, true to the old joke, cannot find out what he is supposed to do in his new job.

Although this story has lost some of its wit, the music has not. In *Strike Up the Band*, Gershwin had begun to move away from musical comedy; with his score for *Of Thee I Sing,* he went one step further. This was comic opera outright. The music is more ambitious than show tunes. "Who Cares?," "Love Is Sweeping the County," and the title song almost demand to be seen onstage, sung by a chorus and in

*For* Of Thee I Sing, *librettists George S. Kaufman and Morrie Ryskind satirized presidential politics by inventing a candidate who campaigns on a platform of "love" (opposite) and vows to take as his First Lady the winner of a national beauty contest. When he decides instead to marry his secretary, Mary, the country is unsettled. But after he wins the election, Mary's giving birth to twins (below) boosts his popularity and he settles any remaining unhappiness by having his Vice President marry the beauty queen. William Gaxton and Lois Moran were President and Mrs. John P. Wintergreen and Victor Moore played a befuddled Vice President Throttlebottom.*

costume. Gershwin was growing surer of the difference between stage and popular music. One could not help but wonder just how far he would progress.

Nobody would have guessed he'd go as far as *Let 'Em Eat Cake,* which was Gershwin's last Broadway musical if you consider *Porgy and Bess* an opera. The sequel to *Of Thee I Sing, Let 'Em Eat Cake* opened in 1933 at Broadway's Imperial Theater with almost all the original leads reassembled. William Gaxton was again Wintergreen and Victor Moore once again was the hapless Throttlebottom. The show's first scene made it clear, though, that this wasn't to be more of the good cheer, rousing tunes, and harmless satire that had swept its predecessor to the first Pulitzer Prize for a musical.

For this show was about fascism in America. It dealt with the truth of the Depression, rather than with escape from it, and demonstrated how unemployment and despair could be exploited by demagoguery. Ryskind and Kaufman had again provided the book, in which this time John P. Wintergreen loses his reelection campaign to John P. Tweedledee ("Vote for Tweedledee—What's the Difference?"). The "Wintergreen for President" rallying cry becomes "Wintergreen for Dictator." *Let 'Em Eat Cake* was entertaining Broadway with the suggestion that America might buy totalitarianism! Audiences were not amused and the show failed.

Gershwin considered the music for *Let 'Em Eat Cake* his best yet, calling it "the composer's claim to legitimacy." It is indeed ambitious, at times as operatic as the *Porgy and Bess* to come. The only popular tune to emerge from the show is "Mine." Yet music, extended and dramatic, is the very fabric of the work. Dialogue and plot continue within sung material. Many of the musical exchanges are vitriolic variations on comic opera; overall, the score is clashing and grinding, its harmonies nasty and even dissonant, its melodies sardonic. Gershwin said, "I've written most of the music for this show contrapuntally, and it is this very insistence on the sharpness of a form that gives my music the acid touch it has. . . . " Indeed, in its very overture this music is cutting; the cheerful marching in *Of Thee I Sing* has turned savage.

Incredible as it may seem, until 1977 Gershwin's publisher believed that all of *Let 'Em Eat Cake*'s music but the overture had been lost. After the show's depressing New York reception, nobody had expressed much interest in it. When the composer's original manuscript was finally found in the Gershwin Archives of the Library of Congress, it revealed the musical sophistication he had achieved in 1933. Notated in Gershwin's own hand, the *Let 'Em Eat Cake* score is a blueprint for orchestration, a blizzard of notes, as if the composer had been cramming in all the music he could before his time ran out.

This strange musical is not an overlooked masterpiece. It is often silly and sometimes incoherent, but it is a singular work—the Marx Brothers gone Brechtian. Moreover, Gershwin's music makes astonishing progress toward the serious musical theater that Kurt Weill and Ira Gershwin subsequently explored in *Lady in the Dark,* a type of musical that neared realization with Bernstein's *West Side Story* and the musicals of Stephen Sondheim many years later.

Gershwin's final work for the theater was the extraordinary *Porgy and Bess*. No other composer for the American theater has written anything in its class. Even now, no one can agree on what genre it belongs to, but whether it is called opera, "folk opera," or musical, it is magnificent.

*Porgy and Bess* is based on the Dubose Heyward novel *Porgy,* which had been adapted into a successful drama before arriving in

*At the end of* Let 'Em Eat Cake, *ex-Vice President Throttlebottom (Victor Moore) is led to the guillotine by ex-President, now-dictator Wintergreen (William Gaxton, left). Throttlebottom's crime was being too fair an umpire in a baseball game between Congress and the Supreme Court.*

*Todd Duncan and Anne Brown played the original Porgy and Bess. Duncan was an opera singer who at first dismissed Gershwin as a pop songwriter. Duncan was surprised that Gershwin could even play the piano.*

this, its most famous form. As a story of the crippled Porgy, the sexy Bess, and the brutal Crown, it has the ingredients for passionate tragedy in the grand opera tradition. It also reflects the racial stereotyping of its period in its condescending treatment of rural black southern people. Time has given it some help in that respect. In certain passages it has a mythic, surreal sense of bygone America reminiscent of the paintings of Edward Hopper. That is as much as one can rationalize the libretto's racial slant. Heyward himself wrote the libretto, and he and Ira Gershwin provided the lyrics. While some were written by Heyward alone, others by Ira Gershwin alone (including "It Ain't Necessarily So," "There's a Boat Dat's Leavin' Soon for New York," and "Bess, Oh Where's My Bess?"), and some were collaborations, it is difficult to tell who did what. They are generally excellent, inseparable from the music.

*Porgy and Bess* begins with a glissando—an upward swoop of strings—that sends a promise of excitement surging through the theater. From there to that glissando's recurrence at the finale, this work is one long rush of the most gorgeous music ever written for the American stage. The music is so familiar to most Americans that it seems almost unnecessary to recount individual titles. The songs of personal emotion—of hope, loss, and love—reach out on long lines of heartfelt melody: "Summertime," "My Man's Gone Now," "Bess, You Is My Woman Now," "I Loves You, Porgy." The rhythmic pieces have a soulful richness that crowned Gershwin's lifelong affair with black music: "I Got Plenty o' Nuttin'" and "It Ain't Necessarily So." Harmony does visceral things to us. We sing melody but we *feel* harmony. "There's a Boat Dat's Leavin' Soon for New York" particularly capitalizes on a harmonic motif that Gershwin uses throughout *Porgy and Bess.* At the song's peak moments (always on the phrase, "That's where we belong"), Gershwin repeatedly manipulates our emotions through changing harmony in a way that no other Broadway composer did before. The rhythmic pulse and the harmonies developed throughout *Porgy and Bess* give it a musical heartbeat, intensified by the orchestrations, which were written by Gershwin himself. Where would "My Man's Gone Now" be without its crushing accompaniment? How could we be devastated by the final "Oh Lawd, I'm on My Way" without its rushing rhythm, its dramatic harmonies, its aching counterpoint, its breathtaking instrumentation?

In this final and culminating work of Gershwin, we find the combination of his musicianship and theatricality at full strength. His mastery of the forces that combine theater and music nails us. We have no recourse but to surrender to his engulfing music.

Gershwin's orchestrations are in the composer's own musical language; they underline and exploit his own harmonies and inner voices; they give him a chance to work with another aspect of music besides melody and harmony—instrumental coloration. Another orchestrator might have done a perfectly creditable job with *Porgy and Bess,* but the music wouldn't have sounded as authentic as it now does. Curiously, in the musical theater, when the orchestrations are done by the composer they do not sound as dated as when done by others. The shows that Gershwin didn't orchestrate have a period sound, while *Porgy and Bess,* "An American in Paris," and the Concerto in F have a timeless orchestral sound.

The original 1935 production of *Porgy and Bess* was a commercial failure, running only 124 performances. Revived seven years later, it ran for 286 performances. Since then, it has become one of

the most frequently performed works in all our musical theater, and has been produced extensively abroad. Unfortunately, many of the revivals were abbreviated versions. Producers have taken great liberties in trimming it, most often by omitting the recitatives—the dialogue sung between arias. This was particularly deplorable since Gershwin made more musical use of the device than did most opera composers, who usually did not give it substantial melodies.

Gershwin spent his final years in Hollywood, writing songs for movies. Far from being mere doodles, "A Foggy Day," "They Can't Take That Away from Me," and "Love Is Here to Stay" were the equals of any songs he'd ever written.

Where might he have gone from there? He spoke of writing a musical about the making of a musical. Almost forty years later, such a musical was produced: *A Chorus Line.* It's not that George Gershwin was ahead of his time. It's that all the possibilities of the musical theater seemed to flow from him. He simply embodied the Broadway musical theater.

*Kittiwah Island (above) is the site of the picnic in* Porgy and Bess, *where the pimp-like Sportin' Life (John Bubbles) sings his amoral creed "It Ain't Necessarily So." His attitude, as it's put in the song's verse, is: "Sun ain't got no shame; moon ain't got no shame/So I ain't got no shame, doin' what I like to do!" Sportin' Life will lure Bess away to "the high life" in New York by telling her that Porgy will remain in jail for killing Crown. Freed and finding them gone, Porgy sets out on his goat cart to find Bess, singing the opera's thrilling finale, "I'm on My Way."*

*Overleaf: A successful 1976 Broadway revival of* Porgy and Bess *by the Houston Grand Opera company at last presented the work uncut.*

231

# IRVING BERLIN

There have been more theatrical composers on Broadway and there have been more sophisticated composers on Broadway but there has never been a more beloved composer—or a better songwriter—on Broadway than Irving Berlin. Of all the giants of our musical stage, he probably had the greatest gift of melody. By his own count he published more than a thousand songs over a career of more than sixty years. He insisted that "most of these songs were bad, or at least amateurish," but, then, he described his exquisite "Remember" as "just another tune."

Berlin considered himself a songwriter, no more, no less. He is the only one of the Broadway greats who had a separate career as a writer of pop songs. He wrote the fewest show scores but there is no question he belongs among the masters. Irving Berlin is, well, Irving Berlin. Because his approach was so straight, Berlin's songs have been criticized as corny. Piano bar sophisticates do not clamor for them. Strange as it may seem to say of America's most versatile and popular writer of song, his day will come. Irving Berlin is the perfect songwriter, a prodigious and amazing talent. His songs reflect our country's idealized image of itself: mountains and prairies, glistening treetops, proud fellows, and girls as pretty as melodies. Perhaps we have rejected that image thoughtlessly. When we listen to his anthems we can understand the myth of America and care for it. He was the only one of the giants unembarrassed about writing holiday songs, creed songs, patriotic songs, and he was unembarrassed because he was ingenuous about them. He was unafraid to deal with truisms; even his disarming melodies amount to valid *musical* truisms. Both the music and the lyrics satisfy us because they are honest, not calculated, and because they are born of craftsmanship.

Berlin composed his share of sophisticated songs; any one of those he wrote for the movies of Fred Astaire would do—"Let's Face the Music and Dance," "Cheek to Cheek," "Top Hat, White Tie and Tails," "Puttin' On the Ritz," and all the rest. But Berlin's trademark is the straightforward melody with the straightforward lyric—a simplicity that leads to the very mark of a classic: inevitability. His own test of a good song is not how ingenious it is but how unlabored it sounds. For him, a good tune is one that can be sung or played by anyone. Berlin's approach to lyric writing is even more direct than his approach to melodies. A good lyric according to Berlin is one that states the title promptly and then *keeps* stating it so that the public will remember it when shopping for records and sheet music. He will find a strong key word for a big note, like "stealing" ("that extra bow") or "billing" ("out there in lights") for "There's No Business Like Show Business," and then work backward so that the rhymes lead up to it. It is this unabashed practicality, the no-nonsense

*Irving Berlin plays for Nanette Fabray while preparing* Mr. President. *He was an inspired melodist and a versatile craftsman who faced his work without pretension. "Brahms wrote music," he said. "I just write songs."*

business of song writing, that typifies the man's unneurotic talent.

Like all composer-lyricists, his words match his music. It's no accident that in "Always" there is a triple rhyme and a pause to set up the title word, and then it is presented with both a musical resolution and a nonrhyme to underline it:

When the things you've planned,
Need a helping hand,
I will understand,
Always, always.

Berlin and Porter are our premier composer-lyricists. Each demonstrates the perfect mating of music and words. The two could not have been more different. Porter sought the dextrous and witty in his lyrics. He was cool, ironic, his heart protected. Berlin opened up, looking for the words on the tips of our tongues. In his music, the well-schooled Porter could create a song through style. Using clever construction he could make the most of his basic melodic material. The untutored Berlin depended on melody alone. His harmonies were only implied, his use of rhythm instinctive. He did not include such details when he played his songs. Porter aimed to please his circle of sophisticates. Berlin measured success by mass popularity. Personally, they could not have been more different. Porter was a lotus-eater, Berlin a worker. Yet, they admired each other—indeed, *liked* each other. Israel Baline, born in Russia, an immigrant to New York's Lower East Side; Cole Albert Porter, a Yale man, mixing in café and even high society. Their noncompetitive relationship was possible because they were secure enough to respect equals and knew that originals cannot have competitors.

Though we speak of Berlin's characteristic simplicity, his music can't be easily identified. He wrote so many different kinds of songs it's hard to believe the same man was responsible for them all. Where is the similarity among the syncopated "Everybody Step," the rousing "Say It with Music," and the innocent "Oh, How I Hate to Get Up in the Morning"? It was such versatility that led to gossip that Berlin had a black songwriter squirreled away, writing his tunes (prejudice had forced many black songwriters to work anonymously).

These stories arose because of the contrast between Berlin's range and his musical illiteracy. He could not read music or write it down. A musician would sit by his side at the piano and notate a finished song as Berlin played it. Nor could he play the piano well. On one occasion, a producer couldn't believe that Berlin had written an awful song he was playing, but suddenly inspired, the producer asked the composer to play "White Christmas." When it sounded just as bad, the new song was accepted on the spot. Berlin couldn't even play the piano in more than one key. He had a special piano that would, with the shift of a lever, change keys.

As a major Broadway composer, Berlin was preceded only by Kern. He wrote his first score in 1914 (for *Watch Your Step*) and continued through twenty-one shows until the 1962 *Mr. President*. Like most of the show writers in the twenties, he specialized in revues, in his case *The Ziegfeld Follies* and the various editions of *The Music Box Revue,* named for his own theater. From these shows came such theatrical numbers as "Shaking the Blues Away"; the archetypal *Follies* song, "A Pretty Girl Is Like a Melody"; the achingly beautiful "What'll I Do?"; and "All Alone," a song any lyricist would stake his reputation on:

*In 1917, Berlin wrote for the Ziegfeld Follies the song that would ever after be associated with it—"A Pretty Girl Is Like a Melody." Musical scores for Ziegfeld's shows were usually written by teams of composers. It was a special tribute to Berlin that for the 1927 edition he was asked to write the entire score. One of its songs was the exhilarating "Shaking the Blues Away."*

*Berlin's revue* As Thousands Cheer *produced the everlasting "Easter Parade," done just the way you'd have wanted. The song is the very model of show music. Everything about it is theatrical—its expansiveness, its aptness for choral singing, its wide range, its soaring quality, its sense of movement.*

*Ethel Waters sang Berlin's show-stopping "Heat Wave" in* As Thousands Cheer, *a revue that took as its format the sections of a daily newspaper.*

Thinking how you are,
And where you are,
And if you are all alone too.     (*The Music Box Revue 1924–1925*)

Berlin wrote only two shows in all of the thirties, *Face the Music*, a minor success, and one of the most successful of all revues, *As Thousands Cheer*. He never tires of telling about the most famous song of that 1933 revue. According to Berlin, *As Thousands Cheer* was in need of a parade number for its finale. He dug into his trunk and came up with a 1918 song he had written imitating Felix Powell's hit song "Pack Up Your Troubles." The song was called "Smile and Show Your Dimple" ("you'll find it's very simple"). By his own admission it was a "terrible" song, but, stealing its first eight mea-

sures, he rewrote the lyric as "Easter Parade." The story exemplifies the importance of the right lyric to a song's success.

Berlin's theatrical inactivity during the thirties, when musical comedies were coming of age, left him unprepared for the era of musical plays to follow. Even in the early forties, he departed from revues for but one book show, *Louisiana Purchase.* Then, in 1942, he wrote the score for the military revue, *This Is the Army.* More or less a sequel to his First World War revue, *Yip, Yip, Yaphank,* it was typical of Berlin's special association with national American life. Although the trappings of *This Is the Army* ring of show business patriotism (it was produced by "Uncle Sam" and opened on the Fourth of July), there is a fundamental difference between Berlin's patriotic music and, for example, George M. Cohan's calculated flag-waving. Berlin

*A revue,* This Is the Army *dealt with military life from a draftee's point of view. Since its cast was all-soldier, the female roles were played by men. Today's increased awareness of homosexuality has made such innocent and traditional comedy no longer possible. That isn't progress.*

rose to various national occasions as if he dwelled in the country's heart. It was only in later years (with *Miss Liberty* and *Mr. President*) that he became professionally patriotic. *This Is the Army* is as accurate a reflection of wartime America as a defense-bonds poster or a Norman Rockwell cover for the *Saturday Evening Post*. Some of its songs were drawn from his *Yip, Yip, Yaphank* ("Oh, How I Hate to Get Up in the Morning") and others were new ("This Is the Army, Mr. Jones"), but all of them reflected the honest we're-in-this-together of America in the war years of the forties. Financed as a war benefit, the show had an extended Broadway run and then toured as a military entertainment. Entirely identified with Berlin—he was even *in* it—it established him as America in song.

Late in 1945 Rodgers and Hammerstein offered Berlin *Annie Get Your Gun* after the death of Jerome Kern. Berlin had misgivings about the project. He wasn't at all sure he liked the Dorothy and Herbert Fields book. He didn't quite believe the producers' excuse that they were "too busy with another project" to write this one themselves. Rodgers, he thought, can write anything, so Berlin concluded that Hammerstein considered *Annie Get Your Gun* too superficial an entertainment for the team. Berlin was also uncertain that he could write lyrics for the rural characters in *Annie Get Your Gun*. Hammerstein assured him, "All you have to do is drop the 'g's. Instead of 'thinking,' write 'thinkin'.'" Berlin gave it a try, going home and writing "Doin' What Comes Natur'lly." Though Rodgers and Hammerstein approved, he still wasn't certain, went home again, and wrote "They Say It's Wonderful." All in a week.

Finally sold, Berlin proceeded to compose one of the greatest scores ever written for a Broadway musical. The catchiness is unend-

*The tremendous popularity of* This Is the Army, *and its success in selling war bonds, established Berlin once and for all as an American institution rather than merely a songwriter. In a way that was more naive than egotistical, he came to believe in this reputation and to feel it his responsibility to write songs and shows about national themes. Here he is at stage center among the arm-wavers.*

Ray Middleton played Frank Butler to Ethel Merman's Annie Oakley in Annie Get Your Gun. *The story Herbert and Dorothy Fields wrote for the show was only craftsmanlike, a romance between rival sharpshooters. Yet, crazy as this sounds, it presented a hillbilly Annie Oakley so naive that Merman could go out and do her show business thing in the part and still be right. This was because as a performer she was as uncomplicated as Annie.*

Opposite, above: *Before Annie Oakley and Frank Butler could become romantically involved they had to compete as sharpshooters. As they matched shooting tricks in this scene, Merman and Middleton sang one of the biggest of* Annie Get Your Gun's *many hit songs—* "Anything You Can Do (I can do better)."

Right: *For* Annie Get Your Gun, *Berlin wrote one of the silliest yet most adorable songs in musical theater history—"I'm an Indian Too." Merman sang "I may run away/with big chief Son of a Bear " with the innocence of an eight-year-old in a school pageant. Not only did she get away with that but it was exactly what audiences came to see her do.*

Far right: *Every star likes a big entrance somewhere in a show, and this was Merman's for* Annie Get Your Gun. *It was in keeping with her style. The moment also became the popular image for the show, turning up on posters and on the cover of the original cast album.*

ing, the wealth of melody dizzying. The score simply tops one song with another. It is musical theater royalty. The show's love songs are "The Girl That I Marry," a lilting waltz and certified classic; "They Say It's Wonderful," a period ballad; and "I Got Lost in His Arms," a melody much better than its lyric. Even the show's comedy songs, "Doin' What Comes Natur'lly" and "Anything You Can Do," were popular hits.

The highlights of the *Annie Get Your Gun* score are its charm songs, the showstopping "You Can't Get a Man with a Gun," "My Defenses Are Down" and "Moonshine Lullaby." Each is unlike the other, none are "like" Berlin, and yet all are unmistakably his. "My Defenses Are Down" is the epitome of a show tune, while "Moonshine Lullaby" is a modestly extraordinary cowboy lullaby.

To top this marvelous score—to top all of the songs in all of the musical theater, perhaps—is "There's No Business Like Show Business." This song is to musicals what "White Christmas" is to Christmas and "Easter Parade" to Easter, not just a tribute but, finally, the thing itself. It is a showstopper not because of the singer, not because of the dancers, not because of the staging or even the theatrical moment, but because of the song's heart. Here is the very spirit of the Broadway musical, perhaps of all theater. It is greasepaint in song.

Berlin expected little of the number. He was so doubtful about its quality that when he first played it for Rodgers, Hammerstein, and the Fieldses, he mistook their silence for disappointment and promptly suggested that he'd write something else for the spot.

In a sense, the song was a throwaway that could have been in any show. Even Berlin wonders whether it would have been as effective if Merman hadn't sung it. Indeed, he wonders whether *Annie Get Your Gun* would have been as great a success without her. The impact of a show, he says, doesn't depend only on the quality of its material. A first-class musical can go unnoticed if it is miscast or misdirected. *Annie Get Your Gun* has worked with other stars—Mary Martin, Dolores Gray, Debbie Reynolds—but, according to Berlin, it might never have gotten the chance without Merman's original, overpowering performance.

When *Annie Get Your Gun* opened on May 16, 1946, musicals were just becoming national rather than strictly Broadway entertainments. The phenomenon of original cast albums and road companies had prompted this change. As a result, Berlin's next musical was not just another show but a public occasion. If *South Pacific* had been the first supermusical (a highly publicized event with a huge advance sale), then Berlin's *Miss Liberty,* which opened three months later in the summer of 1949, was the second. *Miss Liberty* was a supermusical on the basis of its collaborators' reputations. Berlin's librettist was Robert E. Sherwood, one of America's most eminent dramatists. A triple Pulitzer Prize winner for plays now rarely performed—*Idiot's Delight, Abe Lincoln in Illinois, There Shall Be No Night*—he was attempting a musical book for the first time. The director was Moss Hart, the author of many successful comedies, revues, and book musicals, who had never directed a musical before. The choreographer was Jerome Robbins. Berlin's reputation as a patriotic composer even prompted a heightened interest in the show's subject, the Statue of Liberty.

*Miss Liberty* was coolly received. It ran a respectable 308 performances, but such a showing is disappointing for a production so highly touted. Almost thirty years later, still feeling the sting of disappointment, Berlin talked about having its book rewritten. He

blamed Sherwood for being "too good a playwright for that kind of show. He tried to make it too distinguished." Truth is, Sherwood's problem was that he was an inexperienced librettist, unaware of the different needs of a drama and a musical.

The score for *Miss Liberty*, on the other hand, is vintage Berlin. It would be nearly as popular as the *Annie Get Your Gun* score had the show been a hit. Perhaps *Miss Liberty* would have done better had it been written for a star. There are songs in it that have the appeal of almost anything in *Annie Get Your Gun:* "Let's Take an Old-Fashioned Walk," "A Little Fish in a Big Pond." The show has a fine charm song in the Lorenz Hart-like "Falling Out of Love Can Be Fun." In setting Emma Lazarus's poem "The New Colossus," engraved on the statue's pedestal, to music as "Give Me Your Tired, Your Poor," Berlin revealed his admiration for Rodgers and Hammerstein's "You'll Never Walk Alone," but Berlin's song is still a stirring piece. It was just one of an unusually large number of chorus songs for a Berlin show. Since none of the leads—Eddie Albert, Allyn Ann McLerie, and Mary McCarthy—was a major star, perhaps Berlin didn't trust their voices.

He wouldn't risk weak voices the next time out and went straight

*Miss Liberty* was one of the first supermusicals, not only because of its Berlin score but because of its esteemed librettist—playwright Robert E. Sherwood. Instead of responding to the challenge of writing for a new form, Sherwood wrote a thin romantic comedy about a photographer (Eddie Albert) and the girl (Allyn Ann McLerie) he thinks was the model for the Statue of Liberty. Even so, the show wouldn't have seemed that bad had expectations been merely reasonable.

In Berlin's Call Me Madam, *Merman played Sally Adams, the "Hostess with The Mostest On The Ball," a thinly-disguised parody of Washington's Perle Mesta. Miss Mesta had been a celebrated party-giver during the Truman Administration, but, being a Republican, she naturally came into her own when Eisenhower was elected President. She was made Ambassador to Luxembourg, a diplomatic event best remembered for providing* Call Me Madam *with a plot.*

*Berlin's last musical,* Mr. President, *which opened in 1962 starring Robert Ryan and Nanette Fabray, was proclaimed the first show with a million-dollar advance sale. Musicals were on their way to becoming more business than show.*

246

to Merman for *Call Me Madam,* one year later. His collaborators were just as prestigious as those for *Miss Liberty,* but this time the director and the authors had musical theater experience and that made the difference. *Call Me Madam* proved no blockbuster hit nor a musical for posterity, but it was Berlin's second greatest success, running for 644 performances.

The story is based on Perle Mesta, who was a well-known Washington hostess in the Eisenhower years. As Mesta had been named ambassador to Luxembourg, so the show's "Sally Adams" was ambassador to a tiny principality called "Lichtenburg." The authors were Howard Lindsay and Russel Crouse, celebrated for their hugely successful 1939 play *Life with Father,* and librettists for a number of Porter musicals, including *Anything Goes.* George Abbott, at the time the reigning director of musicals, staged *Call Me Madam* and Robbins was again Berlin's choreographer. The combination of these names and Merman was enough to make the show still another supermusical. Like Rodgers and Hammerstein, Berlin would settle for nothing less.

*Call Me Madam*'s score is satisfactory but hardly in the class of *Annie Get Your Gun* or *Miss Liberty.* Its ballads are lovely—"Marrying for Love" and "The Best Thing for You." Its hit was "You're Just in Love," a counterpoint duet.

With age, Berlin's enthusiasm for the musical theater appeared to ebb. He did no shows in the twelve years between *Call Me Madam* and *Mr. President* (1962). By then he was seventy-four years old. Theater composers generally have much longer careers than playwrights, but they, too, finally write themselves out. Porter was sixty-four when he wrote the inferior score for *Silk Stockings.* At sixty-three, Rodgers came up with only a few ingratiating melodies for *Do I Hear a Waltz?* and wrote nothing of much consequence afterward.

*Mr. President* was still another supermusical for Berlin and the most ballyhooed of all. It had a book by Lindsay and Crouse, by then bigger than ever after writing the book for *The Sound of Music.* The director was Joshua Logan, then a Broadway lion for having staged four huge musical successes in only eight years—*Annie Get Your Gun, South Pacific, Wish You Were Here,* and *Fanny*—plus as many hit plays. The leads were Robert Ryan and Nanette Fabray. The casting of Ryan was part of a disturbing trend to give musicals prestige by using dramatic stars. For a show so highly touted it was a disaster. It eked out 265 performances and that only on the remains of one of the first million-dollar advance sales in Broadway history.

*Mr. President* concluded Berlin's active career. He continued to write songs into his nineties, typically insisting that only a few were any good. Anyway, he believed the public's taste in music had so changed that nobody would be interested in a new Berlin song.

We will not see the likes of Irving Berlin again. Another era produced him. Today's musical theater is more sophisticated than his was; it demands from its composers music rather than songs. Yet having invented the American song, Broadway cannot now go and uninvent it. Audiences want tunes. People will always love to sing and Irving Berlin was America singing.

Won't you play a simple melody?

Overleaf: *In the heyday of musical comedy, Broadway was ruled by songs and stars and nobody worried much about the state of the art. Perhaps there wasn't that much to worry about when the stars were like Bert Lahr. The greatest clown America ever produced, extravagant and wild, Lahr left his audiences helpless with laughter as he destroyed pretension with his buffoonery. Here, in the first act finale of the Jule Styne-Comden and Green revue* Two on the Aisle, *he plays Siegfried to Dolores Gray's Brünnhilde in a travesty of Wagnerian opera.*

# THE MODERN ERA

# COMPOSERS: THE MASTERS

Kern, Rodgers, Berlin, Porter, and Gershwin may well have been the giants but they were hardly the only men who set the high standards for Broadway's music. From the twenties to the fifties, similarly if not equally gifted composers were working all around them. But for accidents of career and chance, some of these others might also have ranked at the top. They are all certainly masters. Early deaths, complex personalities, and whimsicalities of fortune cut some careers short. Poor show choices and plain bad luck kept others from being celebrated. Theater composers' names are made by hit shows, not just good songs. Here we have the composers who fill out the body of the early years, as well as those who followed them to bring the musical theater through the war and into the fifties. They all made, developed, and sustained the tradition of show music.

Vincent Youmans and George Gershwin were the golden boys of the twenties composers. Expectations were unlimited for both of them and both were doomed to die youthful deaths. By 1927, at the age of twenty-nine, Youmans had three hit shows to his credit: *Wildflower, No, No, Nanette,* and *Hit the Deck.* His tragedy is that he hadn't the chance to do more. At thirty-five he was an invalid, victimized by tuberculosis. He never wrote another show and died a lingering death twelve years later.

Vincent Youmans is best known for the rousing songs we identify with choruses and production numbers. They are the stuff of the musical theater: "I Know That You Know," "Great Day," and "Hallelujah." Such breathless-with-excitement music is what we still relish in Broadway musicals and we have Youmans to thank for it. He also wrote lovely ballads, the gorgeous "More Than You Know," "Time on My Hands," and perhaps his best-known, "Tea for Two." Its lyricist, Irving Caesar, is fond of pointing out that the song's title is mentioned only once, at the beginning; what's more, the rest of the lyric has nothing to do with tea for two. This, he says, is because it was only a "dummy lyric," one jotted down to give Youmans a form to write to. But the dummy worked so well it was kept.

Youmans squeezed twelve shows into the twelve years of his career. *No, No, Nanette* was successfully revived on Broadway in 1971, thanks to a libretto rewritten by Burt Shevelove. It suggested that self-mocking revisions could make possible the revival of such empty-headed musical comedies. Unfortunately, there are few other Youmans shows apt for such treatment and fewer director-writers with touches as light as Shevelove's.

Like Youmans, Arthur Schwartz is also of the same generation as what I suppose must inevitably be called the Big Five. He is one of the most remarkable examples of an untutored composer writing sophisticated songs. In his youth, Schwartz tried and failed to team

*Bert Lahr became a star with the 1928* Hold Everything. *He made first-nighters weep with laughter as a punch-drunk fighter, along with fellow comic Victor Moore (the chef) and straight man Harry T. Shannon. The score was by Ray Henderson (music), Lew Brown and B. G. DeSylva and it included "You're the Cream in My Coffee." The team had already established itself with the* George White's Scandals *revues, and went on to write such standards as "The Birth of the Blues" and "Black Bottom." Their big book show was* Good News, *with its "Varsity Drag" and "The Best Things in Life Are Free."*

up with Lorenz Hart. In Howard Dietz he found a lyricist nearly as gifted, and the two collaborated on many great songs. Dietz and Schwartz were responsible, as much as anyone (including Rodgers and Hart and Porter) for the style and wit of American theater song. But the revue form they specialized in was short-lived. Their songs have lasted but there are no shows for audiences to continue loving them in. After too long a wait, Schwartz finally did write for book musicals, with Dietz as well as with Dorothy Fields, but the only revivable one is the 1951 *A Tree Grows in Brooklyn*. As a result, Schwartz is better known to aficionados than to the general public. Ironically, his most theatrical song—"That's Entertainment"—was written for a movie (the film version of the revue *The Band Wagon*).

The songs that Arthur Schwartz wrote for revues throughout the thirties span a broad range of styles and reveal a rich gift of melody. They are very definitely theater songs, conceived to be presented in person, onstage, sung and danced in costume, under lighting. While still a youth he wrote "I Guess I'll Have to Change My Plan" and put it in his first revue, *The Little Show* of 1929. This enchanting song is unusually smart for the period. His work in the decade to follow included two solid scores for the successive revues *The Band Wagon* and *Flying Colors*. *The Band Wagon*, considered by many the best of all revues, included "Dancing in the Dark," "New Sun in the Sky," and "I Love Louisa." *Flying Colors* added the exquisite "Alone Together," "Louisiana Hayride," and "A Shine on Your Shoes." He also wrote (for *Between the Devil*) the perfectly lovely "By Myself," a song as consistent with its lyric (by Dietz) as any written by a composer-lyricist.

*A Tree Grows in Brooklyn* was the closest Arthur Schwartz ever

*Opposite: Some forty-six years after its premiere, in 1971 Vincent Youmans's* No, No, Nanette *rode the nostalgia boom to a successful Broadway revival. Audiences were delighted with such familiar oldies as "Tea for Two" and "I Want to Be Happy," but also discovered forgotten songs. Here (from left to right) old pros Jack Gilford and Ruby Keeler join Bobby Van and Helen Gallagher in "Take a Little One-Step."*

*Below, left: Fred Astaire's trademark was top hat and tails, and for the Dietz-Schwartz revue* The Band Wagon, *designers Constance Ripley and Kiviette decked out sister Adele and the whole company to match. Even the fabulous set by Albert Johnson got into the act. The revue, starring the Astaires (below), was one of the best.*

*Based on a popular novel and with a story like* Carousel's, A Tree Grows in Brooklyn *is about the marriage of a nice girl (Marcia Davenport, right) to a doomed ne'er-do-well (Johnny Johnson). To give Shirley Booth's part star size, the character of the wife's sexually liberated sister was built up into the lead.*

came to a hit book musical. It deserved more than 270 performances. This was a musical play in the Rodgers and Hammerstein style and a good example of the genre. Working with Dorothy Fields while Dietz was busy being a Hollywood executive, Schwartz proved himself entirely capable of writing music to suit a story. That is, to use the key word of the time, he knew how to "integrate" a score despite his background in revues.

The music for *A Tree Grows in Brooklyn* grasps the show's period and the score exemplifies Schwartz's melodic gift. It includes strong ballads ("Make the Man Love Me," "I'll Buy You a Star"), ingratiating charm songs tailored to the star, Shirley Booth ("Love Is the Reason," "He Had Refinement," "Is That My Prince?"), and the ebullient production numbers that, perhaps more than anything else, meant *Broadway musical* at the time ("I'm Like a New Broom," "Mine Till Monday," "Look Who's Dancing"). The score for *A Tree Grows in Brooklyn* is nearly dud-free and George Abbott's script is sufficiently straightforward to make the show as revivable as any good old-fashioned book musical. Buoyed by the positive reception to the show, Schwartz again teamed up with Fields and Shirley Booth for *By the Beautiful Sea*. Inevitably, the second seemed a sequel to what was, after all, not *that* great a hit. *By the Beautiful Sea* didn't work out very well and Schwartz finally went back to working with Dietz. The team came up with two failures, *The Gay Life* and *Jennie*, before illness finally curtailed Dietz's career. *The Gay Life* is a depressing example of a good score going down the drain with a weak libretto.

Schwartz continued to consider musicals into the seventies but he was discouraged by fewer producers clamoring at his door, by his inability to find a worthy lyricist, and by the popularity of rock music. Living in London only emphasized his feeling of isolation from the contemporary Broadway. Yet his song catalogue attests to achievement enough. Were the unlucky decisions to work on revues and weak books really bad luck only? Perhaps, rather, theater awareness —a sense of where the stage is going, a nose for possible shows—may be as necessary to a composer as actual musical ability.

A lack of such stage sense hurt Harold Arlen, a man considered the songwriter's songwriter. Though he wrote many tremendous and lasting hits, the ingenuity of Arlen's composing is more appreciated by his fellow composers than by the general public. He never had an out-and-out hit show and that, in a nutshell, explains why audiences do not automatically rank him with the giants. Two of his musicals, the 1944 *Bloomer Girl* and the 1957 *Jamaica,* ran over 500 performances but they were overshadowed by the higher-powered hits of their time, from *Kiss Me, Kate* to *My Fair Lady,* not to mention the Rodgers and Hammerstein shows. Unfortunately, too, Arlen's finest scores were written for failed musicals, *St. Louis Woman* in 1946 and *House of Flowers* in 1954. Once more, good songs alone couldn't carry shows.

Though a first-class composer, Harold Arlen was not a man of the theater. He didn't have show judgment or the plain knack for the stage. His wish to write for the theater may have outstripped his propensity for it. He was not a composer to think in terms of book, production, and characters. He was interested mainly in his music, polishing a song for its own sake rather than the sake of the production. His care may have resulted in many musically perfect songs, but at the expense of theatrical spark.

His choices of lyricists reflected the problem. Though never

*Arna Bontemp's novel* God Sends Sunday *was adapted into the libretto for* St. Louis Woman, *with the help of collaborator Countee Cullen, but the 1946 musical is best remembered for its Arlen-Mercer score.*

*In 1946, Arlen and Mercer's* St. Louis Woman *introduced Pearl Bailey along with (left to right) Harold Nicholas, Ruby Hill, and Fayard Nicholas.*

able to find a steady collaborator, he worked with the best in Ted Koehler, E. Y. Harburg, and Johnny Mercer, and even discovered one in Truman Capote. Yet, none of these had reliable taste in scripts either. Koehler was Arlen's first stage lyricist, collaborating with him on the 1930 edition of the *Earl Carroll Vanities*. They wrote great songs together—"I've Got the World on a String," "Get Happy," and "Stormy Weather"—but Koehler never pursued book musicals and Arlen switched to Harburg, one of the finest of all lyricists. The team wrote three shows together, of which *Bloomer Girl* was the major hit and, at 654 performances, the biggest of Arlen's career. Some fine songs came out of the show—"Right as the Rain," "Evelina," and "The Eagle and Me"—but the team didn't collaborate again until the disappointing *Jamaica*, thirteen years later. Johnny Mercer, with whom Arlen wrote *St. Louis Woman* and *Saratoga*, never achieved a theatrical reputation commensurate with his ability because he, too, thought in terms of the song rather than the show. Like Arlen, Mercer was a poor judge of book material, and the musicals they worked on never stood much chance of success. The *St. Louis Woman* run of 113 performances hardly seems fair, considering such songs as "Any Place I Hang My Hat Is Home," "Come Rain or Come Shine," and "I Had Myself a True Love." However classy, these are pop rather than theater songs, more thoughtful than exuberant and spontaneous.

As for Capote, his lyrics for Arlen's 1954 *House of Flowers* are positively remarkable for a newcomer. They are technically proficient and artistically superior. The credit for the *House of Flowers* lyrics is shared by Arlen and Capote, so it's hard to know who wrote which words. It's likely that Arlen contributed the technique and Capote the poetry. Together, they made this score one of the most beautiful in the musical theater. The show is another of those that has become a cult favorite on the basis of its music but, as with most cult musicals, its revival (off-Broadway) recalled the reason for its original failure: the book.

This musical marked Arlen's peak as a Broadway composer. Its songs, delicately flavored for the Caribbean milieu, included the languorous "I Never Has Seen Snow," "A Sleepin' Bee," and the title song. In a way, though, another number was the score's most significant. Writing specifically for Pearl Bailey, Arlen put together a catchy comic song, "What Is a Friend For?" Here, at last, was theatrical music. When Arlen aimed for a production number, it usually came out for singing, not staging. Like "Two Ladies in de Shade of de Banana Tree," it tended to be oversized but not in the right way for the stage. He just wasn't production oriented.

Harold Arlen's music is associated with blues, peculiarly combining jazz harmonies with what might be called "Jewish warmth." Beginning in 1930, he had written nine scores. The last was produced in 1959, when he was still only in his fifties. Although he began work on various projects, Harold Arlen's music was not heard on Broadway again. Some composers think he might have been the greatest of them all.

It's hard to place Noel Coward in this group. His is, of course, a famous and dear theater name. Because he was so visible and versatile and *good* as a playwright, songwriter, lyricist, composer, and performer, it comes as a surprise to find that not many of his operettas, revues, and musical comedies actually were produced and succeeded on Broadway.

In terms of songs, his best New York musical was the 1929 operetta *Bitter Sweet*, with its "I'll See You Again," "Zigeuner," and the jewel-like "If Love Were All" that is so often taken as Coward's autograph:

> I believe that since my life began
> The most I've had is just
> A talent to amuse   (*Bitter Sweet*)

Yet *Bitter Sweet* ran only 157 performances.

Noel Coward is one of those singular people whose career cannot be categorized. He remained the curious ·outsider, the charming Englishman, perhaps dearer to theater people than to the public. He is not a major figure of the Broadway musical theater and yet he cannot be excluded when dealing with its major figures.

Vernon Duke is the final composer in this survey of Broadway's first generation. He is last because least, but being least in such company is no disgrace. Duke was a musical schizophrenic, writing classical music under his real name, Vladimir Dukelsky. Gershwin thought up the pseudonym "Vernon Duke," and apparently influenced Duke's use of blues harmonies as well as his pen name.

Duke wrote a number of excellent songs for revues throughout the thirties, including "I Can't Get Started with You" (with Ira Gershwin lyrics) and the wonderful "April in Paris" (with Harburg) for one of his first shows, *Walk a Little Faster* (1932). The middle part of this song (the release) is a variation and development of the main

*Noel Coward and Gertrude Lawrence play an English music-hall team in the lovable "Red Peppers" from the group of playlets by Coward comprising* Tonight at 8:30. *The song is the zany "Has Anybody Seen Our Ship?" and with it, Broadway achieved a level of smart gaiety that has since gone unmatched.*

melody. Such developing is a sure sign of a trained musician at work and makes a song more of a whole. Three years later, for *Thumbs Up,* Duke wrote a companion piece to "April in Paris," the Gershwin-like "Autumn in New York." He also wrote the lyrics, which are typical of the composer who is unaccustomed to writing lyrics: They are self-consciously literary and overly dense. "April in Paris," with its French harmonies, and the bluesy "Autumn in New York" make a unique and lovable pair.

Most of Duke's theater work was done in the thirties and early forties, during which he wrote nine scores. After a twelve-year absence he returned to Broadway in the fifties with two revues, *Two's Company* and *The Littlest Revue,* neither a success. His most successful book musical was the 1940 *Cabin in the Sky,* with its hit song, "Taking a Chance on Love" (lyrics by John Latouche and Ted Fetter). Otherwise, no significant musicals mark Duke's career.

The second generation of theater composers must begin with Burton Lane and Hugh Martin, not only because they are two of my favorites but because they spring from the same tradition as those who preceded them. Born in the century's teens, Lane and Martin form the connecting link between the first generation of musical theater composers and those who matured in the forties. If Kern and Gershwin had musically married, Hugh Martin and Burton Lane would have been their children, and professionally troubled children they were.

Hugh Martin is a man truly of the theater. He'd been a performer and later became a vocal arranger—one of the finest vocal arrangers of the Broadway stage. This is an invaluable background because vocal arranging deals with the very difference between pop and stage music. Martin was one of the most promising of show composers and had a first-class collaborator in Ralph Blane. Their first musical was a beauty and a hit: *Best Foot Forward* in 1941. Its boisterous opening number, "Buckle Down, Winsocki," set the tone for years of opening numbers to come. The show was smooth enough to more or less hold up in revival, providing the setting for Liza Minnelli's stage debut in 1963. The publicity over Judy Garland's daughter overshadowed "You Are for Loving," an exquisite ballad that Martin and Blane added to the revival.

*The young Katherine Dunham (above and at right), later to be acclaimed in modern dance, snuggles up to Dooley Wilson in* Cabin in the Sky. *Among Vernon Duke's songs from the original production was the classic "Taking a Chance on Love."*

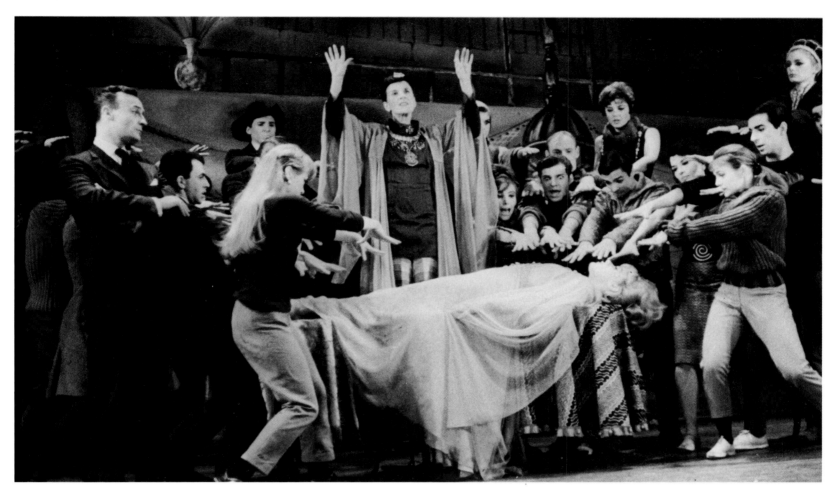

Martin and Blane are best known for a movie score, *Meet Me in St. Louis,* with its "The Boy Next Door," "Have Yourself a Merry Little Christmas" and, of course, "The Trolley Song." They never quite matched that when writing for Broadway, though Martin on his own had middling successes with *Look Ma, I'm Dancin'!* and *Make a Wish.* When the team broke up, Martin collaborated with Timothy Grey on *High Spirits,* an adaptation of Noel Coward's *Blithe Spirit.* Since Martin gave Grey equal credit on both music and lyrics, it is difficult to know who is responsible for what. There are good songs in *High Spirits*—"You'd Better Love Me While You May" and "Go Into Your Trance"—but they do not match the quality of Martin and Blane's earlier work. Hugh Martin has written no shows since. The frustration of his career, one of the musical theater's mysteries, is downright depressing.

Burton Lane's career is almost as strange. He was signed to write the score for *The Greenwich Village Follies* when he was *fifteen!* Although the show never materialized, he was soon contributing songs to revues. There were, at one stretch, four shows using his material when he was in his twenties. By then he'd also written "(I Like New York in June) How About You?" a song so good it would have been enough for any composer. Though encouraged by Gershwin, for whom he was a rehearsal pianist, Lane is rather a musical descendant of Jerome Kern. It is class lineage in either case.

He was a worker in his youth, contributing (with Howard Dietz's lyrics) to such revues as *Three's a Crowd* and *The Third Little Show.* In 1940, he teamed up with E. Y. Harburg (they were introduced by Ira Gershwin) to write the musical comedy *Hold on to Your Hats.* Four years later, Lane wrote the score for an Olsen and Johnson revue, *Laffing Room Only.* Though it ultimately produced a hit song for

*Bea Lillie, the wonderful English comedienne, made her last Broadway appearance as the medium Madame Arcady in Noel Coward's musical adaptation of his* Blithe Spirit, *retitled* High Spirits. *The ghost of Elvira (Tammy Grimes) is being levitated in the hope of exorcism so that her husband Charles (Edward Woodward, at left) can live, unpestered, with his second wife. The Hugh Martin-Timothy Grey song for this scene is the catchy "Go Into Your Trance."*

*In this famous scene from* Finian's Rainbow, *Senator Billboard Rawkins (named for the notorious Southern bigots Senator Bilbo and Congressman Rankin) is turned black by a magical bolt of lightning. From a modern perspective, the liberal intentions of this satire seem themselves offensive—being turned black for a joke, a punishment. Such plot devices have made* Finian's Rainbow *virtually unrevivable.*

*Michael Kidd's choreography for* Finian's Rainbow's *"When the Idle Poor Become the Idle Rich" looks as fresh as ever. The show was Kidd's first assignment as a choreographer.*

Alan Jay Lerner's book for On a Clear Day You Can See Forever *was an original story about a student (Barbara Harris) who recalls, under hypnosis, a previous life in the 18th century. Singing Lerner and Burton Lane's "Tosy and Cosh" here, as her former self, she reminisces about elegant suitors.*

which Lane also wrote the lyric—"Feudin' and Fightin'"—the show didn't take off. Strangely enough, after so busy a youth, Lane then became the reluctant giant among Broadway composers. He wrote only two shows in the next thirty-three years, *Finian's Rainbow* and *On a Clear Day You Can See Forever.* His explanation is that movie commitments kept him from doing some shows and weak books kept him from doing others, but these excuses are too facile for such a long period of inactivity. Whatever the real reason, it is plain from the work Lane did do that he is prodigiously gifted. Even having written just two shows, he ranks at the top. Had he done more he would surely be as celebrated as Rodgers.

*Finian's Rainbow* has one of the best of all Broadway scores, with lyrics by E. Y. Harburg at the peak of his form. To list some of the songs is enough to set the mind to humming: "When I'm Not Near the Girl I Love," "How Are Things in Glocca Morra?," "Look to the Rainbow," "If This Isn't Love," "Something Sort of Grandish," "Old Devil Moon." There is no other show, not even *My Fair Lady,* that produced so many song standards. Lane's ingenuity is astounding for a self-taught musician. He wrote a minuet for "Something Sort of Grandish," a verse that doubles as a release for "Look to the Rainbow," a melody that climbs the scale like a ladder for the exuberant duet "If This Isn't Love," and a series of tricky, bluesy, modulating harmonies for "Old Devil Moon." "When the Idle Poor Become the Idle Rich" is a production number whose rousing melody can't be drowned out by a shouting chorus. The *Finian's Rainbow* score simply cannot be overpraised. The show has an outdated political book by Harburg and Fred Saidy but it worked when it counted most—when the show was first produced.

On the other hand, the libretto of *On A Clear Day You Can See Forever* (1965) was bad from the start. Alan Jay Lerner's original story was devised to argue and celebrate the virtues of extrasensory perception. This approach did not work; it restricted the show with its lecture-demonstrations of what can't be demonstrated; it forced the show to argue with a skeptical audience.

However, Lane's score for the show is almost the equal of *Finian's*'s score. Lane writes for book musicals. He writes songs for plot. Perhaps such book-show songs are growing old-fashioned, but Lane is so theatrical, and so *good,* that this old-fashioned is like chocolate or fireplaces. We take what we get. *On a Clear Day* begins with "Hurry! It's Lovely Up Here," which introduces the mood of what is about to transpire. This lilting soft-shoe number is positively exquisite. The soaring ballads "She Wasn't You" and "Melinda" (a stunning waltz) are peformed back-to-back. "What Did I Have That I Don't Have" is a mock torch song, bluesy and from the belly. "Wait 'til We're Sixty-Five" is another waltz, but this time set to the syncopated rhythm of Kern's "Waltz in Swing Time." Lane's orchestrator on the show was Robert Russell Bennett, the grand master who had worked for Kern and Rodgers, and the music deserved him. But what do these song titles mean to the general public? Nothing. And why? Because they couldn't stand apart from a foolish show. Lerner's lyrics didn't make sense outside the story (they seldom made sense inside it). A marvelous lyricist, Lerner was handicapped by this show's subject matter. The only song from this score that has endured (and it's one of Lane's biggest hits) is the title song, "On a Clear Day You Can See Forever." Only when hearing this music without the lyric can one appreciate the wealth of its melody.

It had been eighteen years between *Finian's Rainbow* and *Clear Day.* After *Clear Day* it was twelve years before Lane wrote another show, *Carmelina,* in 1978. His collaborator was again Lerner, and one thing can be said with certainty about any Burton Lane score: practically everything in it will be golden. His work, though for few shows, ranks with Broadway's very greatest.

Kurt Weill is atypical of Broadway composers. He had established his reputation in the German theater, collaborating with Bertolt Brecht on several classics, *The Threepenny Opera* being the most famous. Weill was a trained composer—indeed, the author of two symphonies. It seemed as though his orientation toward high music and theater was too high for Broadway; the original Broadway production of *The Threepenny Opera* ran a mere twelve performances in 1933.

After immigrating to the United States in 1935, Weill tried to continue the political theater he'd done with Brecht by collaborating with Paul Green on the 1936 musical *Johnny Johnson.* Though this

*Bertolt Brecht and Kurt Weill's* The Threepenny Opera *is a cynical fable likening capitalists to gangsters. A true Brechtian style was faithfully adopted for the German work's Broadway premiere (below) in 1933, but New York critics judged it by the standards of musical comedy and found it so wanting that it closed after 12 performances. The finale of* The Threepenny Opera *features a "victorious messenger" who appears in the nick of time to rescue the hero-thief, Macheath, from execution—to emphasize that no such things happen in real life.*

work has a strong score written in Weill's ironic cabaret style, its production by the Group Theater was not a success. It deserves a stern rewrite so it can be revived for, like so much political theater, it plays like so much propaganda.

With *Knickerbocker Holiday* two years later, Weill tried to achieve an American sound. His inclination in book material was still toward the political. Maxwell Anderson's stiff, pamphleteering, hugely boring script about colonial Manhattan didn't help. *Knickerbocker Holiday* was lucky to play 168 performances, but it did produce the beautiful "September Song."

It was with *Lady in the Dark* that Weill made his major contribution to the Broadway musical theater. The period was alive with change. In 1940, Rodgers and Hart's *Pal Joey* introduced cynicism to the wonderful world of musical comedy. Three years later, *Oklahoma!* set the theater to talking about integrated lyrics and ballet sequences. Sandwiched between these two productions, *Lady in the Dark* pioneered the use of long musical sequences. Of these three shows, *Oklahoma!* had the greatest appeal during wartime years. It was cheerful and besides, though the least sophisticated, it was, overall, the best show. But *Lady in the Dark* was the most interesting in terms of structural innovation, which is why it seems more contemporary decades later.

Moss Hart's book for *Lady in the Dark* was based on the then new phenomenon of psychoanalysis. Drawn from Hart's four years of experience on the couch, it deals with Liza Elliott (played by Gertrude Lawrence), a fashion magazine editor whose problem is that she can't make up her mind—about magazine covers, about men. With the help of her analyst, she examines her dreams and finally understands her troublesome trauma.

*Burton Lane's* Carmelina *was an old-fashioned, romantic book musical with a libretto by Alan Jay Lerner and Joseph Stein, about an Italian woman (played by Georgia Brown) who, years after the war, is still collecting child support payments from no fewer than three American ex-GI's. Her Italian suitor was played by Metropolitan Opera basso Cesare Siepi, here singing the entrancing "It's Time for a Love Song." Was it time for such songs again on Broadway, gorgeous Lane melodies and knowing Lerner lyrics? It's always time. Would 1979 audiences sit still for a musical play in the fifties Rodgers and Hammerstein style? If it's good.*

*In* Lady in the Dark, *the men in the life of successful magazine editor Liza Elliott (Gertrude Lawrence) included three movie stars-to-be: Victor Mature (right) as a vain actor; Macdonald Carey (center) as a tough ad man; and Danny Kaye (left) as a photographer.*

*Musical numbers for* Lady in the Dark *were concentrated in four dream sequences: "The Glamour Dream," "The Wedding Dream," "The Childhood Dream," and here, "The Circus Dream," which was the best. Gertrude Lawrence is at the far left, the acrobat beside her is Victor Mature, and over at the right is ringmaster Danny Kaye.*
*Kaye (below) got to sing the tongue-twisting "Tchaikovsky," for which he became famous.*

*Left: A 1977 revival of* The Threepenny Opera *at Lincoln Center starred Raul Julia as Macheath and Ellen Greene as Jenny, the role created in Berlin and played at both the New York premiere and in a 1954 Marc Blitzstein hit revival by Lotte Lenya, Kurt Weill's widow. This revival meant to present the work as originally intended. Though Ralph Mannheim's translation was truer than Blitzstein's, this time the production style had nothing to do with Brecht. Ironically, the show was again a success. Weill's score had become a popular favorite, proving that all musicals don't have to sound "Broadway."*

Ogden Nash wrote the lyrics for Weill's biggest Broadway hit, One Touch of Venus, *and collaborated on the script with S. J. Perelman. Those were times when sophistication was actually commercial and America's wittiest writers were working in the theater. Mary Martin got her first star part in this 1943 musical. The male lead was Kenny Baker, the last Irish tenor on Broadway, and their big song was "Speak Low."*

*That's Norman Cordon as a jealous husband carried away in Kurt Weill and Langston Hughes's* Street Scene, *a musical about daily life in New York. The composer hoped this show would make the Broadway musical "a real blending of drama and music in which the singing continues naturally where the speaking stops and the spoken word as well as the dramatic action are embedded in overall musical structure." Weill's theory was sound, but his approach was too operatic. Indeed,* Street Scene *ultimately entered the opera repertory. Bernstein and Sondheim later implemented these ideas for the theater in a more Broadway style.*

The structure of *Lady in the Dark* is more interesting than its story. The show confines its music to three dream sequences. According to Weill, with these "three little one-act operas, I continued the story in musical fantasies when the realistic story stopped." Weill's style of operatic cabaret music was still in evidence, but Ira Gershwin was stage smart and helped to theatricalize it. Weill's other American collaborators could not control Weill's Germanic tendency in music because they were not music people. In fact, most of them weren't even professional lyricists. Conditioned by his experience with Brecht, Weill sought partners who were dramatists or poets: Ogden Nash (*One Touch of Venus*), Langston Hughes (*Street Scene*), and Anderson (*Lost in the Stars* as well as *Knickerbocker Holiday*). The only professional he worked with besides Gershwin was the young Alan Jay Lerner, who had a particularly Americanizing effect on Weill. He wrote his most "Broadway" songs for their *Love Life:* "Here I'll Stay" and "Green-Up Time." In practice, unfortunately, Weill's approach was operatic, as in *Street Scene* (which he considered his most highly evolved work). *Lady in the Dark* is his most important show, and it is still fun to see.

Jule Styne and Frank Loesser are to Kurt Weill what the racetrack is to a dance festival. Their shows initiated the hectic, brassy, pit-orchestra sound that characterized Broadway musicals for the next twenty or thirty years.

Styne and Loesser are the last of America's great pop songwriters to have crossed show business's great divide—from Tin Pan Alley to Shubert Alley, from pop music to theater. The theater composers after them were all stage specialists. Styne and Loesser brought the unpretentiousness of the music business with them.

Originally a lyricist ("Two Sleepy People" with Hoagy Carmichael), Loesser was already an established hit writer ("Spring Will Be a Little Late This Year") when he started work on *Where's Charley?* Both his father and his brother were trained musicians, but his own musical background was rudimentary, although he later studied piano.

Considering that *Where's Charley?* of 1948 was Frank Loesser's first show, the theatricality of its music and its aptness to the Oxford College setting was impressive. The show is based on the Brandon Thomas warhorse *Charley's Aunt,* and it included the song that Ray Bolger made into a way of life: "Once in Love with Amy." *Where's Charley?* has a lovely ballad in "My Darling, My Darling" and a fine production number in "The New Ashmolean Marching Society and Student Conservatory Band." But its neatest and nicest song is "Make a Miracle," a breathless, think-about-the-future duet. It is written as a canon, a form of counterpoint in which the same melody is placed against itself, starting at different times. Despite his limited schooling, Loesser liked fugues. However, he never let such musical cleverness overshadow melody; "Make a Miracle" is one continuous and lilting strain.

The score for *Guys and Dolls,* produced two years later, is Loesser's most celebrated. This musical version of Damon Runyon's

Although Guys and Dolls *had some of the standard ingredients of musical comedy—two pairs of lovers engaged in on-again, off-again romance—there was nothing typical about it and it enchanted New York. From its Broadway argot (derived from Damon Runyon's short stories), to its syncopated opening number (a trio of horseplayers sing "A Fugue for Tinhorns"), to its parade of gorgeous, funny, singable songs—the show was pure delight. The plot bounces from Forty-second Street to Havana and back again and is too complicated to summarize, but a few key scenes are shown here. At the top left is the climactic first act crap game (held in a sewer) in which the romantic hero, Sky Masterson (Robert Alda), gets Lady Luck on his side and wins*

Broadway fables deserves its reputation, for it catches exactly the hectic rhythm of thirties Broadway street life and even raises it to a mythic level. The curtain rises on a bustling Times Square, and the show's opening scene is a headlong rush from the tinhorn gamblers' fugue ("I've got the horse right here") to the Salvation Army chorale ("Follow the fold and stray no more"). The duet "Marry the Man Today" is another canon and the show's best song, I think. Then there is "Adelaide's Lament," musically and lyrically ingenious, telling how a man's reluctance to marry is reason enough for a girl to have a psychosomatic cold:

> La grippe, la grippe, la post-nasal drip
> With the wheezes and the sneezes
> And a sinus that's really a pip!
> From a lack of community property—
> And a feeling she's getting too old,
> A person can develop a bad, bad cold.  (*Guys and Dolls*)

"Adelaide's Lament" is a showstopper whose comic appeal masks both a verse of almost operatic ambition and a series of dissonant harmonies hardly familiar to theatergoers' ears. Loesser had a way of treating such music in a Broadway style, making it accessible. Similarly, his casual lyrics belied their dexterity.

*Guys and Dolls* also has its share of conventional songs, the ballads "I'll Know" and "I've Never Been in Love Before," and the production number "Luck Be a Lady Tonight." "Sit Down, You're Rockin' the Boat" is typical of spitituals common to musicals at the time, but it is a superior example. Overall, the variety of songs in the show is mind-boggling, from the shrugged shoulders comedy of "Sue Me" to the jazz modulations of "My Time of Day." Here is one of the great scores and, with Abe Burrows's book, one of the great shows.

With only two musicals under his belt, Loesser undertook to write the book as well as the music and lyrics for no less than a Broadway opera. Then again, since *Guys and Dolls* and *Where's Charley?* had just run almost two thousand performances between them, he could pretty much do as he chose. He took as his source Sidney Howard's 1925 Pulitzer Prize–winning drama, *They Knew What They Wanted.* This is a creaky romantic melodrama but its basic story is solid, with emotional peaks not unlike those exploited by Puccini, who was obviously Loesser's model. Howard's play is faithfully followed: Tony, a wealthy, warmhearted, middle-aged Italian vintner living in California, proposes by mail to Amy, a girl he has seen only once. Accepting, she arrives to find that he'd sent not his picture but that of his young foreman. She marries Tony anyway but in her disappointment allows herself to be seduced by the foreman. When Tony learns of her pregnancy he throws her out, but then changes his mind. He and Amy had finally fallen in love.

It is a good story for a musical and Loesser actually improved on the original. He also illustrated it with more than thirty songs: Italian songs ("Abbondanza," "Sposalizio"), ballads ("Don't Cry," "Warm All Over"), charm songs ("Happy to Make Your Acquaintance"), and production numbers ("Big 'D'"). Is it an opera? No, it is a Broadway musical with a great deal of music. There is sometimes too jolting a contrast between such brassy American songs as "Standing on the Corner" and so high-flown a ballad as "My Heart Is So Full of

Robert Weede left the Metropolitan Opera for Broadway's The Most Happy Fella, in which he played a California winemaker who proposes to a much younger woman by mail. Above, at right, he sings the title song after having had his marriage proposal accepted. Jo Sullivan (standing, above) played the mail-order bride; Susan Johnson was her confidante.

Greenwillow was about a quaint young man (Anthony Perkins) in a quaint little town, who was uncertain about marrying for fear he had inherited a quaint wanderlust from his quaint father. Up to its knees in sentiment, the show nevertheless sang out with a lovely Frank Loesser score.

You" (the most Puccini-like song in the score). Yet the composer's personal tone held them together.

The Most Happy Fella had the misfortune to open in the spring of 1956, a bare six weeks after My Fair Lady's spectacular arrival. Because of that, it wasn't hailed as it might have been, though it ran a healthy 676 performances. Without question it is a golden work and one of our musical theater's overlooked ones.

Frank Loesser's only Broadway failure was Greenwillow, which ran for 95 performances in 1960. The show, based on a novel by B. J. Chute, had a coy story that marked a far journey from the free-wheeling Guys and Dolls. Greenwillow became a cult musical because of its rich score, with its offbeat "A Day Borrowed from Heaven," the flowing "Summertime Love," and a particular gem, "Faraway Boy." This last has the delicate flavor of "More I Cannot Wish You" from Guys and Dolls.

The last and biggest of Loesser's hits was How to Succeed in Business Without Really Trying, opening in 1961 and running for 1,417 performances. It is a satire of corporate ladder climbing, told in cartoon style. For a Loesser musical, How to Succeed is short on good music; in fact, its score hardly sounds musical. The show's best-known song is "I Believe in You" and it is the only one with any zing. This sounds like a real theater song but for some other show. Its lyric fits, but the music doesn't. I don't think Loesser had a musical handle on How to Succeed, perhaps because it would have worked just as well without music. A musical must need music.

How to Succeed in Business Without Really Trying *was directed by Abe Burrows and Bob Fosse in a cartoon style. Old-time crooner Rudy Vallee (third from right), though inexperienced in the theater, found the perfect silliness for such caricature. The tone came naturally to Robert Morse (skipping) who became a star playing the superambitious young hero.*

*How to Succeed* was Frank Loesser's last show to reach Broadway but not the last he wrote. *Pleasures and Palaces* was one flop based on another, the Samuel Spewack comedy *Once There Was a Russian*. The musical closed out of town in 1965. Finally, at his death in 1969, Loesser had completed the book, music, and lyrics for still another show, a Mexican musical called *Señor Indiscretion*. It is based on a Budd Schulberg story with the same title and one can't help but be tickled by the prospect of a Loesser score with a Mexican flavor. *Señor Indiscretion* may yet be done.

Though his output was small, Loesser's *Guys and Dolls* and *Where's Charley?* are sure classics and he has to be ranked among Broadway's best.

Harold Rome is a composer - lyricist who cannot be neatly compartmentalized, in era or style. He emerged with the tremendously successful 1937 labor union revue, *Pins and Needles*. A later revue, *Call Me Mister,* celebrated the return of army veterans to civilian life. It was a successful and *very Broadway* revue that introduced a marvelous new star, Betty Garrett. Hailed as a new Merman, her stage career was tragically destroyed by McCarthyism because of accusations not against her but her movie actor husband, Larry Parks.

Rome had another hit four years later, with the 1950 musical comedy *Wish You Were Here.* This show occupies a special niche in the hearts of musical theater makers. It was bombed by the critics but survived destruction, riding on word of mouth to a 598-performance run. It has been a symbol of hope, ever since, to musicals that are panned.

Harold Rome's greatest success was *Fanny* of 1954. Starring Ezio Pinza, Florence Henderson, and Walter Slezak, it was based on a trilogy by Marcel Pagnol. A musical play in the Rodgers and

Opposite: *In* How to Succeed in Business Without Really Trying, *a young opportunist (Robert Morse) cons the president of World-Wide Wickets Company (Rudy Vallee) into thinking that he went to the boss's alma mater and together they sing "Grand Old Ivy."*

*Betty Garrett stopped the show with "South America, Take It Away" in the postwar revue* Call Me Mister.

Hammerstein tradition, this was Rome's best score—good theater songs for a successful, but curiously unremembered show.

Rome's other musicals were only mildly successful. His 1959 *Destry Rides Again* included a gorgeous ballad—"Anyone Would Love You." *I Can Get It for You Wholesale* (1962), adapted from Jerome Weidman's garment business novel, is remembered only for introducing Barbra Streisand. Rome later pulled off a coup in securing the musical rights to *Gone with the Wind,* but despite the renowned title and a 1972 production in London, the show never made it to New York.

Harold Rome was a melodist in the Kern tradition, and the composer of many popular songs. Though his career overlapped eras, he did not change with the musical theater as Rodgers did. He is closer in spirit to the second generation of composers than to the third.

When it comes to writing Broadway overtures, Jule Styne is second only to Gershwin. However, because orchestration had become so much more sophisticated since the thirties, Styne's are more effective. Both men understood the importance of the overture: It sets up the show, galvanizing the audience with a startling sound. It builds up excitement so that the soar of a curtain rising is the only thing that can top it. The overture has long symbolized the feel of Broadway. It is among the grandest of musical-theater traditions. For most shows, the orchestrator pieces out the overture from the main songs. Beginning in 1949, with *Gentlemen Prefer Blondes,* Styne wrote his own, complete with instrumental parts. Those for *Gypsy*

*Playing that "little girl from Little Rock," in* Gentlemen Prefer Blondes, *Carol Channing becomes the toast of Paris and the object of a millionaire's passion. Minutes after this night-club scene, she will step toward the audience, a curtain will drop behind her, she will sing "Diamonds Are a Girl's Best Friend" and become one of the greatest stars in the Broadway theater.*

272

Barbra Streisand's theatrical experience totaled one performance in a flop off-Broadway revue when she was hired for a supporting role, the telephone operator Miss Marmelstein, in Rome's I Can Get It for You Wholesale. Below: *Elliot Gould (at left) in a garment district scene from the show.*

*Based on the memoirs of the burlesque queen Gypsy Rose Lee, the musical* Gypsy *really focuses on the stripper's mother, Rose (Ethel Merman), who pushed two daughters to achieve the stage success that had eluded her. Here, she cold-shoulders a balky receptionist as daughters June Havoc (Lane Bradbury, center) and Gypsy (Sandra Church), along with Mama's latest lover (Jack Klugman), look on helplessly.*

*Opposite:* Though Gypsy *ended up as an orthodox book musical, there are images in it— such as this chorus girl Christmas tree —that suggest what Director Jerome Robbins had in mind in his original plan to make it a concept musical celebrating the American variety stage.*

and *Funny Girl*—with the opening soar of the trumpets and their tension before the torrent of rhythm—are his best.

Styne had made the Broadway plunge in 1947, the year before Loesser. Over the next twenty-five years he wrote sixteen shows, making him the most prolific composer of his era. He started off with a hit in *High Button Shoes* (727 performances), a period piece about New Jersey in the century's teens. The flimsy story deals with a couple of confidence men trying to use a respectable family as patsies in a swindle. But the show is filled with catchy numbers: the lilting and very special "Can't You Just See Yourself in Love with Me?," a lovely ballad in "You're My Girl," the rousing "Papa, Won't You Dance with Me?," and the soft-shoe spot, "I Still Get Jealous."

Styne's next, *Gentlemen Prefer Blondes*, was based on Anita Loos's stories about the not-so-dumb chorine Lorelei Lee. The show is best known for catapulting Carol Channing to stardom. "Diamonds Are a Girl's Best Friend" is the show's best-known song, but it is too careful a specialty turn, baby-feeding its lyrics to the audience. With the other songs in the show, Styne developed the qualities already evident in *High Button Shoes:* an easy flow of melody combined with a growing show sense. "Bye, Bye, Baby" is a relaxed vaudeville turn in the style of the earlier "I Still Get Jealous." "A Little Girl from Little Rock" is another showcase for Channing, revealing Styne's special knack for tailoring a song to a performer. The score's best numbers are "It's Delightful Down in Chile" and "Sunshine," both flat-out theater songs and both, as it happens, victimized in the production by garish chorus arrangements.

With the 1951 revue *Two on the Aisle*, Styne began a long-lasting

collaboration with Betty Comden and Adolph Green, lyricists, librettists, and sometimes both. The team hit their stride with the 1956 *Bells Are Ringing*. We think of it as a typical second-generation musical comedy but it was too good to be typical. The Comden and Green script is an original story about a shy girl (played by Judy Holliday) who works for a telephone answering service, and her romance, first imagined and then realized, with a handsome client (Sydney Chaplin). This is a journeyman story but it was viable at the time because Comden and Green tailored it to the adorable comic personality of their pal, Miss Holliday. Styne picked up the tongue-in-cheek style of his collaborators. He also wrote perfectly in character for Holliday, as he had earlier for Channing and would, later, for Merman and Streisand. "It's a Perfect Relationship" is a swell theater song. The whimsical lyric ("I talk to him, and he just talks to me") is underlined by satiric music which begins in a light mood, turns melodramatic, and ends as, of all things, a conga. "It's a Simple Little System" is a plot song describing how the answering service is a front for a bookie operation, but it is presented as a mock cantata. There are also a couple of first-class ballads in "Just in Time" and the classic "The Party's Over." My favorite from the show is the vaudevillian finale, the show-stopping "I'm Going Back" ("Where I can be me/At the Bonjour Tristesse Brassiere Company/. . . A little mod'ling on the side"). This is a spirited, funny, and irresistible number that showed off Miss Holliday's unique combination of brains and clowning. Judy Holliday, who died in 1965 when she was not quite forty-four, was one of the stage's most special stars and I think "I'm Going Back" is the song to remember her by.

Over the next eleven years, Styne wrote five more shows, four of them flops, with Comden and Green, before the partners realized that they were not bringing out the best in each other. For in the very same stretch, while working with others, Styne wrote two of Broadway's best scores, *Gypsy* with Stephen Sondheim and *Funny Girl* with Bob Merrill. Jerome Robbins, who was responsible for the direction of both shows, relentlessly demanded and received Styne's best efforts. Both of these scores contain Broadway gold. *Gypsy* is a perfect show score, in many ways the most perfect one.

*Gypsy* has only one "trunk" song (a song hauled out of the composer's past)—"Everything's Coming Up Roses," which Robbins remembered being deleted from *High Button Shoes* (it was then called "Betwixt and Between"). One can hardly imagine it in another show, given Sondheim's new lyric and its superb orchestration by Sid Ramin and Robert Ginzler. These two share some of the credit for the final effect of *Gypsy*'s music. Styne has always been choosy about orchestrators; *Funny Girl* was similarly supported by the orchestrations of Ralph Burns.

As for the other songs in *Gypsy*, "Some People" is a uniquely gritty "charm" song. It was Ethel Merman's opening shot and with its headlong drive sent her and the show winging. Styne also wrote an effective ballad—"Small World"—for Merman, no easy trick considering her dominating personality. The duet "Together" for her and Jack Klugman begins so straightforwardly it seems a child's song. But at the release its harmony begins to step up the scale, creating an inner tension. This gives the number's cheerfulness an underlying skepticism. Styne's music, abetted by Sondheim's lyric, shows that Mama Rose, the obsessive stage mother, can never be genuinely exuberant. She is too driven, too frustrated. These songs are adapted to Merman's fire-alarm voice and they represent the

*What is it about Ethel Merman? The lady was never a great beauty, never a comic, never an actress. She acted the way she sang, squaring off with the audience and yelling at it. Only once, in* Gypsy, *did she present a real characterization and that was because the part of the brassy, vulnerable stage mother was tailored to her. But then there was that voice, a physical thing, pushing out from the stage in ever wider, pulsating throbs. She didn't merely introduce* "I Get A Kick Out of You" *and* "There's No Business Like Show Business" *and* "Everything's Coming Up Roses," *she shoved them in our faces, and we loved it.*

*What is it about Merman? It, of course, is the most indefinable, intangible, and important quality a stage performer can have: dynamism. It is hardly coincidental, then, that Merman was associated with the greatest scores of every composer she worked with. She brought out in a composer the reason he wrote for the theater in the first place. Even if one were to concede that Gershwin's* Girl Crazy *was not inspired by her since it was her first show and* "I Got Rhythm" *her debut song, there is still Porter's peak score for* Anything Goes, *Berlin's for* Annie Get Your Gun, *and Styne's for* Gypsy. *These are three glorious scores and each was written for Merman. There is no performer who has so inspired our stage composers because there is none who so magnificently exemplified exactly what the Broadway musical is all about.*

*Barbra Streisand was not an experienced actress when she starred as Fanny Brice in* Funny Girl, *but she had star presence and a spectacular voice. She also had Jule Styne's songs to sing—comedy songs, knock-'em-dead songs, and soaring ballads. Streisand specialized in ballads, and Styne was one of the supreme ballad composers of the modern era. Opposite: A kid of twenty-two, she rears back, alone onstage in* Funny Girl *at the Winter Garden Theater, and socks out "The Music That Makes Me Dance." Out there, alone with the audience, the difference between an actor and a star is the sexual relationship with the audience. This is love on its way to ecstasy. Barbra Streisand, in* Funny Girl, *isn't pretending—she is in a performing delirium and it is the soul of stardom.*

Broadway style of music at full throttle. As for "Rose's Turn," it is in a class of its own. Literally and figuratively, it is *Gypsy*'s ultimate number, a free-form construction picking up themes from other songs in the show and weaving them through craggy and dissonant combinations. This is a nervous breakdown in song. Styne never wrote more powerfully for the musical stage.

But he wrote more for *Gypsy*. "Mr. Goldstone, I Love You" is another song that, even musically, elaborates on Mama Rose's personal quality. Like "You'll Never Get Away from Me," in which she claims to have feelings, it shows her incapable of thinking about anything except getting to the top. "Little Lamb," which Styne had to argue Robbins into keeping in the show, gives *Gypsy* its only tender moment as Rose's daughter June sings of being forced to pretend, for the sake of her vaudeville act, that she isn't getting older. "All I Need Is the Girl," written to give the show's dance lead a solo, is the one song in *Gypsy* that could be considered musical flab. By the time of *Gypsy*, the dance solo had grown obsolete.

If Jule Styne had written no other show, *Gypsy* would have assured his ranking among Broadway's top composers.

*Funny Girl,* like *Gypsy,* is a show-business biography. The subject is Fanny Brice, the singing comedienne who was a Ziegfeld Follies star in the twenties. Styne's lyricist on this 1964 production was Bob Merrill, a composer-lyricist (*New Girl in Town, Take Me Along, Carnival*). Responsibility for only the words seemed to free Merrill to write the best lyrics of his career.

Styne's score for *Funny Girl* isn't as consistent as the one for *Gypsy,* but it does have many great songs. In Barbra Streisand, Styne had not only a powerhouse singer but one just then exploding on the mass market. Doubtless stimulated by so ripe an opportunity to get some hit songs, Styne gave the youngster a tremendous load. She had the kingpin number in the fabulous "Don't Rain on My Parade." This is a most unusual song, an intensified Charleston, and it always stopped the show. She also had three gorgeous ballads in "People," "The Music That Makes Me Dance," and "Who Are You Now?" This last is a very special song with an eerie quality, stretched out and melancholy. Intensely theatrical, it is the kind of song that silences and rivets an audience.

*Funny Girl* came into New York trailing cowbells of disaster. It played endless previews while Robbins worked on it, but it surprised all the insiders by becoming hugely successful, Styne's biggest hit. Ironically, neither *Funny Girl* nor *Gypsy* won a Tony Award for its season's best music. *Gypsy* was beaten out by *The Sound of Music* and *Funny Girl* by *Hello, Dolly!* But if one composer represents the throat-catching, hair-raising excitement of fifties and sixties Broadway musicals, it is Jule Styne. Moreover, such shows as *Funny Girl* and *Gypsy* marked a new approach to serious musicals. The Rodgers and Hammerstein musicals had been gagging on their own sobriety. Styne brought showmanship and energy.

The last of the traditional musical-play composers was Frederick Loewe, and if anyone challenged Rodgers as the master of modern operettas, it was he. Collaborating with lyricist-librettist Alan Jay Lerner, Loewe reeled off a series of hits whose scores brimmed with melody.

After a few false starts—*What's Up?* in 1943, *The Day Before Spring* in 1945—Loewe established himself with *Brigadoon* in 1947: its lively, exciting opening, "Down on MacConnachy Square," and

then the endearing "The Heather on the Hill," "There But for You Go I," "Come to Me, Bend to Me," and "Waitin' for My Dearie." *Brigadoon* was a bit heavy on the endearing. The show's most popular song was also its best—"Almost Like Being in Love," a lilting, soaring song that is eerily reminiscent of Kern.

Four years later, in 1951, Lerner and Loewe came up with *Paint Your Wagon*. It was only a mild success (289 performances) though it had such fine songs as "I Still See Elisa," "I Talk to the Trees," "They Call the Wind Maria," "Wand'rin' Star," and "Carino Mio." But these songs clashed with the show's rural western setting. Loewe was born in Germany and his musical background lay in Viennese operetta. Although *Paint Your Wagon* dealt with Americana, it had Continental music, emphasized by a leading man—Tony Bavaar—with an operatic tenor. Given Lerner's lyrics, such music could pass for Scottish in *Brigadoon* as it later passed for English in *My Fair Lady* and *Camelot*. Broadway audiences did not notice such musical anomalies. But operetta music for a western mining town? Audiences weren't *that* susceptible.

*My Fair Lady* was another story—Shaw's—and it inspired Loewe to compose one of Broadway's most glorious scores. Technical shortcomings of the era make it less the perfect musical than it once seemed—this sort of musical play was already starting to date and the show is basically operetta to begin with—but there's no resisting it. *My Fair Lady* is magnificent musical theater, one of Broadway's ranking achievements, and Loewe's music simply could not be improved upon. It is perfect for the material and one is still awed by it. Loewe solved the problem of having a leading man, Rex Harrison, with a weak singing voice by capitalizing on his rich *speaking* voice. It was not new to have a character speak-sing—Gertrude Lawrence had just done it in *The King and I*—but Loewe made it an actual asset. Again and again, Harrison enchanted audiences with his patter songs: "Why Can't the English?" and "I'm an Ordinary Man," and of course the exhilarating "A Hymn to Him" (better known as "Why Can't a Woman Be More Like a Man?").

Composing with an exacting awareness of character, Loewe

even tailored Eliza's songs—in *musical* terms—to her changing character, from the Cockney "Wouldn't It Be Loverly?" and the angry "Just You Wait" to the refined celebration of "I Could Have Danced All Night" and the finally independent "Without You." As a set of songs for a straightforward musical play, this score is without superior.

Yet if one ignores the lyrics of these songs, Loewe's Viennese throb can be heard in the music. Only when writing "With a Little Bit of Luck" and "Get Me to the Church on Time" for Eliza's raffish father did he suppress it. Of all the wonderful songs from the show, perhaps the most affecting is the most operetta-like of all, "I've Grown Accustomed to Her Face," and yet Loewe so entwined his music with the spirit of the story and the show's unique character that this song seems to be the one that brims *My Fair Lady*'s cup over.

Lerner and Loewe found it impossible to resist the temptation to try to match *My Fair Lady*'s success with another of the same sort: another blockbuster show with star names. For in terms of a new kind of market (cast album sales, movie deals, diverse financial clout), *My Fair Lady* had become the biggest hit in Broadway musical history. This next show was *Camelot*, starring Julie Andrews, who had played Eliza Doolittle in *My Fair Lady,* and Richard Burton. Based on T. H. White's classic *The Once and Future King,* the show had physical splendor. It also had some good songs in "How to Handle a Woman," "If Ever I Would Leave You," and "What Do

*As George Bernard Shaw's upper-class linguist Professor Higgins, Rex Harrison concentrates on the Cockney dialect of flower girl Eliza Doolittle (Julie Andrews).*

*Stanley Holloway brought the authentic style of the British music hall to* My Fair Lady *with "Get Me to the Church on Time."*

When a musical's lyricist is also its librettist, there is usually little choreography. This is because the writer has power enough to keep his script from being cut to make room for dances. Alan Jay Lerner wrote the books as well as the lyrics for both My Fair Lady and Camelot (at right and below) and each show had minimal choreography by Hanya Holm.

*The stars of* Camelot, *Richard Burton (King Arthur) and Julie Andrews (Queen Guenevere), sang together only once in the show—"What Do the Simple Folk Do?"*

the Simple Folk Do?" But though there is a great deal of musicality in White's material and its chivalric period, the show couldn't come to life with *My Fair Lady*'s ghost hovering in the background. A duplication should not have been attempted. After so large-scale a success, it is better to do something simple than a show equally elaborate.

Besides, Loewe was no longer enjoying the rough and tumble of Broadway. Having suffered a heart attack, he decided to have fun. One cannot but admire Loewe's independence in turning his back on Broadway's money and glamour. Thirteen years later, in 1973, he was finally cajoled to return for a project most unworthy: transforming the movie musical *Gigi* (whose score was by Lerner and Loewe) into a Broadway show. Loewe didn't even write a new score for it. The show flopped, and, with that, Loewe gave up on Broadway again.

Overall, Loewe did not compose many shows and certainly didn't blaze any trails. Perhaps he was not the greatest melodist since Kern, as Lerner describes him, but *My Fair Lady* is indeed a classic and Loewe will always be remembered for it. *My Fair Lady* crowned and concluded the era of the musical play as well as the second generation of Broadway composers.

# THE PROFESSIONALS

Everything had been too easy. It was time for a crisis.

The first generation of musical theater composers had refined the quality popular song. They saw stage music as superior popular music. The second generation of composers grew more theatrically aware but they still didn't consider a show score successful unless two or three hits emerged from it. With *On the Town* Leonard Bernstein proved, to his chagrin, that hit songs were not the criteria of a good score. Then, without warning, American taste in popular music changed dramatically to loud, raunchy, danceable rock 'n' roll. The third generation of show composers found that Broadway's music was no longer America's popular music.

This new music—hardly music at all—was so vulgar that at first it was dismissible, yet it had a vitality that showed up traditional pop and theater music as having become repetitious and sterile. Smugly superior, the musical theater refused to stoop to rock 'n' roll, convinced this was but a fad that, if ignored, would go away when America came to its senses. It was sure that musicals' music would go on forever, and why not? The shows were still so popular, so *good*.

Conditioned to look for hits, the composers for the stage still identified with the old pop music, even as it was being embalmed by the purveyors of "mood music." These soft, orchestral, soulless renditions of older songs found their uninvited way into elevators, supermarkets, banks, restaurants, even telephones. This wordless sound—usually in the form of castrated Kern, Rodgers, Berlin, and Loesser—spread like an antimusical cancer at the very time that rock 'n' roll was becoming popular. The oppositions set up between the two were unmistakable: the young versus the old, action versus passivity. The theater, forgetting it had created the vital popular song of which the "mood music" was a mockery, now became the slave of such music. Average audience age began to rise as composers of musicals—once the leaders of popular musical taste—retreated, refusing to recognize the ruffians of rock 'n' roll. Although Elvis Presley popularized rock in the mid-fifties, there was no rock musical until *Hair* in 1968. Musicals became theater for a complacent, Eisenhower America.

No longer writing pop hits, many songwriters panicked. Some of the greatest so despaired of America's altered musical taste that they simply gave up and retired. This was a tragic loss. Some young theater composers-to-be tried their hands at rock 'n' roll but few were successful because in their hearts they believed they were musically slumming. With the traditional connection between the

*Liza Minnelli was not yet ready to carry a whole show when she made her Broadway debut in 1965 along with the song-writing team of Kander and Ebb in* Flora, the Red Menace *(above). The show itself was a commonplace musical comedy about socialism in the thirties. The young team and their star had much to learn. Though gifted, Minnelli proved to be an ordinary actress and, frankly, a klutz. Singing, she imitated her mother, Judy Garland. But friends believe in each other and Kander and Ebb wrote their next show—*Cabaret—*especially for her, only to have Director Harold Prince turn her down. Minnelli grew by performing in nightclubs. She grew doing the film version of* Cabaret; *she grew helping Kander and Ebb out by stepping into* Chicago *when Gwen Verdon was briefly ill; and when the team wrote* The Act *(opposite) for her, she had grown completely. Liza Minnelli had become a legitimate, confident, dynamic, flamboyant, and fabulous Broadway star.*

287

pop music business and the musical theater blocked, composers and lyricists with theater aspirations had to find not only a new, purely theatrical reason for writing songs, but also a new route to Broadway. The one they developed was out of the college musical and through the summer resort. Hotels and camps in the mountains outside New York, such as Tamiment in the Poconos and Green Mansions in the Adirondacks, engaged resident composers and lyricists to write new, Broadway-style shows *every week.* Theater-bound youngsters such as Charles Strouse and Lee Adams, Fred Ebb, Sheldon Harnick, Mary Rodgers, and Marshall Barer got their feet in the show-business door by working at such resort hotels. Weekly deadlines and the immediate need to satisfy audiences provided a sharpening discipline. From there it was but a hop to the New York theater, with a skip over the old way station of hit song writing. Broadway's producers were so anxious to capitalize on the musical theater's popularity that they were then willing to share risks with the newcomers.

Instead of realizing that theater music and popular music were mutually exclusive and had overlapped in the past purely by chance, these third-generation theater composers still longed to write hits; they still considered themselves in the pop music business. We must try to understand this since hit fever infects every Broadway songwriter. It is the reason even the most ambitious musical will abruptly stop to showcase or reprise a song its writers believe to have hit potential. There is *nothing* that satisfies a songwriter team like a hit. This is not merely because of the money, though it can be considerable. It is because of the kick the writer gets from having the whole country singing his song; from hearing it on the radio, hour after hour; from making it in the *music* business.

So the debut shows for this third generation of Broadway music writers—Jerry Bock and Sheldon Harnick's *The Body Beautiful,* Lee Adams and Charles Strouse's *Bye, Bye, Birdie,* and so on—tended to have at least some songs with a rock'n'roll beat. *Bye, Bye, Birdie* was about a rock 'n' roll singer. Other shows had no such excuse. They merely added the rock rhythm to ballads, looking for hits by thinking new (rock) and old (ballads) at the same time. Inevitably, these were bastard songs, defeating a show's integration and making for isolated numbers: "What I Did for Love" in *A Chorus Line* or, even more incongruously, "Tomorrow" in *Annie.*

When not making such tries for hits, Broadway's composers of this generation tended to ignore both rock and time. They pretended that nothing had changed and continued to write the style of show music that had attracted them to the theater in the first place. Few composers were moving forward or were exploiting their own talents or were looking past "songs" to longer and more complex musical forms. It was such music that Leonard Bernstein would ultimately compose as he began the third generation.

Bernstein's career had seemed securely destined for conducting and composing classical music when he began converting his 1944 ballet "Fancy Free" into a musical. He became the best theater composer of his era. Unfortunately, he was a victim of his own versatility. Gifted in so many fields, he had to steal time to write shows. He opened the door to a new musical theater and then, rather than walking through, he chose to go elsewhere. He wrote only five shows in thirty-two years, with a nineteen-year gap between *West Side Story* (1957) and *1600 Pennsylvania Avenue* (1976), but his shows count.

"Fancy Free" is a ballet about three sailors on shore leave. Director George Abbott pushed the impressionable newcomers Betty Comden and Adolph Green toward his style of farce in their libretto. So "Fancy Free" was made into an ordinary musical comedy, *On the Town,* but one with special spirit and a positively precocious score. Its "New York, New York" ("a hell of a town") is a traditional opening number written in an untraditional way, with odd intervals and open tones and fresh, twitchy rhythms. Bernstein had especially wanted a hit—a song the whole country would sing. He pinned his hopes on "Lucky to Be Me," a very Gershwin tune that resembles "Someone to Watch Over Me." It never was a hit. *On the Town* has other ballads—"Lonely Town" and the touching "Some Other Time"—but its best music is *funny.* Unlike pop songwriters, classical composers appreciate the challenge of writing comic music.

From the start—mainly because of his background in classical music—Bernstein was different from other stage composers. His show music, like his classical music, is profoundly influenced by Igor Stravinsky and Aaron Copland. But he uses their style in his own way, filtering it through his own personal sensibility. With *Wonderful Town* in 1953, he began to capitalize on his unusual talent. This show was drawn by Joseph Fields and Jerome Chodorov from their successful play *My Sister Eileen,* about two midwestern sisters recently arrived in New York. Eileen gets all the boys, but the bookish main character, Ruth, gets the leading man. Because of its makeshift book, *Wonderful Town* doesn't hold up in revival, but Bernstein's score does. His opening number, "Christopher Street," is in every way the equal of *On the Town*'s "New York, New York." They are both big city numbers for big city shows and Bernstein's upbeat syncopation catches the rhythm and color of Manhattan (at least, as New Yorkers thought of it at the time). Again demonstrating Bernstein's affinity for funny music, the comic numbers are *Wonderful Town*'s treat: "What a Waste," "Conversation Piece," "Conga!," "Pass That Football."

*Rosalind Russell stopped* Wonderful Town *with "Conga!," a number in which she played a reporter trying to interview a group of Brazilian naval cadets who would rather dance than talk.*

Wonderful Town's "Wrong Note Rag" is a showstopper. In this comedy duet, built around sour notes, Leonard Bernstein found a way to capitalize on the mismated voices of Edie Adams (center, right) playing the sexy Eileen, and Rosalind Russell (center, left) as the intellectual Ruth. Miss Russell gave one of Broadway's memorable comic performances but, unlike the conservatory-trained Adams, she had no voice; her songs had to be written for a less-than-an-octave range.

Once established, Bernstein abandoned musical comedy for comic theater of a decidedly higher order. No other Broadway composer could have written *Candide*. But it was perhaps a mistake for Bernstein to break up with Comden and Green for this show. Without their lyrics, musical sensitivity, and wit, this 1956 mock comic opera suffered from too heavy a hand. Based, of course, on Voltaire's classic satire, it was intended to be the great American musical. A group of cultural heavyweights were lined up alongside the composer: Tyrone Guthrie, the Shakespearean director; Lillian Hellman, the prestigious dramatist; John Latouche, the poet. The only trouble was that literary credentials are of little help in solving second-act problems, Hellman's fidelity to Voltaire's episodes only assured a show lopsided with plotting and scenery. Still, Bernstein outdid himself, providing a satiric score lavish with musical invention. It is dry ("Bon Voyage," "You Were Dead, You Know") and cynical ("What's the Use?"). Its most famous piece is the mock coloratura aria, "Glitter and Be Gay," a fabulous musical exercise. Unfortunately, *Candide*'s lyrics are wordy, as lyrics tend to be when literary people write them. They are funny to read but too densely written for the theater.

Bernstein's stage masterwork is *West Side Story*. The show dances from the opening number until the finale. It required a huge amount of dance music and Bernstein wrote most of it. Unfortunately, he had small opportunity to write the comic music at which he was so adept because *West Side Story* is a serious work, transposing Shakespeare's *Romeo and Juliet* to New York's slums.

The variety and quality of this score and the show's emphasis on singing and dancing rather than on the book made *West Side Story* a watershed musical. Most of the score is made of "numbers," but they are much longer than Broadway was accustomed to. Though Bernstein had stopped trying to write hits, with "Tonight" and "Maria" he got two of them and deserved to, for both are beautiful songs. "America," sung by Anita and the Puerto Rican gang of teenagers (the show's "Capulets"), is a comic number Bernstein did fit into the show, and it is a superior one. Perhaps more Mexican then Puerto Rican (it is influenced by Copland's "El Salón México"), the number's offbeat rhythms save it from being just another list song.

The excitement of the *West Side Story* score comes from its meters, the clipped "Something's Coming," the tense and jazzy "Cool," and the counterpoint of the "Jet Song" against "Tonight." "One Hand, One Heart" and "Somewhere" (so like Stravinsky's "The Firebird") have a sustained tension unique in our theater music. Even "I Feel Pretty" is musically ambitious. It begins simply as a syncopated, hand-clapping Spanish waltz. Straightforwardly enough, it breaks for a release before returning to that "A" theme. Then it moves into a verse. Not strange. Songwriters had long since stuck introductions into the middles of songs. Bernstein's verse, however, moves on to a second theme and then a *third* before finally returning to the song's main body. And then, as if *still* not satisfied, Bernstein injected elements of a canon into the finale. It is quite a piece of theater music and was so divertingly staged by Jerome Robbins that the audience had no time to realize how many musical concepts were being thrown at it.

*Two* Candides *and two* Candides: *Robert Rounseville to Barbara Cook's Cunegonde in the original 1956 production (right), and Mark Baker to Maureen Brennan's Cunegonde in the 1974 revival (above). The show was Leonard Bernstein's first flop but his brilliant score attracted a large cult following. When Lillian Hellman finally permitted her libretto to be rewritten in 1974, Harold Prince staged Hugh Wheeler's new script in an arena setting. With the action spread dynamically throughout the theater, the need for slow, scenic changes was eliminated and the show lightened up. The reborn* Candide *ran 740 performances.*

*English comedienne Hermione Gingold did a hilarious routine with a cello in* John Murray Anderson's Almanac, *one of the last full-fledged Broadway revues. The auspicious debut launched the delightful Gingold on a long American career.*

The entire score is marvelously orchestrated. Because of its musical values, *West Side Story* is one show that will never be musically dated, though its book has not worn well. Bernstein contributed to the orchestrations, collaborating with two of Broadway's best—Sid Ramin and Irwin Kostal. He proved that it *is* possible for a composer to find time to work not only on the dance music but also on orchestrating. One cringes at the thought of *West Side Story* with the usual dance arrangements and a standard orchestrational work-over.

Bernstein's abandonment of Broadway was a decision he had to make. He might have juggled careers the rest of his life. He chose to concentrate on the directorship of the New York Philharmonic. From time to time he began work on a show but none materialized until *1600 Pennsylvania Avenue* in 1976. Intended as liberal propaganda, it was a perfectly awful idea for a show: historic race relations in the White House, comparing the presidents with the servants. There is invariably something irritating in shows written by white people about minority-group problems. This irritant was not eased by dance production and strong music in *1600* as it had been in *West Side Story.* By the time it opened in New York, *1600 Pennsylvania Avenue* had been so patched up there was no telling what it had been meant to be. It was a disaster, closing in a matter of days. Lost in its midst was an ambitious score.

Leonard Bernstein has contributed marvelous music to our theater, a blend of classical technique and Broadway brass. With *On the Town, Wonderful Town, Candide,* and *West Side Story* he gave the theater four solid and original works. Four hits out of five (not counting his 1950 version of *Peter Pan,* which was not a full-scale musical) isn't a bad record. Bernstein was truly ahead of his time; not till the seventies, with the shows of Stephen Sondheim, did the

*The calypso rhythms of the song "Matilda" made Harry Belafonte famous in the 1953 revue* John Murray Anderson's Almanac. *Such clever, good-looking Broadway revues were great fun, but for no good reason at all, their likes may never be seen again.*

Damn Yankees *choreographer, Bob Fosse, modeled his dances on baseball players' swinging and sliding moves.*

musical theater catch up with him. Broadway audiences were not quite ready to give up the musical's traditional fare of short, catchy songs. They had been spoiled by the accessibility, the affability, and the familiarity of the songs written by Broadway's second generation of composers.

The third generation of Broadway composers that began with Bernstein included Richard Adler and Jerry Ross, Jerry Bock, Bob Merrill, and Meredith Willson. Fast on their heels, with the turn into the sixties, came Jerry Herman, Charles Strouse, John Kander, Cy Coleman, Harvey Schmidt, and Sondheim. This was a flood of talent; the musical theater seemed to be thriving.

The first of the new teams to come along in the fifties was Adler and Ross. They wrote two shows and only two shows because Ross died, tragically, at the age of twenty-nine. Sponsored by Frank Loesser, Adler and Ross did *The Pajama Game* on his recommendation. Their score marked a terrifically impressive debut, with rich ballads ("Hey, There"), fresh comedy songs ("Her Is," "Hernando's Hideaway"), originality ("Steam Heat"), and exuberance ("There Once Was a Man"). The team's last score was for *Damn Yankees,* their second show and their second success. Perhaps not a match for *The Pajama Game,* the score of *Damn Yankees* not only had its share of hits ("Whatever Lola Wants," "Heart") but regularly catchy tunes. Adler and Ross were not inclined to write production numbers and their songs had a softer edge than Broadway was accustomed to at the time. This reflected Loesser's influence on them; indeed, *Pajama Game*'s "A New Town Is a Blue Town" sounds uncomfortably like Loesser's "My Time of Day" from *Guys and Dolls.*

*Gwen Verdon played Satan's sexy assistant in* Damn Yankees, *the musical about a baseball fan who sells his soul to become a great player. Here, she does the devil's work, singing Adler and Ross's "Whatever Lola Wants" to Stephen Douglass in hope of getting him to violate his contract and forfeit his soul.*

Adler and Ross took equal credit for both music and lyrics, so it is difficult to know who was responsible for what. With Ross's death, however, Adler was unable to continue on the same level. Writing the music and lyrics for *Kwamina* in 1961 and *Music Is* in 1976, he couldn't come up with melodies. He turned to producing.

Arriving on Adler and Ross's heels, Jerry Bock had a fair success collaborating with George Weiss and Larry Holofcener on the 1956 *Mr. Wonderful*. The show, a vehicle for Sammy Davis, Jr., was little more than a frame around a nightclub act. It produced a couple of hits ("Too-Close for Comfort" and the title song) and was enough to establish the composer. The partnership with lyricist Sheldon Harnick that followed was to have a healthy record of success, including the Pulitzer Prize–winning *Fiorello!* and the landmark *Fiddler on the Roof*. More striking than Bock and Harnick's success was their refusal to repeat themselves. Though their first show, the failed *The Body Beautiful*, was a conventional one, *Fiorello!* the following year (1959) had a bracing freshness. Based on the political life of New York's Mayor LaGuardia, it was directed by George Abbott in his usual brisk style but its warm period treatment lent the show a special flavor. It was a musical with character. Bock demonstrated an easygoing gift of melody and a knack for theatrical size in his music. This was a good show and it will revive well.

*Tenderloin* and *Fiorello!* were as much alike as any two Bock and Harnick shows, probably because Abbott's treatment of period New York was so repetitive. *Tenderloin,* designed by Cecil Beaton, was a gorgeous production. By now sure of himself, Bock provided it with a better score than he had written for *Fiorello!,* one securely in musical character, not just for the story but for the period. His ballads and chorus songs had the strolling sidewalk style and the organ grinder harmonies of turn-of-the-century New York streets. *Tenderloin* was not a success. For one thing, its main character was an unlikable, prudish reformer. For another, this show about sin in "Little Old New York" was staged by Abbott, the man who dislikes anything "dirty." But it was a better show than its brief engagement (216 performances) would suggest.

In 1963, Bock and Harnick worked under the director Harold Prince, and that made a real difference. Unlike Abbott, Prince allowed their show to slow down and savor moments. Bock's music for *She Loves Me* was again adapted to a mood and milieu, this time providing a heartwarming Middle-European quality. He and Harnick wrote twenty-three songs for this show, which was more than the Broadway usual, and though Bock is more a songwriter than a composer, they had special gaiety and charm. While the production had its devout partisans, most theatergoers of the time insisted on

*If anyone personified the exuberance of musical comedy performance, it was the beloved and debonair Jack Cassidy, who never had or provided more fun than when he was kidding himself, playing a golden-haired, silver-voiced, brass-plated ham. On the left with him in* She Loves Me *is another musical theater honey, Nathaniel Fry, and to the right, Ralph Williams and Barbara Baxley.*

brash musicals. *She Loves Me* was better suited to the quieter taste of later times and has become popular in revival.

*Fiddler on the Roof* was a smash hit at once. Bock did not, perhaps, fully rise to the musical challenge of this trailblazing show. Considering its perpetually choreographic staging, its deep emotional roots, and its universal theme, the music might have had longer lines and greater breadth. Still, the composer brought rich Yiddish musical qualities to his score and much of the feeling in *Fiddler on the Roof* is a result of deep sentiment in the music.

Bock and Harnick were hard put to follow this act. While *Fiddler on the Roof* was in the process of setting Broadway's long-run record (3,242 performances), they chose to do an entirely different kind of musical—different from *Fiddler* and different from any others—and wrote its book themselves with Jerome Coopersmith. Or rather, its *books*, for *The Apple Tree* of 1966 was a bill of three one-act musicals: *The Diary of Adam and Eve*, based on the Mark Twain story; *The Lady or the Tiger?*, drawn from the classic Frank R. Stockton fable; and *Passionella*, based on a Jules Feiffer novella. Although a gifted director of plays, Mike Nichols was ill at ease staging *The Apple Tree*, and the novelty of its being three musicals in one made life no easier for him. The show had much that was marvelous (especially *The Lady or the Tiger?*), but it didn't hold together and it didn't have the feeling of a hit despite a decent run of 463 performances.

Bock and Harnick began having personal disagreements while preparing *The Rothschilds*, four years later. Both were unhappy about doing another "Jewish" show after *Fiddler*. *The Rothschilds* ran over 500 performances, making Bock the most successful of the third-generation composers, but it also caused Bock and Harnick to break up. Harnick went on to collaborate with Richard Rodgers on the failed *Rex* and Bock took an extended leave of absence from

*Bock and Harnick's* The Apple Tree *was based on short stories by Mark Twain, Jules Feiffer, and Frank Stockton. The best of them was Stockton's* The Lady or the Tiger?, *in which a soldier (Alan Alda, at center) is forced to choose between two doors which conceal, respectively, a lady and a tiger. Guiding his choice is the Princess Barbara (at right), played by Barbara Harris.*

*In* Take Me Along, *an adaptation of Eugene O'Neill's charming comedy* Ah, Wilderness, *the role of Uncle Sid was built up for star comic Jackie Gleason. Here he sings Bob Merrill's catchy title song along with Walter Pidgeon and the company. Gleason, Phil Silvers, Buddy Hackett, Sid Caesar, and Alan King were of the last generation of comics to consider theater a necessary part of their repertoire.*

*Above: From left to right are Jerry Orbach, Pierre Olaf, and Anna Maria Alberghetti in* Carnival. *Composer Bob Merrill gave the show the charming "Love Makes the World Go Round." Sterling baritones were going out of style, but Orbach's relaxed charm made him one of the most successful leading men in musicals of the sixties and seventies.*

*Above, left: Here is an example, from* Carnival, *of Gower Champion's talent for making stage pictures.*

Broadway. It is a pity the team separated. Their record speaks for itself and they obviously had a positive effect on each other's work, but, like marriage, song-writing collaboration is not always good for friendship.

Bob Merrill and Meredith Willson, both composer-lyricists, also emerged in the fifties. They couldn't have been more dissimilar. Merrill—known as "Bob" to avoid confusion with the Metropolitan Opera baritone—was a product of the school of popular music that had killed popular music, writing such dim-witted novelties as "How Much Is That Doggie in the Window?" The level of his musicianship was in itself enough to make Merrill unique—he picked out his tunes on a child's xylophone! Yet he could not only produce singable melodies but he produced them for a series of successful musicals: *New Girl in Town* (1957), *Take Me Along* (1959), and *Carnival* (1961). Merrill even faced up to the challenge of replacing a known and loved song—"Hi Lili, Hi Lo"—while writing *Carnival*, a stage version of the film *Lili.* His equivalent song, "Love Makes the World Go 'Round," was a similarly childlike waltz that proved equally popular.

Sugar, *with music and lyrics by Styne and Merrill, was an adaptation by Peter Stone of the movie* Some Like It Hot, *about a couple of musicians who inadvertently witness a gangland slaying and then join an all-girl band to escape from the mobsters. Robert Morse (right) and Tony Roberts played the ladies.*

Though no more than a journeyman lyricist, he accepted the offer to write the words to Jule Styne's music for *Funny Girl* in 1964 and rose to the occasion. Many of these lyrics are superb. Working again with Styne on *Sugar,* eight years later, he couldn't duplicate that success. Between these shows, Merrill wrote the complete score for a dud—*Henry, Sweet Henry*—and after *Sugar* he abandoned Broadway to write for films and television. He attempted a theater comeback in 1978 with *The Prince of Grand Street,* for which he wrote the book, music, and lyrics, but the show closed during its out-of-town tryout.

In contrast, Meredith Willson was a classical musician; he had been a radio music director before writing his first show—*The Music Man*—at fifty-five. Yet, not only was that first musical a tremendous success, but he wrote all of it: book, music, and lyrics. What's more, his score is delightful. Perhaps its greatest charm is its midwestern simplicity, something all but unknown on Broadway. For our musical theater's sound was born of show business and is steeped in a Broadway vernacular. Years of artistic inbreeding had made it even more *Broadway.* For in four decades of musicals, too many composers had been influenced by too few composers. Willson's music for marching bands and barbershop quartets and his rhythms drawn from the salesman's spiel brought a fresh kind of show music to New

*No composer ever made a more impressive Broadway debut than Meredith Willson, whose* The Music Man *was not only his first show and a smash hit, but also was crammed full of fresh, ingenious, melodic theater songs. In the title role, Robert Preston, best known at the time for playing heavies in movie melodramas, proved a natural on the musical stage and became an instant star.*

As The Music Man *had done for Robert Preston, Meredith Willson's second show,* The Unsinkable Molly Brown, *made a star of an actor not previously associated with musicals. Tammy Grimes (at the piano, below, and at right) had been a dramatic actress and her gifts turned Molly Brown into a brash, colorful, magnificently lovable caricature—a rich country girl who breaks into Denver society. Harve Presnell (right) was her beau and between his gorgeous baritone and her glorious energy, Meredith Willson's fine score was performed 532 times.*

York. Orchestration gave it the sound of Broadway, but there was a sense of small-town America in this music, an openhearted quality which usually eludes our brassbound musical theater.

*The Music Man* is the story of a con man who comes to a small town in turn-of-the-century Iowa selling marching band equipment that he does not intend to deliver. He falls in love with the town librarian and reforms. This is not a great story, but unlike many shows of its time (1957), it has an inherent musicality. Some of Willson's ideas were plain corny. He seemed proudest of two seemingly disparate songs, the march "Seventy-Six Trombones" and the ballad "Goodnight, My Someone," which proved to have the same melody set to different rhythms. Other songs were fresher, especially such patter numbers as "Trouble" and "The Sadder but Wiser Girl."

*The Unsinkable Molly Brown* had many of the qualities of *The Music Man.* Its libretto placed a period story (about an uninhibited lady with money and no class) in a midwestern setting (Denver) and several of the songs sounded like *Music Man* cutouts. But, again, Willson provided an exuberant, showmanly, and tuneful score. He also showed an affinity for writing lyrics to character, which was surprising considering his theatrical inexperience.

Willson's next—and last—show on Broadway, *Here's Love* (1963), was unexceptional. Based on the film *Miracle on 34th Street,* it traded on Christmas in New York with sticky sentimentality. He tried out another show—*1491*—but its Broadway ambitions were destroyed in Los Angeles. A family tragedy seemed to then discourage Willson entirely and he disappeared from the theater.

*The Music Man* will remain a classic. Though it is conventionally structured, its American qualities have broad appeal and its score is irresistible. Willson's musicianship might have been taken to more challenging theatrical ends, but his very strength—distance from the Broadway scene—kept him out of touch with changes in and ambitions of the musical theater.

As if prophetically, the team of Lee Adams and Charles Strouse made their Broadway debut as the sixties began. It was a decade of commercial success but also of creative stagnation. Adams and Strouse exemplified that.

Charles Strouse is a composer of formidable ability, combining a rich melodic gift and a thorough musical training with stage-sense. His instinct for the musical theater is so strong and so sound that he writes not mere songs but, literally, production numbers. Adams, if not an exemplary lyricist, is as stage-wise as Strouse. Their contribution to any musical tends to be more practical than inspired. Strouse's energetic and spunky score for *Bye, Bye, Birdie* ranked for too many years as his best, when he ought to have been growing. It produced such standards as "Put On a Happy Face," "A Lot of Livin' to Do," and "Kids." Such songs revealed at the outset the composer's affinity for show music—catchy tunes for projectable and energetic numbers. They seemed to come so easily to him that, unlike Bernstein (who has no such natural melodic gift), perhaps he hadn't a pressing need to stretch himself. The comparison with Bernstein is appropriate because few among Broadway's third generation of composers rival Strouse's musical background. Trained at the prestigious Eastman School of Music, he has composed symphonic and chamber music. With such formal advantages, plus his theatrical

*Bye, Bye, Birdie managed to capitalize on and spoof rock 'n' roll simultaneously. "One Last Kiss," sung by Dick Gautier—the show's Elvis Presley figure—even became a pop hit.*

instinct, he might have expanded the limits of Broadway's music. He wrote a near-opera for off-Broadway, and some of his songs are special indeed: "Put On a Happy Face," "Once Upon a Time" (from *All American,* a 1962 failure), "I Want to Be with You" (from *Golden Boy*). Too often, unfortunately, Strouse is content to write merely serviceable songs for blatantly commercial projects such as *Applause,* or simply ill-chosen ones like *A Broadway Musical* (1978). He also seems as willing to accept lesser lyrics as he is to accept less than the best from himself. Among Broadway hits, few shows have had more amateurish lyrics than Strouse's *Annie* (they were written not by Adams but by Martin Charnin). Then again, among Broadway hits of the seventies few could boast songs as tenderly and inventively conceived as *Annie's* "Maybe." So, these are the various and frustrating sides of Charles Strouse.

He seemed to have his chance to grow while working under Harold Prince's direction on the 1966 *It's a Bird, It's a Plane, It's Superman.* Prince's ambitions for the musical theater make him demand the best from his collaborators. Strouse turned out a frequently sophisticated score for this show, but perhaps Prince was distressed by the composer's willingness to be facile. For his next show, *Cabaret,* which might have been the one to challenge Strouse, Prince chose to work with John Kander and Fred Ebb. A stimulated Charles Strouse remained one of the musical theater's best hopes.

Kander had written the music for *A Family Affair,* a 1962 flop whose main distinction was that it was Prince's first show as a director (he was called in during road troubles). Ebb had written lyrics for several off-Broadway musicals. They were brought together by a music publisher, Tommy Valando, who sensed their compatibility. The team's first show was *Flora, the Red Menace* in 1965, directed by George Abbott. The legendary director was beginning to lose his touch, but he taught the young songwriters the fundamentals of musical theater. They also benefited from their continued contact with Harold Prince, the show's producer. Prince was ready to direct full-time, and he engaged Kander and Ebb to do *Cabaret.* This show established them all.

Kander's score for *Cabaret* was, like the show itself, schizo-

*Lee Adams and Charles Strouse have tended in their careers toward commercial projects, such as mating name actors with name plays, however inappropriate the combination. An example was putting Sammy Davis, Jr., into a musical version of Clifford Odets's 1937 play* Golden Boy *(left). Some good songs turned up in this score: "I Want to Be with You," "Night Song," and "This Is the Life," but the show's peaks were the fight scenes staged by Jaime Rogers (at right).*

*The problem in* It's a Bird, It's a Plane, It's Superman *was having the big boy (Bob Holiday) fly. Some things just can't be done on the stage without seeming silly.*

*Director Harold Prince tried to create the effect of a comic strip for the staging of the title song of* It's A Bird, It's A Plane, It's Superman. *The boxlike set resembled "The Telephone Hour" from* Bye, Bye, Birdie, *Strouse and Adams's hit of six years earlier. The new Strouse-Adams song was similar, too, but even with a very sophisticated score the show failed to catch on.*

phrenic. As *Cabaret* was half concept musical and half musical play, so his music adopted a Kurt Weill cabaret style half the time, and a conventional Broadway style for the rest. Kander is more deft at tailoring music to a show than any other composer of his generation. In effect, he writes character *music*—for the character of the production as well as for that of the people in the story. This ability is unusually important for when music is in overall character, we feel the show's mood and story in an emotional way.

Melody is not Kander's strength. He is a musicianly composer but sometimes his technique gets in the way of his impulses. *Cabaret's* title song has a strong melody and "Willkommen," from the same show, is even more singable. *Cabaret's* touching "Meeskite" is as sweet and simple as a nursery tune. But Kander resembles Sondheim in that he seems embarrassed by sentiment (which, as a musician, he equates with melody) and, like Sondheim, is apt to either avoid or mock feelings. His scores for *Zorba* (1968), *The Happy Time* (1968), and *70, Girls, 70* (1971), the team's one outright failure, do not abound with catchy tunes. Kander is apparently more inspired by the challenge of theatricalism. This tendency is exemplified by his scores for both *Chicago* and *The Act.*

*Chicago* is conceived as a thirties vaudeville bill turned savagely ironic. Kander's fine songs—the mock maudlin "Class," the "production number" "Razzle Dazzle," or "My Own Best Friend"—all mimic the music of period variety entertainment. Each of these songs is carried by a strong melody, perhaps because their screen of mockery "protected" Kander.

*The Act,* whose theatrical concept is a Las Vegas floor show, uses the solo nightclub performance as a metaphor for self-sufficiency and as an example of how people develop "acts" to hide personal fears. Kander sought to mythologize the peculiar flavor of songs sung by entertainers in nightclub acts. While he captured admirably the lush banality of nightclub material, Kander seemed to be too preoccupied with style to think of melody. Ironically, the devilish ingenuity of his work went unappreciated.

No composer among this third generation is more melodic than Jerry Herman, and if anyone is Irving Berlin's successor it is he. In 1961, Herman's first hit, *Milk and Honey,* sounded like a throwback to simpler days in the directness and simplicity of its music and lyrics (Herman writes both). "This is the land of milk and honey," words and music, might well have been a Berlin song. Its anthem-like innocence reflects Herman's strength and weakness. He will never be one of those composers who stretches the limits of theater music, but his knack for the show tune is irresistible and his melodies are delicious—they need no justification. Many the trained composer would sell his soul for such tunes.

Herman's great hit was, of course, *Hello, Dolly!* There is some cleverness of song structure in this show, particularly in "Put On Your Sunday Clothes," but the score is essentially a series of show numbers. Although the lyrics are integrated and the music reflects the show's cartoon quality, one could hardly compare Herman's use of music with, say, Sondheim's or Bernstein's. Still, the abundance of melody in *Hello, Dolly!* is very satisfying. It is a fine score.

The song "Hello, Dolly!" is not only one of the most famous and best loved of showstoppers in the modern musical theater but also teaches a lesson that should never be forgotten. This is the lesson of directness. Such a song sounds corny to many a musical theater sophisticate, but no song that comes out and wows an audience is

*One of the saving graces of musical theater is that no matter how sophisticated it gets, the basic foolishness of show business always remains. Opposite, below, is Mimi Benzell, a former opera singer at the udder of a goat, making the best of the 1961 musical* Milk and Honey. *The show was a typical Times Square brainstorm—a musical set on an Israeli kibbutz, romantically pairing opera tenor Robert Weede and Yiddish stage star Molly Picon. Up in the swing, getting ready for a production number, is Tommy Rall in the same show. In the bargain, this was a hit. Credit the strong, singable melodies of composer Jerry Herman, making his Broadway debut.*

corny. Such directness is the essence of showmanship, and without showmanship, there is no musical theater.

The tremendous popularity of "Hello, Dolly!" as a show-stopping number and popular song led Herman to repeat this style of song excessively. Title numbers became his trademark, then his obsession: "Mame" (1966), "Dear World" (1969), and then "When Mabel Comes in the Room" for *Mack and Mabel* (1974).

Although *Mame* was a hit, Herman had his troubles after *Hello, Dolly!* The song "Hello, Dolly!" itself became the subject of a plagiarism suit that was filed and won by Mack David on the basis of his old tune "Sunflower." The resemblance between the two is slight and it is always difficult to prove musical imitation. Many melodies sound alike and some *are* accidentally derivative, for composers unconsciously remember thousands of other songs. When they recognize a similarity they invariably delete the offending song. Broadway composers are much too professional and too proud to keep a song, no matter how effective, once they realize its similarity to another. "Hello, Dolly!," however, was already a big hit song and was worth considerably more money than most songs. Mack David's attorney was the celebrated Louis Nizer. A settlement was reached.

Perhaps this legal setback demoralized Herman. The score for *Dear World* (an adaptation of Jean Giraudoux's *The Madwoman of Chaillot*) was not up to his standards.

Taking five years to recover from that first flop, Herman then produced one of his best sets of songs for 1974's *Mack and Mabel*. A musical based on movie director Mack Sennett's romance with actress Mabel Normand, it tried out in Los Angeles, where it was considered a show with problems but basically sound. By the time

*Jerry Orbach created the role of the Narrator in* The Fantasticks, *the off-Broadway musical that opened on May 3, 1960 and promised to run for an unprecedented twenty years. Based on Rostand's* The Romantics, *this debut musical by Tom Jones and Harvey Schmidt was the soul of economy and musical theater: a bare stage, a few actors, a hat, a prop, a song, and a dance.*

Opposite: Man of La Mancha *opened in Lincoln Center's temporary theater in 1965 and then moved to Broadway, where it ran up over 2,000 performances. Richard Kiley, who played Quixote, is shown here with Ray Middleton, himself a leading man of musicals a generation earlier. Much about Mitch Leigh's score was refreshing—Spanish dance rhythms, novel orchestration—but the composer's inexperience led to senseless song-spotting and popular rather than theater music. Leigh followed* La Mancha's *success with the disasters* Cry for Us All *and* Home Sweet Homer.

*Mack and Mabel* arrived in New York, it had been ruined. Buried in the rubble was a prime Herman score—one that would have become a classic had the show been a hit. How many lovers of musical theater have missed the chance to thrill over the sheer Broadway rhythm and the heart-stopping exuberance of this show's "Movies Were Movies"? How many have never heard the rhapsodic stage-scale ballad, "I Won't Send Roses"? *Mack and Mabel* proved a painful example of a newly developed problem: Intensified economic pressure and the focus of a national spotlight were making a musical's tryout and tune-up process too tense to serve its function.

The failure of *Mack and Mabel,* and of music its composer thought his best so far, depressed Herman tremendously. He worked tentatively in the years that followed, worn down by a musical theater that was losing the fun-of-it while becoming a high-stakes business. In a real way, his career exemplifies what has been happening to the Broadway musical. For though there are better-trained and more ambitious composers than Jerry Herman, of all in the third generation he is closest to the musical theater's original spirit; he is the one most similar to the giants. More than any other composer, he could have won the country's love while satisfying the musical theater's needs. He would surely be back with more shows—his *The Grand Tour* arrived on Broadway in 1978—but one cannot help wondering whether the expense and pressure of the modern musical stage are not smothering the exuberance that is its basic strength.

Tom Jones and Harvey Schmidt are one team that tried to escape this pressure. They emerged in 1960 through a strange but fortuitous accident. A one-act musical that they wrote for Barnard College was expanded into an off-Broadway production which opened to mixed reviews. Ordinarily, such a show would have been lucky to run a few months, but this was *The Fantasticks* and it was still running strong in 1978, after *eighteen* years!

The show had a practical advantage, playing in a theater that was tiny even by off-Broadway standards, but that doesn't explain its incredible duration. Fact is, *Fantasticks* has been done all over the world ever since its premiere, in theaters large and small. No, its real advantage is popular appeal. This free adaptation of Edmond Rostand's *Les Romantiques* has an ingenuous charm and a simple, basic theatricality. It also has a lovely musical score that has produced standards in "Soon It's Gonna Rain" and "Try to Remember." Set to sensitive, craftsmanlike lyrics by Tom Jones, who is a lyricist in the Oscar Hammerstein tradition, these are lovely theater songs. Harvey Schmidt is a Broadway musical natural. He is a natural in a less flattering sense too, being unable to read or write music. A musician must sit by his side and notate as Schmidt plays his songs. However, he is hardly a musical simpleton. Schmidt plays piano excellently and his own arrangements spell out harmonies and inner voices in detail. Much of his work rivals that of more sophisticated composers.

Because of the success of *The Fantasticks,* Schmidt and Jones were engaged by producer David Merrick and wrote two successful shows, *110 in the Shade* in 1963 and *I Do! I Do!* three years later. The former has a particularly fine score that combines Broadway spirit with an American musical language reflective of Aaron Copland. Theater composers in search of a Southwestern sound—*110 in the Shade,* based on N. Richard Nash's play *The Rainmaker,* is set in

Texas—invariably look to the Copland of "Rodeo" and even the less-than-western "Appalachian Spring." Although this show was a fair success, the score was not appreciated. It is among Broadway's better ones. As for *I Do! I Do!*, the composer's contributions were overshadowed by the show's novelty (a two-character musical), by the stars (Mary Martin and Robert Preston), and by Gower Champion's flamboyant direction. This cleanly theatrical show has a lovely, melodic, and stage-carrying score that produced the standard "My Cup Runneth Over" and a stunning ballad "What Is a Woman?" *I Do, I Do!* has remained a staple, revived every summer in theaters across the country.

Schmidt and Jones fancied themselves experimentalists. They took the daring step of abandoning a lucrative Broadway career and opening a workshop where they could experiment in private. Although they developed several works in this laboratory, only one ever made an appearance on Broadway: *Celebration*, in 1969. An allegory, it failed, and for good reason: What Schmidt and Jones considered experimental was really just artsy-craftsy—a search for the meaning of life in leotards. Schmidt's talent in particular was born of and for the brassy Broadway show. As Jerry Herman carries on for Berlin, Schmidt does for Gershwin. There is an excitement to Schmidt's rhythms that cries out for dancers and pit bands. He is a writer of positively invigorating songs. In 1977 he and Jones closed their workshop with the intention of rejoining mainstream musical theater on Broadway. It can only be the richer for their return.

Cy Coleman, the final composer of this third generation, came to the theater relatively late and brought to it a different musical point of view. After some classical schooling, Coleman developed a career as a composer and performer of light jazz, even going so far as to have his own café (Cy Coleman's Playroom). Teaming up with a young and gifted lyricist, Carolyn Leigh, he wrote a number of pop hits for Frank Sinatra and Tony Bennett, including "The Best Is Yet to Come," "Firefly," and "Witchcraft." In this era—the early

Above: *N. Richard Nash adapted his play* The Rainmaker *into* 110 in the Shade, *a rewarding musical about a young woman (Inga Swenson) saved from spinsterhood by a fake rainmaker's inspiring lesson in optimism, not to mention sex. Robert Horton, playing the flashy fraud, was a television star who proved less than potent on Broadway.*

*As a vehicle for television's superstar Lucille Ball (here with leading man Keith Andes), playwright N. Richard Nash wrote* Wildcat, *a romantic musical comedy about oil drilling in Texas. Singing songs by Cy Coleman and Carolyn Leigh, Miss Ball was a great box office attraction but when she left the show prematurely, it had to close. This can be a problem even when a show that is good in its own right is overly dependent on a major star.*

sixties — it was unusual for a composer to succeed at writing non-rock songs, but Coleman succeeded.

He was in his thirties when he turned to the theater. Unlike most of the other composers of the third generation, he wasn't show people. His background was in the music and record business, his associations those of a commercial composer, and he was not steeped in the lore of the stage. Debut musicals are usually filled with the clichés of show tunes. Contrarily, Coleman's first musical, *Wildcat* in 1960 (written with Carolyn Leigh), presented song writing of a pop rather than a theatrical nature. Few of the songs even related to the story (about a romance during an oil rush in Mexican America just after the turn of the century). "That's What I Want for Janie," a sweet and lovely song, was one of the few that did relate. However, the show managed to demonstrate Coleman's knack for catchy, musically informed tunes, whether the upbeat ("Hey, Look Me Over!") or the ballad ("Tall Hope").

*Wildcat* was a fair success on the strength of the box office appeal of its star, Lucille Ball. It would have run longer had her engagement not been curtailed by illness. Coleman and Leigh had even worse luck with *Little Me,* two years later. This was a musical that should have, by rights, run for years. It had a hilarious book by Neil Simon, a marvelous star in Sid Caesar, and a delightful score. Coleman and Leigh had discovered the difference between pop and theater music. Most of Coleman's songs for *Little Me* have a comic tone reflecting the show's tongue-in-cheek approach. "I Love You" mocks the hero's egotism, "Boom-Boom" satirizes a corny French cabaret act, and "Dimples" kids vaudeville routines. These songs are all musically intelligent, melodious, theatrical, and appropriate for the show. Coleman and Leigh had originally written "To Be a Performer" for *Gypsy,* a show they'd hoped to do, but the lively and ingenious number fit neatly into *Little Me* and the stirring "Here's to Us" worked wonderfully as the show's single serious song. *Little Me* received good reviews and had enthusiastic admirers but it lasted only a season.

Although Coleman and Leigh seemed good for each other's work, the team broke up. He couldn't be faulted in his choice of a successive lyricist—the superlative Dorothy Fields—and together they wrote a score, for the 1966 hit *Sweet Charity.* By this time, confidence had given full strength to his melodic instinct, his musical invention, and, most important, his understanding of the stage. *Sweet Charity* had a strong number in the muscular "Big Spender." It found tricky, danceable rhythms in "There's Gotta Be Something Better Than This" though the song is too similar to Bernstein's "America." Coleman developed a cutting, ironic, and highly theatrical edge for a marvelous, pulsating song, "Where Am I Going?" However, he still wrote set pieces of music in the pop style—face it, possible hits—such as "Baby, Dream Your Dream." And when without benefit of a strong directorial hand in 1973 with *Seesaw,* he reverted utterly to the pop vernacular. There were good songs in this misconceived show, which overcame monumental out-of-town troubles to arrive on Broadway at least polished. Coleman's score includes "We've Got It," "You're a Loveable Lunatic," and "Welcome to Holiday Inn." These are all solid, but, except for "It's Not Where You Start," they are essentially pop songs.

*Seesaw* was Dorothy Fields's last show—she died a year after it opened—and Coleman worked on various unproduced projects with various lyricists over the next four years until in 1977 he came up with *I Love My Wife* with Michael Stewart, a long-established librettist who was now writing lyrics. This was an unusual musical, with but four characters and a small, onstage band. Rather than being embarrassed by the show's modesty, Coleman capitalized on it. He even orchestrated the music, a usually overwhelming job, made possible here by the smallness of the band. Small band or no, Coleman is the rare Broadway composer trained enough to orchestrate and concerned enough to do it. *I Love My Wife* was a success, and presented a Coleman relaxed in the theater and willing to experiment.

A mere ten months after *I Love My Wife* began its run, Coleman presented a major opus, a score totally unprecedented for him, one that at last capitalized on his musicianship. This was the score for *On the Twentieth Century*—written with still other lyricists, Betty Comden and Adolph Green—and it was virtually another *Candide*. For Coleman had written what was tantamount to a comic opera. Here was an enormous amount of music that simultaneously mocked and *was* comic opera. One might miss, in this score, the catchy melodies and show business pizzazz that had marked Coleman's previous show songs, but that would be to miss the point of his work here: its rightness for this outrageously hammy story and its significance to the composer's growth. The sheer quantity of music, with its elaborate counterpoint and its writing for groups of singers, demonstrated a Cy Coleman outgrowing his roots in pop music and reaching for new theatrical breadth. Among Broadway's third generation of composers, Cy Coleman has written some of the more contagiously joyous and musicianly scores and his growth is exciting.

Looking back over this generation, one is struck by the time suspension that rock music wrought. Many wonderful scores were written during this era but the mass of people who do *not* go to the theater was generally unaware of them. There are few songs that have entered the public consciousness. Adler and Ross, Bock, Merrill, Willson, Strouse, Kander, Herman, and Schmidt are gifted composers, but they have not become household names. Overall, their work shows Broadway's style of music at a standstill. There is little difference between their music and that of the generation before them. Except for Bernstein, Sondheim, and Coleman, the composers of this generation tended to go over the past rather than move ahead toward the future.

Although rock music had developed into a sophisticated musical form, none of its major songwriters wrote for the theater. Few were asked and the successful ones hadn't motive enough. Most were composer-performers and the record and concert business had become more lucrative than successful shows. Besides, these composers found youthful audiences more enlightened, enthusiastic, and stimulating than the older Broadway audiences. A group of fine young composer-performers arose—Paul McCartney and John Lennon of the Beatles, Randy Newman, Jim Webb, Neil Sedaka, Carole King, Paul Simon, and James Taylor. But our theater missed making contact with these versatile and gifted newcomers because it felt so antagonistic toward rock. The age of rock did introduce Galt MacDermot, composer of *Hair, Two Gentlemen of Verona, Dude,* and *Via Galactica.* Although he is a gifted musician, all of his shows to date are written in a bastard style of rock music that belongs to neither the rock nor the theater world. MacDermot also has not

*In the 1966 hit* Sweet Charity, *John McMartin conducted an innocent courtship with Gwen Verdon before learning she was a taxi dancer. The engaging McMartin, later to star in* Follies, *was among the new breed of musical leading men: easygoing and with a more natural, less robust singing voice than stars of the previous generation.*

Hair *was Broadway's first rock musical and its success unsettled the tight little community of musical theater professionals. A number like "White Boys/Black Boys" (at right), with three girls in one stretchy, sequined dress, was cute but by ordinary standards* Hair *was a mess, disorganized, unintelligible, and unstructured. The show had impeccable timing, however. Middle-class audiences could watch America's revolutionary sixties—hippies, flower children, nudity, and drugs—from a safe and comfortable seat. A 1,700-performance hit, it will never be a part of Broadway musical lore except as a curiosity. Like all the rock musicals and fad theater, it is of the moment and disposable.*

displayed a capacity to criticize his own work—to weed out better songs from lesser ones. *Hair* had its hits but "Let the Sun Shine In" and "Aquarius" are hardly memorable show songs. Burt Bacharach, a soft-rock composer of real talent, wrote one show, the successful *Promises, Promises,* but chose to write movie scores and make night-club appearances rather than stay in the musical theater.

Some new songwriters of a fourth generation did appear who seemed committed to careers in the musical theater. Gary Geld and Peter Udell established themselves with a gospel-style score for *Purlie,* a 1970 success based on the Ossie Davis play *Purlie Victorious.* They followed this up with the even more successful *Shenandoah,*

*They're Playing Our Song opened in 1979 to unenthusiastic reviews but enthusiastic audiences and became a smash hit. Neil Simon is the rare Broadway name who can overcome bad reviews. Even more of a dominating force in this show than in his previous musicals, Simon made* They're Playing Our Song *more a play with songs than musical theater. The show catapulted the dazzling Lucie Arnaz (here with co-star Robert Klein) to stardom. Marvin Hamlisch's songs (with lyrics by Carole Bayer Sager) were disco hit-oriented rather than theatrical but the show's success increased his clout as a stage composer. As a fully schooled musician who apprenticed with Broadway's best (he was the rehearsal pianist for Jule Styne's* Gypsy) *Hamlisch is still at the top of the incoming class.*

*Opposite, above: One of the more unlikely subjects for a Broadway musical was the history of the Declaration of Independence. Librettist Peter Stone and composer Sherman Edwards nevertheless based* 1776 *on those events, somewhat fictionalized, if not exactly musicalized. Starring William Daniels as the stiff-necked John Adams (center) and Howard da Silva (left) as Ben Franklin, the show surprised nearly everyone by running over 1,200 performances.*

*Opposite, below: By 1972, even the rather dull 1950s provided a subject for nostalgia and, like* Hair *before it,* Grease *proved that a rock musical could not only survive the transition from off-Broadway to uptown but could last over seven years in doing so. Undistinguished in nearly every way, the show's success was bewildering.*

which ran 1,050 performances from 1975 to 1977. Though superficially dissimilar, these two shows were in the Rodgers and Hammerstein vernacular. Udell's books and lyrics reflect Hammerstein's worst traits (sentimentality, dramatic obviousness) rather than his best (craftsmanship and stage-sense). Geld's music is a résumé of musical-play song clichés. However, the success of these Geld-Udell shows did suggest that audiences still hunger for melodic, singable songs and sentiments they can respond to.

Marvin Hamlisch's music had these qualities plus theatricality. He was the one newcomer to give show music hope of sophisticated continuity. Hamlisch's debut score for *A Chorus Line* was an impressive structure of contrapuntal mini-operas, specialty numbers, and dance music, all linked by *his own* underscoring. His second show, the hit *They're Playing Our Song,* was less impressive but he remains Broadway's highest hope.

The one promising fourth-generation team to come along was Larry Grossman and Hal Hackady. They wrote two shows, *Minnie's Boys* and *Goodtime Charley,* and both failed, but Grossman showed musicianly show-sense and Hackady is a specially gifted lyricist.

There are not enough of these composers and lyricists to light a future. How long can the third generation continue? How long can scores be written in just the same style as they had been for thirty years? Broadway's composers have demonstrated tremendous lasting power. They love the theater and stick to it. Indeed, they've tended to have longer professional lives than our playwrights. But a theater cannot survive without fresh blood. There has never been a time when the musical stage didn't have a generation of Young Turks, bright new composers and lyricists barking at the old guard's heels.

The time has come, for only one composer has been steadily dealing with the musical theater's growth, and its future cannot depend on Stephen Sondheim alone.

*If there was any composer-lyricist who seemed to be leading a new generation to Broadway in the seventies, it was Stephen Schwartz. Until he failed with two shows, everything he did had been a hit. Indeed, for most of 1974 through 1977, his* Godspell, Pippin, *and* The Magic Show *were running simultaneously! Unfortunately, Schwartz's songs had little to do with his success.* Godspell *(left) was a small-size* Hair, *a monster hit giving the composer his one popular song in "Day by Day."* The Magic Show *(far left) was an amateurish production capitalizing on the fabulous young magician Doug Henning.* Pippin, *which was utterly remade by its director, Bob Fosse, made a star of the spectacular Ben Vereen (below). And Fosse used his skills as a movie director to make a wonderful television commercial for* Pippin *(right). It was the first large-scale use of television advertising for a Broadway musical. After poor reviews and a weak start,* Pippin *was made into a hit with this ad campaign. Ever after, whenever musicals were in trouble, instead of working on the shows, the producers worked on the commercials.*

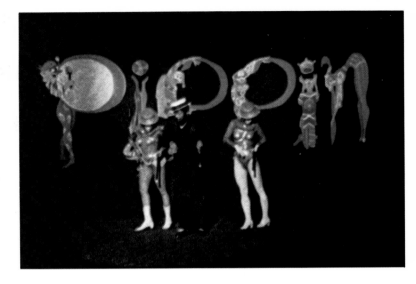

# STEPHEN SONDHEIM

By the age of forty-nine, in 1979, Stephen Sondheim had written the lyrics for three musicals and the complete scores for seven more. With this body of work he established himself as one of the most active composers and lyricists of his era, and surely the most influential.

Sondheim is not a songwriter but a theater composer. He has taken up where Bernstein left off with *West Side Story.* He has established the type of musical theater Kurt Weill had aimed for— "a musical theater," Weill wrote, "which could eventually grow into something like American opera . . . a real blending of drama and music, in which the singing continues naturally where the speaking stops and the spoken word as well as the dramatic action are embedded in overall musical structure." Weill's work sounded operatic when he attempted this. Leonard Bernstein explored it, but chose to spend most of his career in the concert hall. Sondheim has achieved these aims.

His seriousness and musical sophistication have not led to hit songs, and he's had but one, "Send in the Clowns." So Sondheim is not a household name, as were Kern, Berlin, Porter, Gershwin, and Rodgers. He will never be idolized as they were; his tunes will never be whistled in the street. Yet he is doubtless the dominant composer and lyricist in the musical theater of his time.

Born to a well-to-do family and raised in the brittle milieu of the garment industry and show business, Sondheim studied music at Williams College before going on to postgraduate work under Milton Babbitt, the noted modern composer. In his adolescence he had an informal—and, he claims, his most valuable—period of study with Oscar Hammerstein II, a family friend. When the fifteen-year-old Sondheim brought Hammerstein his first show, the older man tore it apart and then proceeded to give the youngster a series of musical-writing assignments. Hammerstein dealt with each carefully and constructively. Though Sondheim's astringence seems to have little in common with the warmth of Hammerstein's lyrics, the newcomer never denied his debt to the veteran. The score of *A Funny Thing Happened on the Way to the Forum* is dedicated to Hammerstein.

Sondheim made his Broadway debut when he was twenty-seven years old, writing lyrics to Leonard Bernstein's music for *West Side Story* in 1957. These lyrics did not always prove technically smooth, apt for the characters, or gracefully expressed. But writing them established him and gave him incomparable professional experience. For the young lyricist was challenged by the rhythmic irregularities of Bernstein's music and its demands for multiple lyrics set to musical counterpoint. Writing words for a trio in the "Tonight

*Columbia Records' president, Goddard Lieberson, studies the music for* Anyone Can Whistle *with its composer-lyricist Stephen Sondheim during the recording session. Recognizing the importance of this score, Lieberson insisted that it be recorded even though the show's brief run had freed Columbia of any legal obligation to do so. (Record companies agree to make original cast albums only if musicals play a minimum number of performances.) Lieberson's love of the theater made him better at making such albums than any other record producer of his time. Sondheim dedicated the published score of* Anyone Can Whistle *to him.*

Ensemble" prepared Sondheim for his later shows when, technically secure, he could concentrate on more felicitous expression in setting counterpoint to words. Moreover, there were enough good lyrics in *West Side Story* to make his talent obvious, such as those set to the exciting "Something's Coming":

> Could it be? Yes, it could.
> Something's coming, something good,
> If I can wait!
> Something's coming, I don't know what it is
> But it is
> Gonna be great!     (*West Side Story*)

Sondheim hoped to be given his first chance to compose with *Gypsy,* but the star, Ethel Merman, demanded an established composer. So Jule Styne wrote *Gypsy,* one of the greatest of Broadway scores. Sondheim gave it as fine a set of lyrics as was ever heard in a musical. In terms of simplicity, directness, emotion, and songfulness, they may be Sondheim's best. Styne's music for *Gypsy* represents vaudeville raised to an archetypal level. Sondheim's lyrics catch its drive:

> Some people sit on their butts,
> Got the dream—yeah, but not the guts!
> That's living for some people,
> For some humdrum people,
> I suppose.     (*Gypsy*)

The feeling and spirit there count for even more than the neat triple rhyme of "some humdrum."

One shrinks from choosing a high point in the *Gypsy* lyrics because they are so rich, and yet the finale, "Rose's Turn," can't help but stand alone. It may well be the most powerful single number—or "turn"—in all of our musical theater. Here, Sondheim's lyric is one long, sweeping stream of consciousness:

> Well, someone tell me, when is it my turn?
> Don't I get a dream for myself?
> Startin' now it's gonna be my turn!
> Gangway, world,
> Get offa my runway!
> Startin' now I bat a thousand.
> This time boys I'm taking the bows and
> Everything's coming up Rose—
> Everything's coming up Rose's
> Everything's coming up Roses
> This time for me!     (*Gypsy*)

These lyrics, only a portion of the number, have but one rhyme, the ingenious "thousand" and "bows and." Lyrics don't *have* to rhyme. Stephen Sondheim is a virtuoso rhymer but he knows that rhymes call attention to melody and harmonic resolution. This would detract from a charging, rhythmic piece like "Rose's Turn," whose aim is to present frustration and emotional breakdown in musical terms. It is a mad scene, all right, but as done on Broadway. Sondheim's intelligence, musical background, and show-sense undoubtedly helped push Styne to write the electric music that goes with it.

Despite his ambition to compose, after working on *West Side Story* and *Gypsy,* two of Broadway's most popular and respected shows, Sondheim was labeled a lyricist. Harold Prince came to the rescue by giving him his first production as a composer: *A Funny Thing Happened on the Way to the Forum* in 1962. This was one of the rare offbeat musical comedies to succeed. None of that success accrued to Sondheim. Although the show won the theater's prized Tony Award as the best musical of that year, Sondheim wasn't even *nominated* for one as a composer.

Except for his earlier, unproduced *Saturday Night, Forum* was the only Sondheim score written in the traditional manner—that is, as musical numbers inserted between book scenes. Still, the songs reflected the show's theme: the connection between the ancient Roman comedy of Plautus and our burlesque stage. This is an excellent score and the rare comic one from its composer. Influenced by the playful humor in the Burt Shevelove - Larry Gelbart script, Sondheim wrote funny words, funny music. It was a show for buffoonery and clowning, for the breadth of the burlesque sketch, for:

Funerals and chases,
Baritones and basses,
Panderers, philanderers,
Cupidity, timidity,
Mistakes, fakes, rhymes, mimes,
Tumblers, grumblers, fumblers, bumblers,

(*A Funny Thing Happened on the Way to the Forum*)

Sondheim's music captured the skip of brainless young lovers, the breastplated grandeur of Wagnerian heroines, and the pomposity of military heroes. The show's success encouraged Sondheim to stick to composing and led to the production in 1964 of *Anyone Can Whistle.* This has become a cult show, the sort that would have run forever if everyone who claims to have seen it had actually bought tickets. Misunderstood and unappreciated, it closed a week after its Broadway premiere. Efforts to revive *Anyone Can Whistle* will always be hampered by Arthur Laurents's book dealing with nonconformity and the delightfully insane. However, the original's production technique and its brightness and verve (for which Laurents deserves much credit as well) were invigorating on a Broadway mired down in stodginess. Sondheim's music and lyrics, like the youthful work of Porter and Coward, burst with spirit and wit. The whole radiated more sheer energy than any subsequent work of his. It is also the most "Broadway" of his scores, spirited and brassy, capitalizing on the pit-band vernacular. The score contained long sequences of interwoven story, music, and dance that foreshadowed the Sondheim to come. There was no way of telling where Laurents's book left off and Sondheim's lyrics began, or when Herbert Ross's wonderful dances were becoming Laurents's direction.

Sondheim wrote much of the show's dance music. This is no rehash of melodies as compiled by a dance pianist. Most of the waltz variations in *Whistle*'s "Cookie Chase" are Sondheim's. He was also writing freer and less restrained music than he would for his later shows. This is music for the musical comedy stage, informed by a classical background. Whatever the flaws of its book, *Anyone Can Whistle* is an outstanding musical because of its precocious spirit and the ambitious structure of its score, its dances, and its staging.

*The first number in* Company *establishes its wry tone. The subject is the competitiveness in marriage. A wife is demonstrating karate to her husband and the first thing you know he's on the floor, and is shortly wrestling with a guest. Their friends sing cheerfully, "It's the little things you do together/That make perfect relationships."*

After the calamitous fate of the show, Sondheim was advised to stick to writing lyrics. Although he had no such intention, nobody was much interested in his composing for the next five years. This discouragement and his friendship with Laurents led to one more assignment strictly as a lyricist, this time for Richard Rodgers, and it would be his last. The show was *Do I Hear a Waltz?* (1965), an adaptation of Laurents's play *The Time of the Cuckoo. Do I Hear a Waltz?* is a conventional musical play. Rodgers provided several lovely melodies and Sondheim's lyrics were craftsmanlike, but only one song, "We're Gonna Be All Right," had any life to it. *Do I Hear a Waltz?* had a very modest success.

It is noteworthy in only one respect. Sondheim's lyrics for this show are warm, and they are the last such lyrics he wrote for a long time. He seems to draw warmth from others. His later shows are all characterized by a chilly, disengaged mood; their lyrics, though dextrous, are cool, skeptical, and analytical, unlike even his own lyrics for *Saturday Night, Forum,* and *Anyone Can Whistle.* When Sondheim's music is emotional his accompanying lyrics are mocking, as if to say, "Pay no attention to that softhearted strain. It isn't me." His detachment has deprived him of wide popularity and denied his shows the emotional transport necessary to the smash hit.

Between 1965 and 1970, determined to become strictly a composer-lyricist, he rejected the countless lyric-writing projects that inevitably were offered on the basis of *Gypsy* and *West Side Story.* Then in 1970, Sondheim teamed up with Harold Prince, a partnership that was perhaps inevitable between the old friends. Musicals are always collaborative ventures, but the Prince-Sondheim partnership reduced the number of personalities to blend. It was a novel collaboration, a producer-director and a composer-lyricist. With Robbins retiring from Broadway, they were prepared to advance the principles he'd developed.

Their first collaboration was *Company,* which proved a truly new kind of musical. Its concept is marriage, its image the glass and chromium of New York. The book is a series of short plays organized by their author, George Furth, into a mosaic. There is no "story" but, rather, a series of related situations involving a bachelor, Robert, and the five married couples who are his friends. The show opens and ends with their surprise birthday party for him. Between are cinematic flashbacks describing these various marriages, Robert's life as a bachelor, and the issue he must confront: If this is marriage, does he want it?

Sondheim found a musical motif for *Company* in the click-buzz of a telephone's busy signal, a sound symbol for the jittery nerves of New York, and that sound starts his overture. Although *Company,* among all of Sondheim's musicals, might well have the least musical milieu, he gave it one of the best of all his scores. *Company*'s music, like most great scores, seems a whole rather than a collection of songs. It has a consistency of style and, as with other composer-lyricists, the words and the music have a unity of temperament. Sondheim's challenge in writing it was considerable: With no chorus, the actors had to sing all the songs and, being actor-singers rather than singer-actors, they could not be called upon for difficult vocalizing. This didn't leave much room for ambitious musical sequences, but Sondheim did write an extended piece for Robert's lecherous-by-proxy friends ("Have I Got a Girl for You?") leading into his own musings about a dream girl ("Someone Is Waiting," a beautiful

waltz). The jumpy nerves that characterize the show gave Sondheim perhaps too many opportunities to show off his lyric-writing expertise. Both "Another Hundred People" and especially "Getting Married Today" are marvelous and breathtaking patter songs but they are exhibitionistic and call attention to the lyricist's virtuosity at the expense of character. As is, some of the show's lines are so intricate they seem written mainly to impress other lyricists:

> Should there be a marital squabble,
> Available Bob'll
> Be there with the glue.     (*Company*)

These are faults of ingenuity and shouldn't be overly criticized. Most lyricists err on the side of sloppiness, which is certainly more deplorable. Sondheim's lyrics are often so dense with words that only perfect pronunciation can get them through, but when that happens the effect is dazzling. What's more, those lines just quoted come in the midst of a marvelous production number for this company of eleven; a playfully "big" number for an intimate, yet full-size musical. The number begins with the loping "Side by Side by Side," which has a lovely and strong melodic line. It then swings into a flag-waving, musical comedy number in which Robert's friends celebrate the warm fun of friendship, asking "What Would We Do Without You?" What Robert thinks they'd do is "just what you usually do" and the number leaves him alone and without company. Any way he slices it, marriages don't look good to him, from the competitiveness in "The Little Things You Do Together" to the wifely boredom

*As Robert, the bachelor around whom* Company *revolves, Dean Jones is alone—as usual—despite the presence of his friends. They are downstage, making merry as they wonder "What Would We Do Without You?" and don't even notice that he isn't there.*

321

expressed toward the end in the electric "The Ladies Who Lunch." It is such pessimism toward marriage and the hero's inability to love a woman that make his heterosexuality suspect. Depending on one's sensitivity toward this, a subtle element of homosexuality might be considered a distracting aspect of *Company*.

Musically, "Side by Side"/"What Would We Do Without You?" is a takeoff on vaudevillian "getaway" numbers. Musical satire is always around the corner in Sondheim's work. He indulges this taste too frequently and it grows tiresome. It might be a result of his retentive musical mind or a reflection of his disinclination to be emotionally expressive. Mockery, after all, is a form of self-disguise.

*Company* is a musical with all its elements woven into a fabric. It is seamless, its components indivisible. Here is a genuine breakthrough, demonstrating that a musical's libretto could be different in kind from a dramatic play. It has a musicianly score, and still a theatrical, Broadway excitement. *Company* ranks with *Show Boat* and *Oklahoma!* and *West Side Story* and *Fiddler on the Roof* as a milestone of the musical theater.

After *Company*, Prince came through on his promise to produce an earlier Sondheim work, *The Girls Upstairs*, retitled *Follies*. James Goldman wrote a straightforward story about a reunion of ex-Follies girls. It concentrates on two of them who are unhappily married to a pair of stage-door Johnnies. Prince's production, as co-staged with Michael Bennett, dealt surrealistically with age and the memory of youth. The only thing that connected their production concept with Goldman's book was Sondheim's prodigious twenty-two-song score. One group of his songs is comprised of archetypal numbers that supposedly came from the old Ziegfeld Follies (satires again). "Beautiful Girls" is of course modeled on *the* Follies song, Irving Berlin's "A Pretty Girl Is Like a Melody." "The Story of Lucy and Jessie" is mock Porter; "Losing My Mind" is based on Gershwin; "Broadway Baby" mocks DeSylva, Brown, and Henderson (authors of such like songs as "The Birth of the Blues"), though it sounds more like Harry Warren's "Lullaby of Broadway."

Another group of *Follies* songs deals with the present. These songs, written in a modern style, have a tone similar to *Company*'s music. "Waiting for the Girls Upstairs" has older characters singing as they watch the ghosts of their youth—played by other actors. It is a long number, running over five minutes, and exemplifies Sondheim's unique talent for writing dramatic musical sequences, opera in the Broadway style, with musical staging in mind. Nor do his lyrics take a back seat to such composing. One of the ex-Follies girls is trapped in a luxurious, embittered marriage and gets off a devastating tirade, building up emotional steam as it speeds ever faster:

> Could I leave you
> And your shelves of the World's Best Books
> And the evenings of martyred looks,
> Cryptic sighs,
> Sullen glares from those injured eyes?
> Leave the quips with a sting, jokes with a sneer,
> Passionless love-making once a year?
> Leave the lies ill-concealed
> And the wounds never healed
> And the games not worth winning
> And—wait, I'm just beginning!     (*Follies*)

Sondheim has no contemporary who could outdo such verbal flamboyance. Probably, none has the taste for such vitriol anyway. These lyrics are brilliant, if perhaps too clever to be wise. To underline their fury, he puts them to a swirling waltz in the style of Maurice Ravel. It is a striking display of setting words *against* music and there are other examples, in *Follies*, of a Sondheim now at the peak of his powers. The show's culminating number places the contemporary characters in a surreal and nightmarish Follies sequence. They run through songs that are musically of the Ziegfeld Follies and lyrically autobiographical. Here is the idealized memory of youth, cracking down the center, as the *Follies* poster illustrates. In all respects, then, this score is the Broadway musical stretched to its limits. Whatever the flaws in its script, the show stands as one of our musical theater's supreme achievements.

Coming on the heels of *Company* and *Follies*, *A Little Night Music* (1973) seemed tame in its aspirations and pretentious in its identification with Mozart (the title is a translation of his "Eine Kleine Nachtmusik"). A worldly operetta, it is based on the 1956 Ingmar Bergman film *Smiles of a Summer Night*. With this show, Sondheim fulfilled his longtime desire to write a musical entirely in three-four time. To even a tutored ear, the variations on this time signature (not all waltzes) do not grow wearisome. Quite the contrary, they provide a subliminal pattern. His score is particularly modeled on "Valses Nobles et Sentimentales," an exquisite set of waltzes by Maurice Ravel, though it has many other musical references. Once more, Sondheim is being a musical mimic. Nevertheless, this is a score of ravishing beauty.

Instead of an overture, it begins with a quintet of *lieder* singers—not story characters but a kind of Greek chorus—gathered around a grand piano (the music takes off on Brahms's "Liebeslieder Waltzes"). An opening group of three pieces, "Now," "Later," and "Soon," sets out the diverse attitudes toward sex among the members of the story's family. These songs are even longer than those in *Follies* and their lyrics are more elaborate. The first of the series, "Now," establishes that the main character, Frederick, has an immediate need for a sex life. He considers, in a set of witty, (perhaps overly) literary lyrics, the possibility of seducing his virginal second wife with suggestive reading:

| | |
|---|---|
| In view of her penchant | And Stendhal would ruin |
| For something romantic, | The plan of attack, |
| DeSade is too trenchant | As there isn't much blue in |
| And Dickens too frantic | "The Red and the Black." |

(*A Little Night Music*)

"Later," which follows on the heels of "Now," is a musical soliloquy by Frederick's son Henrik, a young man suffering a sex drive too urgent to delay. Completing this introduction to the story's family is "Soon" by Frederick's inexperienced young wife, who feels herself on the brink of sexuality. These three approaches to the matter of sex finally resolve into a counterpoint trio that intertwines the three songs. This is opera for the theater. The sequences are followed by back-to-back numbers, one gala—"The Glamourous Life"—and the other pensive—"Remember?"

The score of *A Little Night Music* is so thoroughly involved with the production that there are few set pieces—freestanding songs—

Overleaf, top: *In* A Little Night Music, *Desirée (Glynis Johns) has been discovered by her stuffy military lover (Laurence Guittard) while renewing an old friendship with Fredrik (Len Cariou), who doesn't seem ruffled at all.*

Overleaf, bottom: *"A Weekend in the Country" was the closest* A Little Night Music *would get to a production number. This elaborate musical sequence captured in words and in musical spirit the dangers, traps, complications, and elegant dizziness of romantic short-circuits at the country chateau of Desirée's mother, Madame Armfeldt.*

323

The handwritten manuscript pages are labeled **1**, **2**, **3**, **4**, **5**.

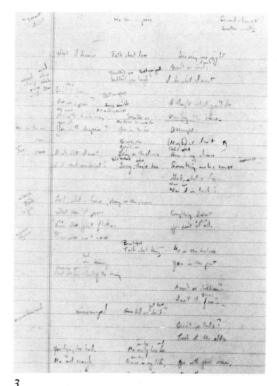

Reproduced here are Stephen Sondheim's studies for the lyrics of "Send in the Clowns" from **A Little Night Music**—rare, tangible examples of the stages a lyric (and its lyricist) must go through. In these drafts—made in pencil on yellow pads—Sondheim moves from a general description of what the character is trying to communicate to specified rhymed phrases and then on to formal verses. "Send in the Clowns" was written for the actress Glynis Johns, so the melody had to be restricted to a narrow vocal range and written in short phrases, allowing her plenty of breathing space. The song also had to fit the story and the character.

1. Sondheim began with free-associations for the character which became an interior monologue. These associations hit so close to the mark that a line of the finished lyric was notated virtually intact by the end of the first sheet.

2. The interior monologue became a series of wry rhetorical questions and ironic observations. Sondheim began to concentrate the thoughts into short phrases. The notion of disguises also emerged.

3. By now, the rhythmic pattern of the song had been set ("What I de-serve," "Talk a-bout love," etc.). This rhythmic pattern suggested a melodic line to Sondheim. Here, too, the disguise element was combined with the idea of farce (vain regrets) and the result became the song's central image: clowns.

4. The form and substance of the lyric are now clear and the song is nearly finished. What remains is "fine-tuning"; to be sure that each word chosen is the right one, that the ideas are fully expressed.

5. Lyric completed, the full song is put to paper for the first time.

but there are some: "Every Day a Little Death," "The Miller's Son," and "Send in the Clowns." "The Miller's Son," it seems to me, sounds like too many other songs for its own good. "Every Day a Little Death," however, is a jewel. There is a consuming sadness in its inventive melody reinforced by the echoing (or canon) structure. The lyrics capture Sondheim's gloom very honestly. When he speaks of life's daily pinpricks of death, nobody is more eloquent:

> Every day a little death
> In the parlor, in the bed.
> In the curtains, in the silver,
> In the buttons, in the bread.
> Every day a little sting
>
> In the heart and in the head.
> Every move and every breath,
> And you hardly feel a thing,
> Brings a perfect little death.
>
> (*A Little Night Music*)

326

"A perfect little death." It is hard to imagine anyone but Sondheim writing that.

It is equally hard to imagine any of Sondheim's contemporaries writing the likes of *Follies* or *Night Music*. His combination of musical and theatrical ambitiousness is unique. But he seemed to overstep his ambition in writing a score for a Japanese musical. The theme of *Pacific Overtures* is the destruction of ancient Japanese culture by Westernization, demonstrated through the ritualism of Kabuki theater. It was an unusual choice for Sondheim, who avoids artiness and is loath to use the theater as a forum for messages. Though he doubtless could have, Sondheim did not try to write his music on the Oriental scale but instead aimed for a Western version of Eastern music. He achieved this through what seemed a tremendous effort of intellect and will, so involving his music with this show's production scheme that it became aural scenery. His lyrics for *Pacific Overtures* represent still another step in the development of scenic songs and his music is tremendously effective in the context of the show. But there comes a point in such thorough integration at which one begins to lose the special contribution that music can make. These songs have so intellectual an intent that they lose the visceral appeal of music.

Through all of these major scores, beginning with *Company*, Sondheim was formidably supported by virtually an alter ego in Jonathan Tunick, perhaps the finest orchestrator in musical theater history.

Stephen Sondheim sits at his piano with the door open beyond him—the door not only to his future but to the future of the Broadway musical. He seems incapable of the safe or conventional. He might well be discouraged by the greater success of lesser shows than his or by the failure of mass audiences to respond to his major efforts. His work represents the musical theater's greatness during his time, and his future is its future.

Opposite, top and bottom: *In* Pacific Overtures, *Mako played the Reciter, a figure from Kabuki Theater, a kneeling chorus of one. He bitterly describes Japan's transition from Eastern customs and traditions to Western rock 'n' roll brashness in a modern technological world.*

Sweeney Todd, the Demon Barber of Fleet Street *starred Angela Lansbury and Len Cariou. This production used a fabulous setting— a real iron foundry adapted by designer Eugene Lee. Sondheim wrote nearly continuous music—so much that the show approached opera. Though as complex and scenic as ever, this score was notably warm and melodic. But marvelous as Sondheim's music and Harold Prince's staging were,* Sweeney Todd *was unsatisfying. It had no theater purpose.*

# BLACK MUSICALS

A book about Broadway musicals shouldn't have a section devoted exclusively to black shows. This book wouldn't have such a section were things racially right in our theater. Instead, musicals about or by black people would be scattered among the musicals about or by white people, Jewish people, Irish people, city people, country people. Black performers would be dealt with among all performers, as they should be.

But things are *not* racially right in our theater. We might no longer put up with a show called *A Trip to Coontown,* the 1898 production that began the sorry phenomenon of the all-black musical, yet in the racially sophisticated seventies, we put up with its contemporary equivalent. If our theater is no longer blatant in its racism, and no longer presents blackface mammy singers, the practice of selling color still persists. Productions are *still* identified as "black musicals" and we cannot pretend that a show cast solely with black performers *isn't* a "black musical." Nor can we pretend that race isn't part of the show.

Broadway has maintained a tradition of black musicals for as long as there has been a musical theater. Black revues were produced intermittently on Broadway throughout the twenties and thirties. Racism was so ingrained a part of American life that producers had no qualms about giving these shows such titles as *Chocolate Dandies, Brown Buddies,* and *Blackbirds,* which was the best known of them. *Blackbirds of 1928,* the most successful of several editions of this revue, starred the great tap dancer Bill Robinson. Ethel Waters and Lena Horne appeared in other editions. There was once, in London, even *Whitebirds,* starring Maurice Chevalier.

Seldom was an all-black revue written or produced by blacks. An exception was the *Shuffle Along* series in 1921, 1932, and even as late as 1952. These had music and lyrics by Noble Sissle and Eubie Blake. Bill Robinson and Josephine Baker appeared in various editions; at the time, such shows were the main way for black performers to escape the ghetto-vaudeville circuit. Baker managed her escape with dignity only by fleeing to Paris, where she was treated as an exotic. The celebrated Florence Mills had to settle for singing songs like "I'm a Little Blackbird Looking for a Blue Bird" in shows with titles like *Dixie to Broadway* (1924). The careers of Bill Robinson and the legendary comedian Bert Williams were contingent on their playing the Uncle Tom—that is, performing obsequiously. Williams's early credits included such humiliations as *Bandanna Land* (1908) and *Mr. Lode of Koal* (1909). Although Williams eventually became a Ziegfeld Follies star and Robinson became a star in Shirley Temple movies, their careers were strictly limited, and the conditions on them were stringent.

*Casting only blacks in a show that is white in story and spirit abuses the work as well as the actors. *Hello, Dolly! *is inescapably a white musical about upper middle class white people. Casting Pearl Bailey, as great a performer as she is, was a purely commercial gimmick.*

Opposite: *Here is the famous "Waiters' Galop" from* Hello, Dolly! *Gower Champion's choreography has become legend, among the finest in Broadway history. The two versions are identical except for the racial difference of the dancers. That is why the black version must be considered a race show. Race is its distinction.*

A Trip to Coontown, *produced in 1898, was the first all-black book musical. As the white musical theater moved up from revues, so the black musical theater graduated from minstrel shows. (The seated chorus girls are in white-face.) Times were such that whites and blacks spoke commonly of "darkies" and "coons" and "niggers."*

*Bill "Bojangles" Robinson was fifty before Broadway finally discovered him. Here he is dancing "Doin' the New Low-Down" in* Blackbirds of 1928, *his first show. Robinson was one of the greatest and most beloved of black stars. Before reaching the peak of fame, if not dignity, as baby Shirley Temple's movie dancing partner, Robinson appeared only in black shows like this one. Of all the* Blackbirds *revues, it was the most successful.*

Like the mainstream musical theater, black musicals turned to book shows in the forties. Produced, written, and composed by white men, these invariably patronized blacks. The 1940 *Cabin in the Sky,* a modest variation on *Porgy and Bess,* was such a show. More common was the black version of materials written for white characters, including *The Hot Mikado* (Gilbert and Sullivan's *The Mikado*), *Carmen Jones* (Bizet's *Carmen*), and *Golden Boy* (the Clifford Odets play). Whether speaking of these or of later "black versions," such as *Hello, Dolly!* and *Guys and Dolls,* the practice is theatrically as well as racially offensive because it violates the integrity of the original work. How can one make sense of a black Yonkers middle class singing show tunes in *Hello, Dolly!* or of black Damon Runyon characters in *Guys and Dolls?* We cannot and do not accept the characters as being black even when they are being played by black actors. Instead, we watch a different show—a black show—for the production's main characteristic has become the actors' race.

The seventies' boom in black musicals was set off by *Hello, Dolly!* in 1967. With business beginning to sag four years into the show's run, its producer, David Merrick, replaced the company with an all-black cast headed by Pearl Bailey. The *Dolly* box treasurer once more started putting out the sold-out signs and saw something new on Broadway—black customers. It took other producers little time to notice the change, for in the past black shows had been produced for *white* audiences. A slapdash musical called *Buck White* was hurried to Broadway, starring a bloated and stage-frightened Muhammad Ali (then Cassius Clay), who was barred from boxing at the time because of his political and religious beliefs. The show didn't last long but the rush to black musicals—*Purlie, Raisin, The Wiz, Bubbling Brown Sugar, Guys and Dolls, Timbuktu*—was on.

Not all of these musicals presented black performers in white material. Even going back to the thirties, there were some musicals

*Black versions of white musicals came into style on Broadway in 1939. That year there were actually two competing versions of* The Mikado, *Gilbert and Sullivan's classic operetta. Audiences had a choice of* The Swing Mikado *or* The Hot Mikado *(below) starring Bill Robinson (in the flowered derby) as the black, therefore hot, mikado. This version, produced by the super-showman Mike Todd, featured abstract, modernistic sets and lots of jazz dancing (bottom).*

Carmen Jones (1943) was an adaptation of Carmen by Oscar Hammerstein II, who set his version of Bizet's opera among southern blacks. Escamillo, the matador, became Husky Miller, the boxer, and so on. Why blacks? Though opera audiences accept melodramatic plots, Hammerstein presumably thought that Broadway would buy the story's lust and murder only if the characters were black. Hammerstein had good intentions but an unerring instinct for the racial gaffe.

Opposite, above: *Until Pearl Bailey came along, Lena Horne was Broadway's token black star. Here (above and at top, in* Jamaica) *is a beautiful woman with a unique voice and magnetic presence. It is a pity she was cast only in all-black shows.*

Opposite: Jamaica *was one of several black musicals written by the blues-oriented Harold Arlen. Even in 1953, a white American actor wouldn't have been cast as the black Lena Horne's romantic lead, but a Mexican (Ricardo Montalban) was okay. The fine actor, and later playwright, Ossie Davis is on the right.*

332

written specifically about black people with music in the black vernacular. *Porgy and Bess* is, of course, the first to come to mind. One can argue for or against the legitimacy of Gershwin's version of indigenous black music. Without a doubt, the Dubose Heyward libretto is condescending toward blacks. It seems fair to judge from the traditional rejection of *Porgy and Bess* by black audiences that the work, however great it is, does not come through to them as authentic.

*Lost in the Stars* was about blacks in Africa, but as written by Maxwell Anderson and Kurt Weill in 1949, it has little of the black African about it. It is more like a stilted European opera. Harold Arlen was one composer who persistently sought black materials for musicals—*St. Louis Woman* in 1946, *House of Flowers* in 1954, and *Jamaica* in 1957—but not for exploitative reasons. There is perhaps an element of the exotic in Arlen's approach to black subjects, as the titles of these shows suggest, but his approach is essentially musical and appreciative.

The first hit black musical in the presumably liberal, modern era was the 1973 *Raisin*. It was drawn from the pioneering Broadway play *A Raisin in the Sun,* written by black playwright Lorraine Hansberry. So, this musical was about black people and their racial

Purlie *was a breakthrough, the first black musical to deal with racial problems. The show was based on the play* Purlie Victorious, *written by the actor Ossie Davis. Though its score was written by a white team—Gary Geld and Peter Udell—they often succeeded in capturing the gospel idiom.*

Opposite, top: *In music, dancing, and dialogue,* The Wiz *used the black idiom consistently and engagingly. The beautiful Dee Dee Bridgewater was a different kind of witch, while Ted Ross played the Cowardly Lion and Tiger Haynes the Tin Man.*

Opposite, below: *Stephanie Mills played Dorothy (standing in the stylized doorway) in* The Wiz, *and while it was sometimes difficult to accept urban ghetto music in a Kansas setting, when a show is going right, nothing seems wrong.*

problems, which not only made black actors necessary but also provided it with a built-in black audience, Broadway's first such audience in significant numbers.

On the positive side, then, in addition to at last giving work to black performers (if not black musicians or stagehands) and desegregating audiences, the heightened fashion in black musicals accomplished something else: It opened the door to musicals dealing with the black experience. But they were still *created* almost entirely by whites.

*The Wiz* sounded, in prospect, like still another white story being made into a black show for the sake of exploitative, racial novelty. However, librettist William F. Brown rewrote Frank Baum's *The Wizard of Oz* in ghetto street argot and Charlie Smalls provided the show with soul-style disco music. George Faison choreographed the company using ethnic dance steps. This was a black show, by blacks, for all audiences, and a frequently exhilarating show. Black artists who attempted more serious musicals about their people had tougher going. In 1971, Melvin van Peebles (a novelist and moviemaker with little stage experience) wrote the book, music, and lyrics for a powerful and angry show called *Ain't Supposed to Die a Natural Death.* It was the one Broadway musical to confront the audience with the unpleasant facts of ghetto life. Comfortable theatergoers, expecting cheerful black singers and dancers, found themselves being held responsible for a real crime in a real world. "I put a curse on you," one of Van Peebles's characters snarled to the audience at the show's end. The character was a mother and she wished on the audience's white children what had happened to her own—the

heroin addiction, the joblessness, the wasted lives born of frustration and futility. Only then could parents understand the black situation. Broadway audiences hardly took to *Ain't Supposed to Die a Natural Death.*

A big and very beautiful show called *Doctor Jazz* set out, a few years later, to be similarly angry in tracing the corruption and commercialization of black jazz by whites. Paul Carter Harrison, a writer with an unusual understanding of the musical theater, ran into many of the problems that Van Peebles had faced. By the time *Doctor Jazz* arrived as a flop, Harrison had been replaced, his book watered down, and his concept aborted. It was left to *Bubbling Brown Sugar* (a title sarcastically modeled on the old *Chocolate Dandies* and *Blackbirds* revues) to make a hit based on its period black music and entertainment styles. This 1976 musical abused whites in only an innocuous way even though it was dealing with a time period (the twenties and thirties) when the celebrated Harlem night spots were barred to black customers. *Bubbling Brown Sugar* emphasized the joy rather than the tragedy of period black entertainment. Though it had a flimsy book and an amateurish feel, its musical numbers were so ingratiating that they carried the show to considerable success. Two years later, *Ain't Misbehavin'* (using Fats Waller's music) also celebrated black musical styles of the thirties, only more artistically and more successfully.

It is necessary to appreciate the talent of the many marvelous performers in the black musical past, even as we are troubled by the embarrassments and insults they suffered. We must also try to

Opposite: *Avon Long appeared in* Bubbling Brown Sugar *thirty-five years after he played Sportin' Life in the first major revival of* Porgy and Bess. *The handsome lady is Josephine Premice, and the song is "Honeysuckle Rose." The plot of* Bubbling Brown Sugar *concerned a pair of white innocents taken on a tour through Harlem—and its history—by a pair of old-timers.*

*Melvin van Peebles wrote, composed, and directed* Ain't Supposed To Die a Natural Death *in 1971. He hoped a black musical could be more than* A Trip to Coontown *with soul music. Broadway didn't appreciate the show's anger or understand its humor. The number shown below, done by Garrett Morris and Barbara Alston, was "Lily Done the Zampoughi Every Time I Pulled Her Coattail."*

*Ain't Misbehavin' was one musical about blacks and with a black subject that wasn't a race show. This tremendously popular, Tony Award-winning musical was based on the career and songs of Thomas "Fats" Waller, a songwriter and performer who had to affect the manner of a servile clown—an "Uncle Tom"—to survive in show business. Ain't Misbehavin' used no dialogue, yet it was theater rather than a concert or cabaret act. It was staged and choreographed with consistent style. Here was black life and black music as if lifted from the pages of a Second World War era rotogravure. And in the Fats Waller-Andy Razaf song "Black and Blue," it sorrowfully and soberly presented the lack of racial pride that too many black shows throughout Broadway history had reflected:*

> *I'm white inside*
> *But that don't help my case*
> *'Cause I can't hide*
> *What is on my face*

*The audiences watched the young black performers singing these words—words emphasized by the absence of orchestral accompaniment. The performers did not look as if they hated Razaf for having written the words. They did not look as if they hated Waller for having sung them. On the contrary, they appreciated what earlier black entertainers had gone through, and what they had to do to survive. But the cast did force the audience to watch them sing these words, and no other words were necessary. This is how musical theater can present powerful themes and, in particular, it is comment enough on the history of black musicals on Broadway.*

understand the mentality that created even the most offensive of the old shows, for only by accepting the reality of such productions as *A Trip to Coontown* can we begin to have a valid understanding of America. Oscar Hammerstein II's various treatments of the black people now smack of a hypocritical, fumbling, and deplorable sort of liberalism. It was Hammerstein who intended to write a musical *Porgy* for Al Jolson in blackface. It was Hammerstein who persistently dealt with interracial romances that somehow couldn't work out. But in his time he was progressive. Prevalent racial attitudes were *worse*.

It is very easy for a white person to advise a black actor that if he can't get a part in a standard production of a show he shouldn't take a part in a race-oriented version of it. Such advice is cheap to give and expensive for the work-starved actor to take. Whatever we may think of race shows, they do give actors work. But the black actor should not be saddled with a choice between work and dignity. Broadway must realize the importance and significance of desegregating itself and making black theatergoers feel welcome there. Black composers and authors should be free, strictly on the basis of talent, to do the writing, not just for black shows, but for any shows; they should be allowed to compete; they should write on all subjects, not just those concerned with race. It is astounding that despite the mammoth contributions of black singers and musicians to the performance of American popular music, only Duke Ellington and Fats Waller made names for themselves as songwriters, and only because they performed their own music. Unbelievable as it may seem, until the seventies, Ellington was the only black composer ever to have written a modern book musical (*Pousse-Café*, a 1966 failure). In the realm of popular music, Marvin Hamlisch had to remind the public that Scott Joplin and not he (the orchestrator-arranger) had written the grand ragtime music used in the movie *The Sting*. Only that film's popularity made possible, finally, a Broadway production of Joplin's opera, *Treemonisha*, nearly sixty years after his death.

Music publishers and theatrical producers have persistently denied black composers access to the public. Waller had to sell great songs ("On the Sunny Side of the Street," "I Can't Give You Anything but Love") to white songwriters in order to make a living. Throughout American history, music was as segregated as the country was. Even today, rare indeed is the Charlie Smalls who has the chance to write the score for a hit show like *The Wiz*. This is the disgrace of American popular and theater music.

Hopefully, the racial practices of the modern stage will become more just and not appear as loathsome to the future as those of the past appear to the present. Perhaps then it will be unnecessary for some future book about the musical theater to have a special section devoted to black musicals.

# FINALE

The theater belongs to the world, but the American musical belongs to Broadway. Drama and comedy do not need Broadway to exist. They have existed for four thousand years and will exist forever, whatever happens to New York's commercial theater. But the musical cannot survive away from Broadway. It is a child of that theater. Nor can Broadway survive without the musical. A hit musical provides its life juices, lights up New York, and keeps *all* the playhouses busy. A season without a smash musical just isn't a proper season, which depresses not only Broadway but the whole town. For the musical is one of those things that makes New York New York. Take away the musicals and Broadway is just a couple of side streets.

The Broadway musical stands with one foot at the brink of fulfillment, the other at the rim of extinction. Its best examples were never better, yet the spirit seems endangered: the productivity, the activity, the ferment, the optimism, the energy. A previously undreamed-of commercialism threatens to drain the musical theater of its fun and to make it less a theater for theatergoers than one for the mass market.

The craft of musical making is within a hairbreadth of perfection. The traffic management of performers has long since been mastered. Remote-controlled winches now move bulky scenery with an effortless flow. Computerized switchboards have made child's play of complicated lighting. Amplification has made full underscoring and the constantly musical musical possible. The most troublesome problem—that of the book—is near solution, now that concept musicals have led to scenarios especially designed for the musical stage rather than "musical plays" borrowed from drama.

The trailblazing work of composers Leonard Bernstein and Stephen Sondheim has led to sophisticated music in the Broadway vernacular, music expanded from the song to the elaborate musical sequence. The choreographer-directors have made shows that interweave story, song, and dance. The musical theater has grown up as a craft; its artists can now concentrate on the pictures rather than on the paints.

But with the technique mastered, where's the joy in musicals? Some of the musical theater's most devoted adherents feel that its soul is dead—that it has become too big a business. Million-dollar investments and multi-million-dollar profits have brought high-powered managements in place of the showmen and entrepreneurs who once produced Broadway's shows. These new managements take the attitude that too much money is at stake to rely on mere quality for success; they feel that audiences can be sold anything with the right marketing strategy. More time is now spent fixing a musi-

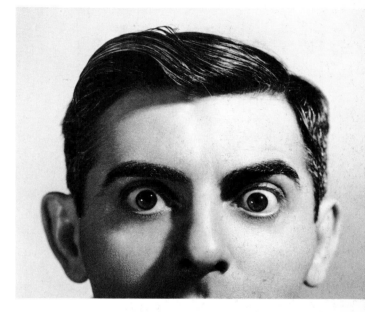

*One can only put it this way: In his era—the twenties and thirties—Al Jolson was the greatest entertainer who ever lived. He was basically a "mammy singer," a graduate of minstrel shows still working in blackface, but he didn't like working with other stars in revues. Eddie Cantor (above) was less egotistical and didn't mind, in fact he starred in countless Ziegfeld Follies. Cantor would skip across the stage while clapping his hands and staring bug-eyed at the audience. For some reason they adored this, and the routine kept Cantor working for thirty years. He had star power, the onstage life that is stifled in the reproduced show business of today's movies and television. Star power is the vital spark between performer and audience. Did anyone have this spark as Al Jolson did? He had a confidence, an exuberance, a compulsion to perform, and a stage life so animal and even terrifying that audiences felt the man possessed. People who saw Jolson spoke as if they'd seen a Martian. His shows were book musical comedies—Sinbad, Bombo, The Wunder Bar— but they were merely set-ups for his specialty songs, such numbers as "Swanee" and "My Mammy" and "Rock-A-Bye Your Baby with a Dixie Melody." When Eddie Cantor finally saw Jolson perform, he said his own work was unsettled for months afterward. Any major star, even one as modest as Cantor, is competitive, but Cantor was frank: "I can't compete with Jolson."*

*Though it is their excitement too, the tragedy of stage performers is that, like butterflies, their beauty is extravagant; it lives for the moment, and then it is gone. They leave no legacy, no record to replay. They glitter in the spotlight and disappear. Who was Fanny Brice? The singer of "My Man" and "Rose of Washington Square"? The Yiddish dialect comedienne? The star of vaudeville and burlesque and seven editions of the* Ziegfeld Follies? *Fanny Brice was one of the greatest of Broadway musical stars. There is no way for those who never saw her work to know her work, and that is something to remember when watching the great performers. They do everything, risk everything, in that transient and dangerous moment in the spotlight.*

cal's television commercial than on fixing the show itself. What's more, the commercials have been succeeding.

But only commercially. The abundance of long-running shows does not mean an abundance of *good* shows. Is *Grease* as good as *The King and I, The Magic Show* as good as *Guys and Dolls*? A long run once meant a smash hit with a gotta-see-it excitement about it. This is no longer true. The standards of professionalism that "Broadway" once signified have become lax. Shows become profitable through marketing, not by wowing the audience. But theater is a love affair between the stage and the audience. When the love goes, the theater of it goes, and there is no love in show marketing. It makes customers of audiences.

There are other troubling signs. Because of inflation, fewer musicals are produced than ever before. Choruses of singers and dancers have become financially insupportable. American taste in popular music has long since shifted from Broadway songs to rock 'n' roll. Young people make up a minority of Broadway audiences, and there is no fourth generation of composers and lyricists crowding the wings. The choreographer-directors may be growing too powerful, for as dancers they minimize the importance of professional writers, of words, of thought; and as co-producers they are tending to cut out anyone who might share in the huge profits of a hit. That is even more discouraging to the composers, lyricists, and librettists who might write for the musical theater. Finally, retrospectives and revivals are in abundance. It would be good if respect for classic musicals had spurred the revivals of shows like *The King and I, Fiddler on the Roof*, and *Hello, Dolly!* with their aging original stars, but unfortunately these revivals smell of the quick buck, the summertime music tent, and the celebration of yesterday as if there were no tomorrow.

If inflated costs and a marketing approach are threatening to take the fun out of musicals, audiences do not seem so ready to forget their special thrill. On its revival in 1977, many flaws showed up in the construction of *The King and I*, yet the Rodgers and Hammerstein masterwork remained valid. When Yul Brynner and Constance Towers whirled around the stage at the peak moment of "Shall We Dance?" the thrill still pulsed through the audience. And when the overture was struck up for a *Porgy and Bess* revival in 1976, the electricity was still in the air. And when Michael Bennett sent his *Chorus Line* out for the finale, there was no exit through which to flee the heart-stopping excitement. The stuff of musicals is still there for show makers to give and audiences to receive.

Those who fear that the musical's great days may be over look back on the songs of Rodgers and Kern and Gershwin and Porter and Berlin. They warm to the memory of even the ordinary musicals of the forties and fifties. They yearn for the overtures that pushed them up the first hill of a theater rollercoaster to set them up for the steep drop, the whirl around curves, the plummets and rises and emotional rushes and tears, flying along from the opening number to a sweeping finale. Nothing could compare to the unique, exhilarating experience of the musical. Are those the thrills of the past?

Not long ago, the musical had a tradition of the "eleven o'clock number." It was called that because a musical, which began at 8:30, was thought to need a peak moment just before the end—that is, at eleven o'clock. The theory was that if the audience could be overwhelmed just then, it would remember the whole show because of that emotional explosion. Whether this was show savvy or superstition, it led to many of the musical theater's great moments. The eleven o'clock number could be big: "Hello, Dolly!" It could be intimate: "I've Grown Accustomed to Her Face." But it was always a surefire success.

The eleven o'clock number was a beloved and exciting tradition. Starting as they do nowadays, at 8:00, Broadway shows end before eleven, for their customers' convenience. Have musicals similarly calculated themselves out of the excitement that made their success? Without risk—without the reach for a thrill—a musical just isn't a musical. Before it's over, a musical has to lift the audience out of its seats, put the audience in shock. A business does not work that way. The theater can't act like a business and be theater. Products don't have show-stopping qualities.

The musical must either change or die, but as a theatrical genre its soul must remain intact. There may be no place, anymore, for the star vehicle and no stage, anymore, for the likes of Jolson and Merman and Lahr, of Eddie Cantor or Fanny Brice, but the show cannot go on without their spirit or without the spirit of pit bands and jugglers and comedians and chorus lines. The musical theater is the Al Jolson who did not feel alive unless he was electrifying an audience with his showmanship. The musical theater is the Ethel Merman so innocently obsessed with gripping the audience that she felt no embarrassment as she strode downstage, planted both feet squarely beneath her, reared back, and blasted the back wall of the balcony. The musical theater is the Bert Lahr who roared onstage from the wings, clowning and bellowing, finding his own life as he took audiences away from *their* lives, releasing them in an explosion of helpless, joyous laughter. Out there, onstage, alone in the spotlight, such stars dance for the public. They come to that ocean of faces unafraid, giving themselves up to the heaving mass, eager—even desperate—to work their gifts on this most dangerous of beasts, which will either swallow them whole or crest them to dizzying triumph.

The musical stage may have outgrown such showcasing of individual performers in pursuit of more sophisticated aims, but any audience is capable of becoming that oceanic beast at any time. If the musical theater ever loses the dynamism to transport that beast, its heartbeat will have stopped. Since our own hearts have come to beat in the same rhythm whenever the lights darken over an orchestra pit, something within us would die as well. For ultimately, the Broadway musical is a metaphor for the ecstasy we are capable of creating and experiencing; it offers us an emotional orgasm. The Broadway musical is not a passive theater. Its audiences are transformed as they are being made love to. They sing and dance as they make their way up the aisles while the walkout music is being played. They are not out of the theater yet. The music goes on, and as it goes on they take the show with them. Not yet out of the theater, they are still wearing the show on their faces. On the sidewalk they are different from the other people. They're fresh from peaking, not quite back to real life.

Well, it was only a show: music, lyrics, libretto, costumes, lighting, actors, dancers. Yet, something bigger had been made, something liberating. This had been no drama, not a comedy. Theater, yes, but a special kind of theater with only one name fit for it: the Broadway musical.

# INDEX

Page numbers in **bold** indicate references to illustrations.

Broadway musicals, of course, do not all become hits. Most flops also have the style, polish, and energy of more successful shows—but with something amiss. They are the Broadway musical in negative form, with a perverse flamboyance of their own, for they cost so much and fail so spectacularly. To the general public, it seems lunatic that producers, directors, and stars should lack the judgment to see millions of dollars go down the drain, sometimes after a single performance. It's what makes show business like no business.

The musical theater community is mesmerized by the phenomenon of flops because not even the biggest names are immune to them. Failure can happen to anyone. Sometimes a good show fails and a poor one runs three years. Because of such unpredictability and risk, musical theater people sometimes wish for their colleagues' failure. If the flop happens to someone else, the thinking seems to go, it won't happen to you.

Bad musicals are like "industrial shows," those Broadway-style musicals financed by corporations to entertain customers and introduce products. Industrials are made by Broadway people; they have the exuberance and bravura of full-fledged musicals. But there is no artistic impulse for their existence; just as with flops, they haven't the magic that is the key to any new hit, the key that is different for every show.

The photographs spread throughout this Index are of shows that lacked the magic—musicals that failed on Broadway, musicals that never reached Broadway, even industrials. They are here, not as an afterthought, but because they, too, have the spirit of Broadway musicals and because the threat of failure is as much a part of the musical theater myth as the fantasy of being a smash hit.

*Juliet Prowse starred in the 1975 Milliken Breakfast Show, the most lavish, best-produced, and most famous "industrial" show.*

345

*Composer Mitch Leigh was savaged while trying to follow up his* Man of La Mancha. *Two disasters followed:* Cry for Us All *and this one-performance bomb* Home Sweet Homer *starring Yul Brynner.*

*Composer-lyricist Stephen Schwartz had been leading a charmed existence, his first three shows all being hits. With the out-of-town closing of* The Baker's Wife (*starring Topol, center*), *he paid his dues.*

Having become a star with Gentlemen Prefer Blondes, *the wonderful Carol Channing next found herself in a splashy vehicle about silent films—*The Vamp. *Diamonds may be a girl's best friend, but an actress is better off with good material.*

*Judy Holliday's last musical was* Hot Spot, *a show about the Peace Corps that ran about a month. Richard Rodgers's daughter Mary wrote the music. A gifted composer, she chose to retire. Martin Charnin wrote the lyrics. He went on to direct* Annie.

The credentials of **Prettybelle** were impeccable: a score by Jule Styne and Bob Merrill, fresh from success with **Funny Girl**; the director was Gower Champion and the star Angela Lansbury. But the chemistry of musical-making is such that the most established practitioners seem to start from scratch each time. **Prettybelle** closed on the road.

It was unheard of, but producer David Merrick closed **Breakfast at Tiffany's** during New York previews. He announced that he was sparing the public so poor a musical. This was grandstanding at the expense of those who had worked hard on the show, such as the stars Mary Tyler Moore and Richard Chamberlain.

Marissa Pell watched her great chance in the title role of Mata Hari *go down the drain in Washington, never making it to a New York opening night.*

Bette Davis had bad luck with musicals. The revue Two's Company *didn't fare well in 1952.* Miss Moffat *(based on the film* The Corn Is Green*) closed during out-of-town tryouts.*

The modern era of superflops began with Kelly, *which closed after its opening night performance at a loss of $650,000. The creators of this show, about a fellow who jumped off the Brooklyn Bridge for publicity, claimed that their Brechtian ambitions were thwarted by crass, insensitive producers.*

*Jerry Lewis and Lynn Redgrave were the stars of* Hellzapoppin, *a 1977 version of the 1938 revue. The famous title was bought, the famous stars signed, and the money accordingly raised. The only thing missing was a show. This was a million-dollar disaster, closing on the road in Baltimore.*

# ACKNOWLEDGEMENTS

There are people who helped me with this book. Nai Chang is the master artist-craftsman who designed it, page by page, and made it more beautiful than I imagined any book could be, especially my own. Lory Frankel was my first copy editor, and everything she took from one section and promised to save for another, by God, she saved. Libby Seaberg took over for her, and then along came Ellen Grand. Lois Brown spent dreary hours in dusty photo archives for me, and Judith Tortolano arranged for the authorizations to reprint lyrics. Arlene Alda was with me for a month, backstage at *Annie*, taking the pictures for the section "Running a Show Through." Jeffrey Apter did research on the text and Terry Miller did that too, plus picture collecting, besides being a walking encyclopedia and my constant critic. Robin Wagner took time in the midst of preparing *On the Twentieth Century* to collect blueprints and sketches and models of his sets. For the section on costume design, Patricia Zipprodt made available not only her files but also her formidable store of knowledge. Then there are the other professionals, the composers and lyricists and librettists and directors, who talked shop with me over the years, sharing enthusiasm and knowledge. I have those showmakers to thank not only for talking but for doing, since without their musical theater a book on the subject would hardly exist. And last, I'd like to express my profound gratitude, as well as my respect and affection, for Robert Morton, my editor. Stubborn, exasperating, and invariably wrong, wrong, wrong, he is that modern rarity, a real book person—someone whose criticism is aggravating because, in fact, it is right, right, right. Such a person is indispensable.

# PHOTO CREDITS

The Publisher especially wishes to thank Joseph Abeles and Martha Swope for their exceptional cooperation and generosity.

On the jacket: *A Chorus Line*, photograph by Martha Swope.

Endpapers: The following show posters courtesy of The Museum of the City of New York: *Can-Can, Bye, Bye, Birdie, Chicago, Porgy and Bess, How to Succeed in Business Without Really Trying, Kiss Me, Kate, My Fair Lady, Oklahoma!, Funny Girl,* and *Hello, Dolly!* Remaining show posters courtesy of Artcraft Lithograph & Printing Company, Inc. Photography by George Roos.

Set designs, drawings, and models for *On the Twentieth Century* by Robin Wagner.

Costume designs on pages 82 top and 83 top left by Patricia Zipprodt.

Cartoons on pages 6 and 7 by Al Hirschfeld, from *The World of Hirschfeld*, published by Harry N. Abrams, Inc.

Photographs by Arlene Alda on pages 1, 38–39, 150, 152, 153, 154, 155, 156 bottom, 157, and 160 © 1979 Arlene Alda. All rights reserved.

Joseph Abeles Collection: 28, 30–31, 42–43, 44–45, 48–49, 50–51, 52, 67, 83 bottom, 84, 86, 96, 97, 98–99, 104, 107, 108, 109, 110, 112–13, 114–15, 116–17, 117, 118–19, 119, 126, 127, 133, 134–35, 135 top, 141, 142, 144, 146, 148, 149, 168–69, 174, 196, 197, 198, 199, 234, 246 bottom, 250 top, 257, 259, 262, 268 bottom, 269, 270, 272, 273 top, 274, 275, 276, 278, 282, 283, 284, 284–85, 285, 287, 293, 294, 295, 296, 297, 298–99, 300, 301, 302, 303, 305, 306, 307, 308, 309, 313 bottom, 319, 320, 321, 328, 329, 333, 334, 336, 345, 346 top, 347, 348, 349, 350 top;

Arlene Alda: 1, 38–39, 150, 152, 153, 154, 155, 156 bottom, 157, 160;

Bert Andrews: 137, 337;

Ash/LeDonne, Inc.: 315;

Columbia Records: 316;

Jerry Cooke, *Life* Magazine, © 1949, Time, Inc.: 212;

Culver Pictures: 11, 92, 93, 94, 162–63, 165, 171, 181, 215, 217, 218, 220, 223, 228, 245, 249, 255, 258, 330, 340, 341, 342;

Eileen Darby: 21, 46–47, 103, 147 bottom left, 147 right, 248, 252, 258–59, 265, 273 bottom;

Eliot Elisofon, *Life* Magazine, © 1960, Time, Inc.: 128;

Bob Golby: 17, 100, 101, 147 top left, 191, 192, 193, 194, 195, 213, 214, 256, 266, 266–67, 268 top, 271, 281, 291 right, 292;

Milton H. Greene: 279;

Seth Joel: 73, 76 top, 77 top right, 77 middle right, 79 top, 80 top right, 81 top;

Mark Kaufmann, *Life* Magazine, © 1964, Time, Inc.: 25, 26–27;

Carl Kravats (courtesy Nolan Scenery Studios, Inc.): 75;

Dick Moore & Associates, Inc.: 350 bottom;

Ralph Morse, *Life* Magazine, © 1939, Time, Inc.: 200;

Museum of the City of New York: 12, 177 bottom, 178, 264 top;

Stephen Sondheim: 325;

Martha Swope: 2–3, 4–5, 8, 34, 69, 72, 76 bottom, 77 bottom, 79 bottom, 80 left, 80–81, 82 bottom, 83 top right, 121, 122–23, 129, 130–31, 135 bottom, 136, 138–39, 145, 156 top, 158–59, 232–33, 286, 291 left, 298 top, 310–11, 311, 313 top, 314, 314–15, 324, 326, 327, 335, 338, 346 bottom, 351;

Theatre Collection, New York Public Library: 14–15, 41, 56, 57, 60, 61, 62, 63, 65, 88, 89, 90, 90–91, 105, 124–25, 166, 167, 170, 170–71, 172, 172–73, 177 top, 179, 180, 182, 182–83, 183, 184, 185, 186, 186–87, 187, 188, 189, 202, 203, 205, 206, 207, 208, 209, 210, 211, 224, 224–25, 226, 227, 230, 231, 236–37, 238, 238–39, 240, 240–41, 242, 243, 246 top, 250–51, 251, 253, 254, 260, 263, 264 bottom, 280, 289, 290, 331, 332;

*Theatre World:* 261;

Jay Thompson: 312;

Robin Wagner (courtesy Nolan Scenery Studios, Inc.): 78 bottom;

Hank Walker, *Life* Magazine, © 1957, Time, Inc.: 106;

Wide World Photos: 40.

The Publisher also wishes to thank the following unions for their cooperation in helping Arlene Alda to photograph *Annie* backstage:

Actors' Equity Association
Local 802 AF of M
Local 1 IATSE
Local 764 TWAU

# SONG CREDITS

The following song excerpts used by permission. All rights are reserved and international copyrights secured.

"Adelaide's Lament" by Frank Loesser, © 1950 by Frank Music Corp., © renewed 1978 by Frank Music Corp.

"Always" by Irving Berlin, © 1925 by Irving Berlin, © renewed 1952 by Irving Berlin; reprinted by permission of Irving Berlin Music Corp.

"Anything Goes" by Cole Porter, © 1934 by Warner Bros., Inc., © renewed.

"Arthur" words by Fred Ebb, music by John Kander, © 1977 by The Times Square Music Publications Co.

"Big Spender" by Cy Coleman and Dorothy Fields, © 1965, 1969 by Cy Coleman and Dorothy Fields; Notable Music Co., Inc.

"Bill" by Jerome Kern, P.G. Wodehouse, and Oscar Hammerstein II (from the musical production *Show Boat*), © 1927 by T. B. Harms Co., © renewed.

"By Myself" by Howard Dietz and Arthur Schwartz, © 1937 by DeSylva, Brown and Henderson, Inc., © renewed, assigned to Chappell & Co., Inc.

"Cabaret" © 1966 by The Times Square Music Publications Co.

"Comedy Tonight" by Stephen Sondheim, © 1962 by Stephen Sondheim; Burthen Music Corp., Inc., owner of publication and allied rights; Chappell & Co., Inc., sole selling agent.

"Come Rain or Come Shine" by Johnny Mercer and Harold Arlen, © 1946 by A–M Music, © renewed; all rights controlled by Chappell & Co., Inc.

"Could I Leave You?" by Stephen Sondheim, © 1971 by Herald Square Music Co., Rilting Music, Inc., and Burthen Music Co., Inc.

"Dancing in the Dark" by Cole Porter, © 1931 by Warner Bros., Inc., © renewed.

"Dear Friend" lyrics by Sheldon Harnick, music by Jerry Bock, © 1963 by The Times Square Music Publications Co.

"Do, Do, Do" by Ira Gershwin, © 1922 by New World Music Corp., © renewed; used by permission of Warner Bros. Music.

"Every Day a Little Death" by Stephen Sondheim, © 1973 by Rilting Music, Inc., and Revelation Music Publishing Corp. (ASCAP).

"He Had Refinement" by Dorothy Fields and Arthur Schwartz (from the musical production *A Tree Grows in Brooklyn*), © 1957 by Dorothy Fields and Arthur Schwartz.

"Hello, Dolly!" music and lyrics by Jerry Herman (from the Broadway musical *Hello, Dolly!*), © 1963 by Jerry Herman; all rights throughout the world controlled by Edwin H. Morris and Co., a division of MPL Communications, Inc.

"Hello Twelve, Hello Thirteen, Hello Love" lyrics by Edward Kleban, music by Marvin Hamlisch (from the Broadway musical *A Chorus Line*), © 1975 by Marvin Hamlisch and Edward Kleban; all rights controlled by Wren Music Co., Inc., and by American Compass Music Corp.

"Her Is" by Richard Adler and Jerry Ross, © 1954, 1955 Frank Music Corp.

"If Love Were All" by Cole Porter, © 1929 by Chappell & Co., Ltd., © renewed; all rights for the U.S. and Canada controlled by Warner Bros., Inc.

"I Get a Kick Out of You" by Cole Porter, © 1934 by Warner Bros., Inc., © renewed.

"I Get Carried Away" by Betty Comden and Adolph Green, © 1946 by Warner Bros., Inc., © renewed.

"I'm in Love with a Wonderful Guy" by Richard Rodgers and Oscar Hammerstein II, © 1947 by Richard Rodgers and Oscar Hammerstein II, Williamson Music, Inc., owner of publication and allied rights.

"In the Still of the Night" by Cole Porter, © 1937 by Chappell & Co., Inc., © renewed.

"I Talk to the Trees" by Alan Jay Lerner and Frederick Loewe, © 1951 by Alan Jay Lerner and Frederick Loewe; Chappell & Co., Inc., owner of publication and allied rights.

"I Wish I Were in Love Again" by Richard Rodgers and Lorenz Hart, © 1937 by Chappell & Co., Inc., © renewed.

"It Never Entered My Mind" by Richard Rodgers and Lorenz Hart, © 1940 by Chappell & Co., Inc., © renewed.

"It's All Right with Me" by Cole Porter, © 1953 by Cole Porter; Chappell & Co., Inc., owner of publication and allied rights.

"It's De-Lovely" by Cole Porter, © 1936 by Chappell & Co., Inc., © renewed.

"Just One of Those Things" by Cole Porter, © 1935 by Warner Bros., Inc., © renewed.

"Let's Not Talk About Love" by Cole Porter, © 1941 by Chappell & Co., Inc., © renewed, assigned to John F. Wharton as Trustee of the Cole Porter Musical and Literary Property Trusts; Chappell & Co., Inc., owner of publication and allied rights.

"Love is Sweeping the Country" by Cole Porter, © 1931 by New World Music Corp., © renewed; used by permission of Warner Bros. Music.

"Mister Cellophane" by Fred Ebb and John Kander, © 1975 by Unichappell Music, Inc., and Kander & Ebb, Inc., administers Kander & Ebb, Inc.

"My Lord and Master" by Richard Rodgers and Oscar Hammerstein II, © 1951 by Richard Rodgers and Oscar Hammerstein II; Williamson Music, Inc., owner of publication and allied rights.

"Now" by Stephen Sondheim, © 1973 by Rilting Music, Inc., and Revelation Music Publishing Corp. (ASCAP).

"People Will Say We're in Love" by Richard Rodgers and Oscar Hammerstein II, © 1943 by Williamson Music, Inc., © renewed.

"Rose's Turn" by Stephen Sondheim and Jule Styne, © 1959 by Norbeth Productions, Inc., and Stephen Sondheim; Williamson Music, Inc., and Stratford Music Corp., owners of publication and allied rights throughout the world; Chappell & Co., Inc., sole selling agent.

"Sabbath Prayer" lyrics by Sheldon Harnick, music by Jerry Bock, © 1964 The Times Square Music Publications Co.

"Some People" by Stephen Sondheim and Jule Styne, © 1959 and 1960 by Norbeth Productions, Inc., and Stephen Sondheim; Williamson Music, Inc., and Stratford Music Corp., owners of publication and allied rights throughout the world; Chappell & Co., Inc., sole selling agent.

"Something's Coming" by Leonard Bernstein and Stephen Sondheim, © 1957 by Leonard Bernstein and Stephen Sondheim.

"Something Sort of Grandish" by E.Y. Harburg and Burton Lane, © 1946 and 1947 by Players Music Corp., © renewed, assigned to Chappell & Co., Inc.

"Tall Hope" lyrics by Carolyn Leigh, music by Cy Coleman (from the Broadway musical *Wildcat*), © 1960 by Carolyn Leigh and Cy Coleman; all rights throughout the world controlled by Edwin H. Morris and Co., a division of MPL Communications, Inc.

"There's a Small Hotel" by Richard Rodgers and Lorenz Hart, © 1936 by Chappell & Co., Inc., © renewed.

"There's No Business Like Show Business" by Irving Berlin, © 1946 by Irving Berlin, © renewed 1973 by Irving Berlin; reprinted by permission of Irving Berlin Music Corp.

"This Is New" by Ira Gershwin and Kurt Weill, © 1941 by Chappell & Co., Inc., © renewed.

"To Be a Performer" lyrics by Carolyn Leigh, music by Cy Coleman (from the Broadway musical *Little Me*), © 1958 and 1962 by Edwin H. Morris and Co., a division of MPL Communications, Inc.

"Triplets" by Howard Dietz and Arthur Schwartz, © 1937 by DeSylva, Brown and Henderson, Inc., © renewed, assigned to Chappell & Co., Inc., © 1953 by Chappell & Co., Inc.

"You Did It" by Alan Jay Lerner and Frederick Loewe, © 1956 by Alan Jay Lerner and Frederick Loewe; Chappell & Co., Inc., owner of publication and allied rights.

"You're the Top" by Cole Porter, © 1934 by Warner Bros., Inc., © renewed.

"(What Did I Do To Be So) Black and Blue" by Fats Waller and Andy Razaf, © 1929 by Mills Music, Inc., © renewed, assigned to Chappell & Co., Inc. (Intersong Music, Publisher) and Mills Music for the USA.

"What Would We Do Without You?" by Stephen Sondheim, © 1970 by Herald Square Music Co., and Rilting Music, Inc.

"When I'm Not Near the Girl I Love" by E.Y. Harburg and Burton Lane, © 1946 by Players Music Corp., © renewed, assigned to Chappell & Co., Inc.

The following script excerpts used by permission; all rights are reserved:

*A Chorus Line*, conceived, choreographed, and directed by Michael Bennett; book by James Kirkwood and Nicholas Dante, music by Marvin Hamlisch, lyrics by Edward Kleban; a Joseph Papp New York Shakespeare Production, in association with Plum Productions.

*Hello, Dolly!*, book by Michael Stewart, music and lyrics by Jerry Herman, © 1964 by Stewart Robinson, Inc.; © 1966 by Michael Stewart.

*Little Me,* book by Neil Simon, music and lyrics by Cy Coleman and Carolyn Leigh, © 1977 by Neil Simon, Cy Coleman and Carolyn Leigh.

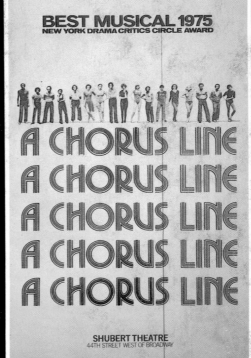

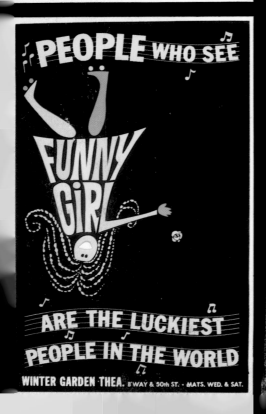

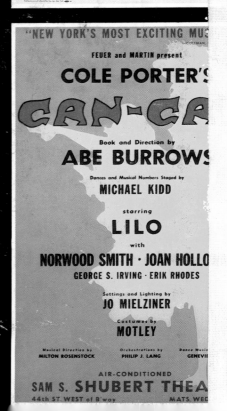